The Muslims
of America

Religion in America Series

Harry S. Stout
General Editor

A PERFECT BABEL OF CONFUSION
Dutch Religion and English Culture
in the Middle Colonies
Randall Balmer

THE PRESBYTERIAN CONTROVERSY
Fundamentalists, Modernists, and Moderates
Bradley J. Longfield

MORMONS AND THE BIBLE
The Place of the Latter-day Saints
in American Religion
Philip L. Barlow

THE RUDE HAND OF INNOVATION
Religion and Social Order
in Albany, New York, 1652–1836
David G. Hackett

SEASONS OF GRACE
Colonial New England's Revival
Tradition in Its British Context
Michael J. Crawford

THE MUSLIMS OF AMERICA
edited by Yvonne Yazbeck Haddad

The Muslims
of America

Edited by
YVONNE YAZBECK HADDAD

OXFORD UNIVERSITY PRESS
New York   Oxford

Oxford University Press

Oxford   New York   Toronto
Delhi   Bombay   Calcutta   Madras   Karachi
Kuala Lumpur   Singapore   Hong Kong   Tokyo
Nairobi   Dar es Salaam   Cape Town
Melbourne   Auckland   Madrid

and associated companies in
Berlin   Ibadan

Library of Congress Cataloging-in-Publication Data
The Muslims of America / edited by Yvonne Yazbeck Haddad.
p.   cm. — (Religion in America series)
Includes bibliographical references.
ISBN 0-19-506728-2
ISBN 0-19-508559-0 (pbk.)
1. Islam—United States.   2. Muslims—United States.
I. Haddad, Yvonne Yazbeck, 1935–
II. Series: Religion in America series
(Oxford University Press)
BP67.U6M87   1991   297'.0973—dc20   90-44510

2   4   6   8   9   7   5   3

Printed in the United States of America
on acid-free paper

ACKNOWLEDGMENTS

This book brings together studies on the religion of Islam as it is experienced in a variety of contexts in North America, in recognition of its expanding minority status in the United States and Canada. The papers collected in this volume were first presented at a conference devoted to the "Muslims of America," held in April 1989 on the Amherst campus of the University of Massachusetts, which was jointly sponsored by the Department of History, the Near East Area Studies Program, and the Arabic Club of the university. The project was supported by grants from the National Endowment for the Humanities, the Department of Education, the Arabian American Oil Company, Five College Incorporated, and Mobiloil Corporation. Resources at the University of Massachusetts were also provided by the Arabic Club, the Office of the Chancellor, the Department of History, the Faculty of Humanities and Fine Arts, the International Programs Office, the Faculty of Social and Behavioral Sciences, and the Near East Area Studies Program. The viewpoints and beliefs expressed in these papers are those of the individual authors and do not necessarily reflect the opinions of the sponsoring organizations.

The organizing committee of the conference wishes to express particular thanks to the following individuals: Joseph Duffey, chancellor of the University of Massachusetts; Murray Schwartz, dean of the Faculty of Humanities and Fine Arts; Glenn Gordon, dean of the Faculty of Social and Behavioral Sciences; and Barbara Burn, director of the International Programs Office. Special acknowledgment is made of the contributions of Elizabeth Brewer, assistant dean for Area Studies and codirector of the conference, who was involved in all aspects of the undertaking since its inception. Robert Engle, conference coordinator, and Alice Izer and Kathleen Moore oversaw all local arrangements in connection with the conference.

Gratitude is expressed to the chairs and respondents of the many panels conducted in the course of the conference. The chairs and respondents from the University of Massachusetts include Roland Sarti, chair of the Department of History; Elizabeth Brewer, assistant dean for Area Studies; Anna Tsing, professor of anthropology; Walter Denny, chair of the department of art history; W. Barnett Pearce, professor of communication; Adnan Haydar, director of the Near East Area Studies Program; Anwar Syed, professor of political science; Robert Griffith, professor of history. Other chairs and respondents include John A. Petropulos, Amherst College; Jonathan Lippman, Mount Holyoke College; Willem Bijlefeld and David Kerr, Hartford Seminary; Robert Haddad, Smith College; Allan D. Austin, Springfield College; and Barbara Aswad, Wayne State University.

The final form of the present text is the result of the efforts of many people. Jane I. Smith and Elizabeth d'Amico provided editorial assistance for all of the papers. Alice Izer typed several versions of a number of manuscripts, and Kathleen Moore maintained general organizational oversight of the collection as a whole. Gratitude and thanks are extended for all of these contributions, without which neither the project nor this volume would have been possible.

CONTENTS

CONTRIBUTORS

Qutbi Ahmed, a doctoral candidate at the Institute of Islamic Studies, McGill University, Montreal, Canada, is the director of the New York office of the Muslim World League and the former president of the Islamic Society of North America.

Nimat Hafez Barazangi was educated in Damascus University, Columbia University, and Cornell University. Her research and teaching interests center on multicultural pedagogical problems. She has published several papers on Muslim children's education, Muslim Arab youth, and Muslim/Arab women. Currently she is designing an action plan for Islamic education in North America based on the results of her dissertation.

Frederick Mathewson Denny, professor of religious studies at the University of Colorado at Boulder, is the author of *An Introduction to Islam, Islam and the Muslim Community, Islamic Ritual Practices: A Slide Set and Teacher's Guide* (with A. A. Sachedina) and numerous scholarly articles on Islamic subjects. He has traveled extensively in the Muslim world and is currently conducting research on Islam and Muslim communities in North America.

John L. Esposito, professor and director of international studies at College of the Holy Cross in Worcester, Massachusetts, is the author of *Islam and Politics* and *Women in Muslim Family Law*. He is the editor of *Islam in Asia: Religion, Politics and Society; Voices of Resurgent Islam; Islam and Development: Religion and Sociopolitical Change*; and coeditor of *Islam in Transition: Muslim Perspectives*. He has authored scores of journal articles on Islamic revival and Islam in the modern world. He has traveled extensively throughout the Muslim world and is involved with organizations working with Muslims in the United States.

Byron Haines is the former director of the Office of Christian–Muslim Relations at the National Council of Churches. He is the author of several articles on Muslims in the United States and a coauthor of *Christians and Muslims Together.*

Yvonne Yazbeck Haddad, professor of history at the University of Massachusetts, Amherst, is the author of *Contemporary Islam and the Challenge of History*, and coauthor of *Islamic Values in the United States* and *Islamic Understanding of Death and Resurrection*. She is the coeditor of *Islamic Impact* and *Women, Religion and Social Change*. She has been engaged in research on the Muslim community in the United States for the last ten years.

Marcia Hermansen, associate professor of religion at San Diego State University, has authored numerous articles on Islam in the subcontinent and is engaged in research on American women who convert to Islam and marry immigrants. She has written several articles on Islam and women.

Steve A. Johnson lectures in Islamic studies at Christian Theological Seminary and is an instructor in the English department at Indiana University–Purdue University at Indianapolis. He is the former editor of *Islamic Horizons* and author of the booklet *Da'wah to Americans: Theory and Practice*, as well as many articles on Islam.

Beverly Thomas McCloud, an assistant professor of Islamic studies at De Paul University, has been studying the role of women in the African American Muslim community.

Kathleen Moore is a doctoral candidate in the department of political science at the University of Massachusetts, Amherst.

Sulayman Nyang, chair of the department of Afro-American studies at Howard University, is a former editor of *Journal of Muslim Social Sciences*. Dr. Nyang has authored several articles on Muslims in the United States and is a coauthor of a forthcoming book on the Muslim community.

Larry A. Poston is chairman of the department of Missiology at Nyack College, Nyack, N.Y.

Abubaker Al Shingiety, a doctoral candidate in the department of communication at the University of Massachusetts at Amherst, is the former secretary general of the Union of Sudanese Writers and former editor of the monthly *Islamic Horizons*.

Jane I. Smith, vice president and academic dean at the Iliff School of Theology in Denver, Colorado, is the author of *The Precious Paper* and *The Concept "Islam" in the History of Qur'anic Exegesis*. She is the coauthor of *The Islamic Understanding of Death and Resurrection*, the editor of *Women in Contemporary Islamic Society*, and coeditor of *Introduction to Religions of the East: A Reader*. She has written numerous journal and encyclopedia articles on Islam.

Carol L. Stone is a research scientist at Indiana University School of Medicine in Indianapolis.

John O. Voll, chairman of the department of history at the University of New Hampshire, Durham, is the author of *Historical Dictionary of the Sudan*, *Islam: Continuity and Change in the Modern World*, and coauthor of *The Sudan: a Profile in Unity and Diversity*. He has written countless articles on Islam in the Sudan and in the modern world.

The Muslims
of America

Introduction:
The Muslims of America

Yvonne Yazbeck Haddad

The conference on the Muslims of America grew out of a desire to expand the scope of scholarly investigation of the growing Muslim community in the United States, heighten public awareness of the Muslim presence, and provide better understanding of the ways in which Muslims experience the United States and adapt to their institutions, as they become increasingly an indigenous part of America.

American Muslims are experiencing both exhilaration at the opportunity to increase their numbers and develop their institutions and frustration and dismay as they continue to experience prejudice, intimidation, discrimination, misunderstanding, and even hatred. It is increasingly important, therefore, to take a fresh look at some of the ways in which they have succeeded in creating a distinct identity and establishing an Islamic community in North America. The dramatic growth in the number of Muslims in the United States has come about at a time when anger is rising among many American citizens toward Muslims overseas as well as hostility toward and discrimination against American Muslims. The situation of Muslims in America must be understood in terms of the dynamics of their relationship to their environment in the United States and its influence on the development of Islamic ideas throughout the modern world.

Interest in the Muslims of America has grown in relation to their increasing presence in urban areas as well as the development of their distinctive institutions across the country. These include more than 600 mosques/Islamic centers, two Islamic colleges, scores of parochial day schools, several hundred weekend schools, women's organizations, youth groups, and professional and civic organizations. The leadership of the Muslim community has been predominantly in the hands of lay volunteers concerned about the maintenance of their heritage and the perpetuation of the faith by the next generation. In the last decade they have been able to organize several printing presses, book distribution centers, and national and regional denominational magazines to help guide the faithful in maintaining Islamic beliefs and practices in what is

3

often an alien environment.[1] Regular television[2] and radio[3] broadcasts feature programs on Islam and the Arab heritage; tapes (both audio and video) of sermons and speeches are distributed through national networks.

The American media, in the form of newspaper reporting[4] and some television programming[5], have begun to take note of these developments. Scholarly interest has been limited, either within the Muslim community itself or from social scientists concerned with ethnographic investigation and the social, economic, and psychological adjustment of immigrants to their North American environment. American scholars of the humanities have tended to view Muslims in the United States as of marginal interest because of their small number as compared to the worldwide Muslim community.[6] Their importance has been overshadowed by the tempestuous American relationship with Middle Eastern countries.

The dramatic growth of the Muslim community in the United States is a recent phenomenon, taking place primarily over the last three decades in response to changes in American immigration laws and the demands of the labor market. The majority of recent Muslim immigrants are university graduates, part of the "brain drain" of persons who have joined the ranks of American professionals. (There are, for example, an estimated six thousand Muslim medical doctors in the United States.) They are economically integrated into the American middle class but appear to be increasingly alienated by American attitudes toward Islam and Muslims.

The impact of American Muslims on the ideological formation of contemporary Islam generally and on Muslim people overseas has been overlooked. In the last four decades, the United States has become a center of Islamic intellectual ferment as an increasing number of Muslim students (estimated at times to be over a hundred thousand a year) have enrolled in American colleges and universities.[7] Their understanding of Islam and its role in the world is being shaped and reshaped in the American milieu. Muslim intellectuals and leaders who have become a significant part of the American academic scene have been able to provide an interpretation of Islam relevant to life in the United States as well as to the modern world. Their writings and ideas have been exported by students returning to their home countries to assume leadership positions in the Muslim world. In this manner the opinions and interpretations of American Muslims have influenced persons in the Middle East, Africa, and Southeast Asia. Their Islamic worldviews have also been attractive to many indigenous Americans, both black and white, who have converted to Islam in the last four decades.[8]

Initial investigation suggests that the number of Muslims who participate in Islamic institutions in America is small, but such participation can be seen to increase during periods of stress. Recent international events and the reactions of the American public to them seem to have stimulated Muslims to become involved in community activities on social, political, and educational levels. Much of this activity is designed to influence the views of the general American public—specifically to blunt the negative image presented by the press. Also, many in the generation of Muslim young people who took advantage of the immigration laws in the sixties and seventies are now seeking institutional support for educating their children in the traditions of their forefathers.

The American experience has presented Muslims with a special challenge. They have unprecedented freedom to experiment with forms and structures for the separation of religion and state away from the watchful eyes of wary governments and the criticism of traditionalists. At the same time, this freedom is fraught with the danger of innovation and deviance; the great range of options available in the American context carries the threat of sectarian division and fragmentation. The essays in this volume are intended to initiate scholarly investigation of such questions as whether a common understanding and interpretation of the Muslim experience exists in the United States; in what way and to what degree the "imported" Islamic heritage, whether Iranian, Arab, Turkish, or Pakistani, affects the redefinition of Islam in the American context; how American Muslims in different areas and at different times have been able to organize Islamic institutions while maintaining their full participation in the American mainstream; and how Muslims have drawn on their heritage, their theological structures, and their attendant religious institutions, in either the traditional or some refashioned form, to create a cohesive milieu in the United States.

If it is true that intellectual and institutional activity becomes more intense during periods of crisis, does Islam either function as a kind of refuge or take the initiative in the quest to provide meaning and relevance in an ever-changing environment? Are Muslim intellectuals active in seeking a creative reordering of life and a cohesive worldview? Do they perceive their role as providing community stability and integration, or are they marginal actors outside the arena of power who strive to stem the tide of apathy and erosion of support among members? Studies in this volume focus on the range of ways in which Muslims have responded to the challenge of maintaining their identity and living out their faith in the American context.

The volume is organized into six sections, taking the reader from specific details and descriptions through material that is more suggestive and interpretive. In the first section Gutbi Mahdi Ahmad discusses the organizational structures of American Muslims, primarily Sunni, providing historical background, reasons why Muslims have chosen to configure themselves in formal organizations, and an overview of the major groups in North America today and the constituencies they serve. The essay concludes with an introduction to some Islamic subgroups, including the American Muslim Mission, Darul Islam, and the Ansarullah. Next Carol Stone offers a detailed projection of the number of Muslims living in America today, extrapolating from 1980 Census Bureau emigration statistics. Looking at proportions of Muslim populations across the world and estimated numbers of immigrants, she calculates that there are some 4 million Muslims in the United States today, with the largest communities in California, New York, and Illinois.

In the second section Byron Haines and Abubaker Al Shingiety deal with ways in which Muslims have been, and continue to be, perceived by non-

Muslims in the American milieu. Haines traces the attitudes of Christian groups to Islam and Muslims through an analysis of documents published by or on behalf of a variety of churches and denominations. He sees a general decline in anti-Muslim rhetoric and in many cases an attempt at more objective understanding, though in some cases the old "conversion" polemics still pertain. Implicit in his presentation is a projection of implications for present and future relationships between Christian churches and the community of Islam. Shingiety uses the Nation of Islam as a case in point to illustrate his thesis that there is a dialectical relationship between the way the West views and represents Islam and the image Muslims have of themselves. He sees the Nation as typical of those groups that attempt to break away from the American ethnocentric model and move to a more "orthodox" position in a broader historical and geographical context.

Three contemporary Islamic scholars who have made a significant impact on the American academic community are the subject of the third section. John Esposito presents the life and thought of the late Palestinian scholar Ismail al-Faruqi, tracing his movement from Arabism to a more comprehensive view of Islam as the integrating factor for all aspects of culture, doctrine, and faith. Esposito stresses the importance of Faruqi's Western training and his broad familiarity with Christian theological diciplines for both his scholarship and his role in interfaith discussion. By integrating thought and action, knowing and doing, Faruqi was an eloquent spokesperson for Islam in the American educational establishment.

Seyyed Hossein Nasr, Iranian expatriot and prolific interpreter of Islam, in his many roles as apologist, philosopher, mystic, and interpreter of the physical sciences is presented by Jane Smith. Nasr argues throughout his writings for what he calls Islamic traditionalism over against modernism, rationalism, evolutionism, and fundamentalism. Deeply versed in Western philosophy, theology, and psychology, he sees all contemporary religion as having moved from its grounding in what he calls *scientia sacra*.

The life and work of Fazlur Rahman, the recently deceased Pakistani scholar, are described by Frederick Denny. Three aspects of Rahman's thought—the philosophical–theological, moral–ethical, and religious–communal—are presented as integrated aspects of his personality and his life as a scholar. An articulate interpreter of Islam, Rahman concentrated particularly on the understanding and interpretation of the Qur'an and its themes, philosophical theology, ethics, and the question of Islam and modernity. Denny gives special emphasis to Rahman's twin legacies of intellect and morality.

The next section of the volume presents various aspects of Islamic activity. Steve Johnson discusses political involvement both among groups of Muslims and between Muslims and non-Muslims in the larger society. He suggests reasons for some Muslim groups' opposition to political activity in America, distinguishing between Muslims and Arabs as political activists and noting the difficulty some Muslims have in associating with Christian Arabs in political organizations. Various ethnic groups are characterized as to the degree of their participation in the American political scene. Next Larry Poston attempts to describe American Muslims in terms of their philosophies of *da'wah*, or mission. He sees a basic division between those who are interested only in making sure the Islamic community remains true to its ideals (the "defensive pacifists") and those who wish to convert non-Muslims to the faith (the "offensive activists"). He explores the historical background of Muslim missionary movements in America, examining the roles of such groups as the Ikhwan al-Muslimin, the Jama'at-i-Islami, the Muslim Student Association, and others that actively promote *da'wah*.

Kathleen Moore discusses the fate of Muslims who have come up against the American legal system. Her detailed study of Islam and the U.S. Constitution examines the rights of Muslims to the free exercise of their religion in prison. Among the issues considered are diet, dress, grooming, conduct of prayers, and other religious activities in the general context of potential discriminatory treatment.

In an examination of Islamic education in North America Nimat Hafez Barazangi posits four underlying presuppositions that distinguish Islamic and Western worldviews and shows how these affect philosophies of education. She presents the results of interviews of forty immigrant families in five major American cities concerning education and the transfer of Islamic values. Barazangi encourages a new approach to the education of North American Muslim children designed to help preserve Islamic identity in Western society.

Beverly Thomas McCloud and Marcia Hermansen discuss aspects of the role of Muslim women in the American context. McCloud treats Sunni African–American women, drawing on her oral history research in a community in Philadelphia. Looking specifically at issues and problems confronted by African–American women who choose to convert from Christianity to Islam, she presents four categories of converts in the persons of four individuals (fictional but synthesized from personal conversations) who reveal a range of responses to the issue of what it means to be a convert to Islam. Hermansen then discusses ways in which American Muslim women choose to express their Islamic identity, with specific reference to women's religious meetings and marriage arrangements. The discussion covers life-styles, dress, and other "patterns and symbols of acculturation." Hermansen concludes that immigrant women in America tend to affirm their identity as Muslims in a number of characteristic ways, including participation in Muslim women's organizations.

The last section of the volume contains three essays dealing with identity issues faced by American Muslims. John Voll distinguishes between two types of such issues—those affecting Muslim minorities in any country at any time and those specific to Western postindustrial or postmodern society. He calls on Ismail Faruqi's image of Muslims as making a *hijra* or emigration to the West, projecting the vision of America as a kind of modern Medina with the potential for a similar transformation of society. Yvonne Haddad traces the changes in American foreign policy that have taken place over the last four decades in relation to the Middle East and their impact on how American Muslims frame their own identity. A steadily increasing sense of frustration and disillusionment has led to a growing number of persons in this country actively committed to an Islamic

identity. Also considering challenges facing Muslims in the United States, Sulayman Nyang posits four specific needs: to maintain an Islamic identity, to defend
Islamic institutions, to build Islamic economic structures, and to find ways to
participate in American political life. Although clear differences exist among
Muslims, he says, rituals and values hold them together. Nyang also distinguishes
between what he calls the assimilationist and the simulationist Muslim, the first
setting Islamic identity over against identity as an American and the second
finding ways to reconcile both affiliations.

It is clear that these studies are the beginning of what must be an even more
farreaching effort. Much work remains to be done on such topics as Islamic
society in relation to American social and diplomatic history, the ways in
which a new community is formed by individuals from a variety of national
and social backgrounds, the role(s) of the mosque, the development of Islamic
leadership, attempts to create an Islamic economic system, the establishment
of Islamic businesses to meet specific Islamic needs as well as ethnic prefer-
ences, the integration of black Americans into an Islamic system, and the integration of Muslims into the American black culture.

The present volume is the first of what must be ongoing efforts to organize
and present the research of a wide range of scholars dedicated to an examination of Islam in the American context.

Notes

1. For a list of available material, see Yvonne Haddad, "Muslims in America: A
Select Bibliography," *The Muslim World* 76 (1986): 93–122.
2. The producers of two television programs are seeking national outlets for their
products. These include "The Arabic Hour," which is produced in Boston and telecast
in Chicago, Los Angeles, and San Francisco, and a new weekly series on Islam
produced in Los Angeles. There are other groups with local access, including a youth
group in Virginia.
3. The most widely heard radio personality is Warith Deen Muhammad, the leader
of what used to be called the American Muslim Mission, whose weekly broadcasts are
carried by over thirty stations. Other local programs are heard in New York City and
Houston.
4. Stories have recently appeared in *The Atlanta Constitution and Journal*, the
Philadelphia Inquirer, the *New York Times*, the *Orange County Register*, the *San
Francisco Examiner*, the *Washington Times*, and the *Chicago Sun*.
5. Radio Canada of Quebec and WNBC have carried stories about Muslims in the
New York area, as have "CBS Morning News," Monitor TV, CNN, and WCBS. Issues
have been discussed by Morton Downey and Phil Donahue, and on "60 Minutes."
6. There are an estimated 3 million to 4 million Muslims in America, more than the
total membership of the Episcopal Church or of the United Church of Christ. The number
of Muslims in the world is estimated at eight hundred fifty million to one billion.
7. For example, there were twenty-eight thousand Iranian students studying in the
United States in 1978.
8. Such persons are estimated at about one million.

I

THE MUSLIMS
OF THE UNITED STATES

1

Muslim Organizations in the United States

Gutbi Mahdi Ahmed

Much research has already been done on Muslim organizations in America. The changing pattern of organizations in the Muslim community, however, necessitates a fresh look at the subject. I therefore pick up the discussion where other reviewers have left off to offer some insights into the recent changes in the pattern of Muslim organizations in the United States.[1]

Early Immigrants' Local Organizations

Early Muslim immigrants started arriving in small numbers around the turn of the century and continued in relatively increasing waves throughout the first half of the century. These immigrants were often characterized as adventurers attracted to the New World for its economic opportunities. Unlike many of their contemporary European counterparts, they did not come to make America their home. Their intention was to make as much money as possible quickly and then return to their homeland. Many, however, failed to realize their dreams and eventually returned, disenchanted, to their home countries. Those who were more successful and were able to adjust to the American way of life generally found in their kin relationships and trade partnerships forms of association that made any other kind of organization unnecessary.[2]

Tempted by their success in business and their ability to adjust, some decided to stay permanently and send for their families to join them. Stories of their success attracted their relatives and others from their villages to emigrate to the United States. A more visible community started to crystallize at this stage, composed of extended families from the same place and living in the same city. Among the best known of these families were the Ajrams who settled in Cedar Rapids, Iowa, founding one of the first mosques there, the Barakats and Alwans who helped build the Toledo mosque, the Khalids who settled in Detroit where, with others, they built the Detroit mosque, and the Jizainis who built a mosque in Michigan City, Indiana. There were also the

11

Khan family who organized the Punjabis in Sacramento, California, and built the first mosque on the U.S. West Coast, the Diabs who built the Chicago mosque, and the early Albanians of Detroit and the Tartars of Brooklyn, New York, who began mosques in their respective areas.

These people organized in response to certain social incidents and pressures. The death of a relative led to the serious consideration of acquiring a grave lot to be used as a Muslim cemetery. The marriage of a daughter outside the faith led to the early organization of youth groups to bring the young together. Children's ignorance of the parents' language and religious beliefs accelerated the efforts to start a Sunday school. Such problems and the cultural challenges they presented led to self-consciousness and the search for identity. The Christmas celebration, for example, prompted families to celebrate Milad al-Nabi (the birthday of the Prophet) as a way for parents to respond to the desires of their children for such festivity. These kinds of factors, particularly the cultural needs of the second generation, pressured families into building mosques and organizing the earliest forms of Islamic associations.

Apart from serving as the "last line of cultural defense," these local organizations did not do much in aggressively contributing to the development of their communities, either socially or spiritually. In fact, they did not take their Islamic mission very seriously. The associations were primarily meant to keep the children from breaking away, as well as to provide a place for families to socialize and for weddings and burials to be performed within the traditional context. Many eventually ceased to exist when they were taken over by the children of the founders. The earliest mosque in America, in Ross, North Dakota, was demolished in 1979. Another at High Park, Michigan, was transformed into a church and many were sold, converted to restaurants, or put to other uses. Those that did survive were not run in the traditional manner as proper mosques. Daily prayers were not observed. Friday prayer either was not organized or was held on Sunday. Mixed dances were held in the mosques accompanied by lavish parties where liquor was freely served. Belly dancers were invited to fund-raising events organized in mosque basements.

The Federation of Islamic Associations of the United States and Canada

By the middle of this century Muslims were still relatively few in number and scattered over the continent, yet they began to feel a need for an umbrella organization. On June 28, 1952, the dynamic leader of the Cedar Rapids Muslim community, Abdullah Ajram (Igram), organized the first national Muslim conference in Cedar Rapids, Iowa.[3] Four hundred Muslims from all over the United States and Canada attended. The main issue on the agenda was the formation of a national organization that could bring together the Muslims of America and coordinate their activities. They formed the International Muslim Society, electing Abdullah Igram as its first president. Little is known of what the new society actually did to serve its purpose, but it continued to hold annual meetings.

The second conference was organized in July 1953 in Toledo, Ohio, and the third in Chicago, Illinois, in July of the following year. During that last conference, the idea of a federation to unite all local Muslim organizations under one umbrella gained the support of the participants, and the Federation of Islamic Associations of the United States and Canada (FIA) was formed; again the members elected Igram as president. Immediately after the conference, the Federation issued its manifesto, which began by saying: "We the members of the Muslim Community of America, in accordance with the Quranic injunction: hold fast to the rope of God all together and do not disperse, declare the creation of the Federation of the Islamic Association of the United States and Canada." The declaration emphasized the educational role of the federation in areas of spiritual, social, and cultural development within the framework of the Islamic principles. It also underlined the federation's public relations mission and its role in promoting better understanding between Muslims and the larger society.

In 1955 the federation held its conference in London, Ontario, signaling the continental structures of its composition and honoring the dedication of its Canadian members, who had been active from its inception. An observer who attended that conference noted its psychological effect on a community that had been cut off from its origins and demoralized by the cultural shock and the dominance of the indigenous culture. Many participants were second-generation Muslims who bore the names James Ali, Alfred Mahmud, Albert Hasson, and so on. There was a report of a Canadian family who embraced Islam during the conference. Hassan Ibrahim, an accountant and a World War II veteran born in America to a Lebanese immigrant and an Italian mother, was elected as its new president. Little is known about the fifth conference, which was held in New York City in July 1956.

The sixth conference was held in Detroit the following year with Kassem Alwan elected as the new president. Son of a Lebanese immigrant who arrived in the United States in 1902, Alwan was an American-born Muslim who served in the United States Third Army during World War II. After the war Alwan worked as a journalist, later started an industry in Ohio, and finally opened a restaurant in Toledo. He was reelected to the presidency at the seventh conference in Washington, D.C., in the summer of 1958. In 1959 the FIA held its ninth conference in Michigan City, Indiana. One thousand people gathered from all over the United States and Canada, choosing Muhammad Khalil (James Calil) as the new president. Khalil was a well-known sportsman from Detroit, whose Lebanese family arrived in the States at the turn of the century. Khalil and Alwan visited Cairo in 1959 where they met with the late President Nasser and were treated as state guests.

Although FIA did little apart from organizing their annual conferences, its success in that organization indicated the new spirit among the American Muslims and the increasing sense of identity and community. The new leader-

ship was characterized by being American-born, educated, in service in the
U.S. Army, and professionally successful. Most present community organizations are struggling with little success to create such leadership from among the
second Muslim generation.

By the early sixties the FIA had to give way to a new organization, which
was better suited to carrying its historical achievement a step further. If the
FIA provided a platform for Muslim immigrants to come together and experience a sense of identity and brotherhood, the time was ripe for a new actor
who would consolidate this experience by giving it a true and authentic Islamic
content. The role found its actor in the recently arrived, more radical, and well-
educated foreign Muslim student.

The Muslim Student Association (MSA)

After World War II, several Muslim student associations were organized on the
university campuses of the United States as overseas students from the Muslim
world arrived for higher studies. By 1963 those associations were active and
close enough to see the need for a national student organization to coordinate
their activities and further their services and outreach. In their first national
conference in Urbana, Illinois, the associations formed the Muslim Student
Association (MSA). In contrast to the FIA's ethnic nature, the MSA represented the diversity and internationalism of Islam. The participants of the
Urbana Conference as well as the first elected executive committee included
Arabs from different countries, Indo-Pakistanis, Iranians, Turks, and others.
Commitment to Islam overrode every other affiliation. Islam was seen as an
ideology, a way of life, and a mission, and the organization was not considered
simply as a way to serve the community but as a means to create an ideal
community and serve Islam.

It is important to consider the nature of the Muslim world at the time the
MSA was founded in 1963. That year Khoumeini was expelled from Iran
during a bloody uprising staged by his Muslim students. The Jama'ati Islami
was banned in Pakistan and Maulana Maududi was sentenced to death. In
Egypt the Ikhwan were jailed and Sayyid Qutb was arrested two years later and
eventually executed. The Masjumi Party was banned in Indonesia and its
leader, Nassir, was thrown into jail. The Algerian Revolution was approaching
its final victory. The students who gathered in Urbana came from these places
and the organization they set up clearly reflected the experience of the Islamic
movement in their respective countries.

An elaborate network with local chapters in every major campus and with
regional and zonal structures was organized. An executive committee at the
center led the organization with the help of several functional committees. The
general assembly met every year at the annual convention to outline the
guidelines of the new policy, and the new executive committee translated it
into their annual "action plan." With increasing membership, experience, and
donations from overseas sources, MSA activities grew and became more

mature and sophisticated. By 1971 the need was already felt for a permanent secretariat, and a rudimentary headquarters was opened in Al-Amin Mosque in Gary, Indiana. In 1973 a full-time executive director was appointed.

In September 1975, at its annual convention in Toledo, Ohio, the MSA general assembly approved amendments to the constitution that changed the MSA's structure and established a general secretariat of full-time workers. The headquarters was immediately organized on a huge farm acquired in Plainfield, Indiana. (The land, covering an area of 500,000 square meters, cost $500,000.) Departments were established for education and publication, training, public relations, finance, and administration. A secretary general and (later) an assistant secretary general headed the general secretariat. Directors of these departments were chosen from the best field workers and former officials, both activists and scholars. Each held a doctorate in his or her respective field.

This period also saw the founding of the North American Islamic Trust (NAIT), an organization that holds the title of MSA properties (mosques, student houses, Islamic centers and service organizations such as the American Trust Publication, International Graphics Press, and Islamic Book Service) and is generally considered the financial arm of MSA. NAIT handled MSA investments, offered small loans to Muslim businesses, and recently handled the promising AMANA Mutual Fund. The Islamic Teaching Center (ITC), another institution founded in the mid-1970s, has departments of correctional facilities, Arabic language, Islamic organizations, liaison, publications, and others. Its mission is essentially Islamic education and training, propagation of Islam, and distribution of Islamic literature.

Many MSA members who graduated, settled, and found jobs in North America continue to be active in MSA. For them it is a kind of school through which they can develop an Islamic personality. Professional specializations are recognized through particular organizations such as the American Muslim Scientists and Engineers (AMSE), the American Muslim Social Scientists (AMSS), and the Islamic Medical Association (IMA). Those who formed community organizations made sure to affiliate them with MSA.

Gradually the MSA image began to dominate community activities and overshadow other organizations. The large numbers of recent Muslim immigrants have found MSA the strongest and most Islamically committed organization, and they have been strongly attracted to it. It became clear that a student, campus-oriented structure was no longer appropriate for this new situation. In February 1977, therefore, the executive committee invited fifty prominent active Muslims from various places in the United States and Canada for a two-day workshop to study and evaluate the situation and advise the MSA on the new strategy. In June of that year a task force was set up to examine and evaluate MSA priorities, programs, and structure and to suggest suitable alternatives. Later, the task force split into three specialized committees: future projections, internal relations, and external relations. The task force presented reports for review by the council of presidents of the affiliate organizations (MSA, IMA, AMSE, and AMSS). The structure of the Islamic

Society of North America (ISNA) was finally approved in 1981 by the general assemblies of the affiliate organizations.

The Islamic Society of North America

Although MSA was the largest, best organized, and most active of Islamic organizations, it was criticized for meddling in community affairs and not confining its activities to university campuses. MSA's response was that the campus membership is also a community of Muslim families and individuals who have the same kinds of problems, and need the same services, as the off-campus communities. Later development, however, showed them that the on-campus and off-campus communities do, in fact, have different kinds of problems and need a different approach. By then it was too late for MSA to become uninvolved, so it responded by changing its structure. The basic change was the creation of an off-campus national community organization, the Muslim Community Association (MCA). MSA and MCA work separately, each in its own field, but are joined at the center in Majlis al-Shura, the legislative body of the Islamic Society of North America (ISNA), along with other constituent organizations.

Under its leadership umbrella ISNA includes specialized or constituent organizations and institutions. These include (1) MCA, a federation of community-based local organizations; (2) MSA, a federation of local organizations on university campuses; (3) professional organizations such as AMSS, AMSE, and IMA; and (4) service institutions established by ISNA such as NAIT, ITC, FID (Foundation of International Development), and CIT (Canadian Islamic Trust, the NAIT counterpart in Canada).

Islamic Organizations in the United States

FIA	Federation of Islamic Associations
MSA	Muslim Student Association
NAIT	North American Islamic Trust
ITC	Islamic Teaching Center
AMSE	American Muslim Scientists and Engineers
AMSS	American Muslim Social Scientists
IMA	Islamic Medical Association
MCA	Muslim Community Association
FID	Foundation of International Development
CIT	Canadian Islamic Trust
MYNA	Muslim Youth of North America
MISG	Malaysian Islamic Study Group
MAYA	Muslim Arab Youth Association
AMM	American Muslim Mission

All these constituent organizations have their own committees and boards. Their administrative, financial, and legal affairs, however, are centralized in the general secretariat of the Islamic Society of North America (ISNA) under the direction of majlis al-shura.

The following chart shows ISNA's various organizational components:

General Assembly of ISNA

Executive Council = Majlis-al-Shura

NAIT, CIT, ITC, FID   AMSS, AMSE, IMA

MCA, MSA

To carry out its work as a grassroots membership organization, ISNA has an executive council consisting of elected and ex-officio members called the Majlis al-Shura, a general secretariat. Majlis al-shura is the legislative body which approves current policies and future plans, requests for affiliations, the annual budget, the president, and the formation of the executive council. The executive council implements the decisions of the majlis and prepares budget proposals and action plans. It supervises the performance of the general secretariat.

The secretariat handles and coordinates all the administrative, financial, and other activities of ISNA and its constituent organizations. Various ad hoc and standing committees are appointed by the majlis and the executive council to perform specialized tasks. The field activities are conducted through elected and appointed bodies in various zones, regions, and local chapters in the United States and Canada. The general secretariat is supposed to have offices in each of the five zones. Some have been closed down due to financial difficulties; only the Canadian zonal office is in full operation.

In addition to giving direction to the Islamic work of its five constituents (MSA, MCA, AMSS, AMSE, and IMA), ISNA has four autonomous service institutions: ITC, NAIT, CIT, and FID. ITC is devoted to the work of educating Muslims and presenting Islam to non-Muslims. Governed by its own by-laws, it is headed by a director general and overseen by a Board of Islamic Trust (CIT). NAIT has a general manager and a relatively large staff to man the various departments in its own headquarters in Indianapolis, Indiana. The FID complements the activities of the professional association in such areas as resource development and training.

ISNA (and its predecessor the MSA) has taken Islamic work in North America a long way from where the FIA left off. The annual conference format organized by FIA has been continued by the MSA and now by ISNA in the form of an annual convention and four zonal conferences, in addition to various conferences organized by ISNA constituent organizations and other affiliates. Symposia on specific topics are also being organized. But while the gatherings of the FIA continued to be mainly social, serving as a kind of register of the visible presence of Islam and Muslims in America, the ISNA conventions function quite differently. ISNA affords the intellectually curious an opportunity to hear and interact with eminent Muslim scholars and leaders from North America and from the Muslim world and gives businesspeople a forum in which to exhibit their goods and services and discuss business together, as well as continuing to provide a time for social meeting and exchange.

But the real difference ISNA has made in the nature of Islamic work is its assumption of a firm ideological structure and Islamic commitment. It also moved to set up grassroots organizations and to provide needed service institutions such as the following: Speaker's Bureau, Film Loan, Schooling and Educational Workshops, Library Assistance Program, Conference Facility, The Housing Cooperation, Muslim Cooperative Projects, Shahada Certificate, Islamic Marriage Certificate, ISNA Zakat Fund, Islamic Correspondence Course, Information for Prison Bureaucracy, Islamic Da'wa Literature, American Trust Publications, Islamic Book Service, Audio-Visual Center, Electronic Data Processing, Islamic Centers Division, AMANA Mutual Fund Trust. Some current Islamic periodicals include *Islamic Horizons, Al-Ittihad, American Journal of Islamic Studies, The Muslim Scientist,* and *The Journal of IMA.*

Many functional committees are involved in various aspects of Islamic work in America, and various national organizations such as the Muslim Youth of North America (MYNA), Malaysian Islamic Study Group (MISG), and the Muslim Arab Youth Association (MAYA) came to foster the ends of ISNA.

ISNA is considered to be *the* national Muslim organization and generally represents the Islamic mainstream. Though many American-born Muslims have joined its ranks, it continues to be seen by many as an immigrant organization. America Muslims generally maintain their own community organizations.

American Muslim Mission

Despite the radical changes that have certainly affected its structure and popularity, the American Muslim Mission (AMM) remains the largest and by far the best organized indigeneous Muslim community. Historically the Nation of Islam, predecessor of the AMM, incorporated the tradition of both the Moorish Science Temple established by Noble Drew Ali and the International Negro Improvement Movement of Marcus Garvey. Ali (formerly known as Timothy Drew) was born in New Jersey, where in 1913 he founded the Moorish Science Temple in Newark. He emphasized the identity of the American Negroes, calling them "Asiatic" and "Moorish" and giving them a nominal kind of Islamic faith. He inculcated in his followers a sense of confidence and pride. He stated that Islam is the religion of the Moors and the Asiatics while Christianity is the religion of the whites.[4] Garvey on the other hand advocated the improvement of Negro social conditions and initiated the "back to Africa" movement.

Elijah Muhammad (born Elijah Poole) was basically influenced by these two movements, although he attributed his teachings to a mysterious personage called Fard Muhammad. Understanding Fard to be in some sense a god figure, he interpreted his own role as that of messenger. In doing so he used the Christian concept of God incarnate, who appeared in the form of a man to recruit disciples and messengers.[5] This, of course, gave a charismatic flavor to his leadership and added a supernatural dimension. Other Muslim organizations have tended to be egalitarian in nature and composition, but the Nation's structure was hierarchic and its leadership strongly centralized. The imam (whether at the local or the national level) provided an authority that helped hold the community together and give it direction. Elijah Muhammad did succeed in building a very strong organization.[6] His success was manifested in five areas:

1. Strong charismatic and centralized leadership commanded the loyalty and obedience of the grassroots.
2. A superbly organized militia, the Fruit of Islam (FOI), composed of militant former servicemen, was created. FOI was charged with the duty of protecting the community, the mosques, and other institutions. It was accused of many infamous doings, including the assassination of Malcolm X. Its various units were headed by "captains" and central leadership was in the hands of the national captain, Captain Raymond Sharif, Elijah Muhammad's own son-in-law.
3. The business organization comprised, among other things, a bank, a fishing company, and a chain of restaurants.
4. The educational institutions named universities of Islam (now renamed Sister Clara Muhammad Schools) ran and continue to run a highly disciplined system of education.
5. The national network of temples (some opened in the West Indies) that, unlike other Muslim mosques, are very well organized under the direction of their ministers in terms of membership and multipurpose functions.

The death of Elijah Muhammad in 1975 and the ascent of his son Warith Deen Muhammad to leadership brought dramatic change. At an earlier stage Warith Deen had been expelled from the movement. In the meantime he kept in close contact with the immigrant Muslims. Despite differences of opinion with his father, however, Warith Deen was Elijah Muhammad's favorite son. On his deathbed Elijah Muhammad called his son in, rehabilitated him, and made him his successor. Imam Warith Deen worked systematically to transform the Nation of Islam into a mainstream Muslim community.[7] In 1976 Warith Deen Muhammad declared that his father was not a prophet and consequently started to replace the theology of the Nation with orthodox Islam. The organization was renamed the World Community of Al-Islam in the West and the black people were called Bilalians after the African companion of the Prophet Muhammad of Arabia. The community mouthpiece *Muhammad Speaks* was renamed the *Bilalian News*. Temples became mosques, ministers became imams, and the Islamic rituals began to be observed. In 1980 the name of the organization was changed again to the American Muslim Mission, and its paper to *The American Muslim Journal* and later to *The Muslim Journal*.

The leadership ceased preaching racial hatred that identified the white man as the devil, relaxed strict discipline, and disbanded the FOI. This did not please the old guard, and many separated under the leadership of Minister Louis Farakhan, retaining the old name, teachings, and form of organization. But Imam Warith Deen continued his plans. In 1985 he decentralized the organization and minimized the authority of the National Council of Imams, distancing himself from the daily affairs of the organization and delegating most of the central responsibilities to the local imams. He instructed his local mosques to integrate themselves into the larger Muslim community.

Imam Warith Deen Muhammad finally succeeded in transforming his father's organization into a mainstream Muslim group acceptable to the Muslim world. Thus, he became an acknowledged leader among the Muslims of America and the international Islamic community, but not without a high price. The Nation's economic empire crumbled following several economic crises and membership dropped sharply as many believers, including some dynamic leaders, left the organization.

Darul Islam

Darul Islam has been the main and the largest indigenous Sunni organization in America, gaining membership rapidly during the sixties. In doctrine it was a typical mainstream movement, though in organization it was a novelty. The name was derived from the classical Muslim division of the world into the realm of Islam (*dar al-Islam*) and the realm of war (*dar al-harb*). Imam Yahya Abdul Karim was accepted as Amir al-Mu'mineen, leader of the faithful, ministries of defense, finance, education, external affairs, social services, mosques, and so forth, were established to provide services for the community. Darul Islam soon became a national organization with some twenty mosques in the New York area alone, and even crossed the border to Canada. Like many black movements of the sixties Darul Islam was a militant movement, with occasional outbreaks of violence.

In the early eighties a Pakistani Sufi shaikh named Jaylani arrived in New York and started teaching in one of the Darul Islam mosques. A few members gathered around him, and news of this shaikh's knowledge and miracles spread rapidly to the other mosques. People started migrating to the shaikh's lectures, and many stayed with him. The community leadership was gradually abandoned in favor of the more charismatic leadership of this "holy man." Eventually Imam Yahya was asked to concede leadership to the more knowledgeable Jaylani and the community fell apart. Those who favored the leadership of Shaikh Jaylani formed a new group, the Fuqara, with a strictly Sufi orientation. Others who stayed with the demoralized Imam Yahya soon disbanded and joined other organizations.

Ansarullah

The Ansar group, which originated in the turbulent years of the sixties, tried to accommodate black nationalism (racism), radicalism, and Islam in one stroke. The self-styled Imam Isa spoke about the world's first civilization, which the black man built in Africa on the banks of the Nile. He then became interested in the Nubians of southern Egypt and northern Sudan as the heirs of that black heritage. Inspired by the success of Elijah Muhammad, he set out to form his own group. Like Malcolm X he visited Mecca, and then went to the Sudan where he paid homage to Al-Mahdi's tomb in Umdurman, met with members of Al-Mahdi's family, and visited Aba Island, the stronghold of the Ansar sect. He took pictures of himself at all these places, and in Brooklyn showed photos of his reunion with his family in the Sudan, claiming to be a descendent of the great Mahdi, the African who defeated the armies of the British Empire. He started organizing young blacks who listened to the amazing reports of his trip and the fascinating history of their own kind. He taught them to dress in the traditional costumes of the Sudanese Ansar and built them a mosque styled after the spectacular tomb of the Mahdi. He changed his own name to Imam Isa Al Mahdi. Later, when the Sudanese Imam Al Hadi Al-Mahdi was killed in the Aba Island rebellion in 1969, Imam Isa again changed his to Assayid Al-Imam Isa Al-Hadi Al-Mahdi.[8] He claimed that Imam Al-Hadi had come to America long ago and married a black American woman, his mother, and then returned to the Sudan after he was born. When these stories reached the Sudan, the Al-Mahdi family were furious. Initially they investigated and decided to file a legal suit against Isa. But after further reflection Al-Sadiq Al-Mahdi, the political leader of the family, decided it would not hurt to have a following in America. In a later visit to the United States he accepted Imam Isa's invitation to his Brooklyn headquarters and, to the indignation of both Sudanese and American Muslims, conferred legitimacy on the organization. In the process, however, Sadiq drew the attention of his host to some of the objectionable doctrines he had been spreading, especially the use of the Bible in their prayers and rituals.

The Ansar emphasized the wearing of "Sunna,"—the long, loose white Sudanese garment and turban for men and a white Arabianlike garment for women with a veil covering the face. Learning Arabic was a high priority; members were instructed to speak only Arabic to their children, so they would grow up knowing the classical language. Music was highly appreciated and the community has its own band. Women have organized their own ballet troupes. The community life centers on the mosque, whose members are generally housekeepers, cooks, guards, teachers, or peddlers.

Imam Isa has always been conscious of the criticism of both the Sudanese Americans, who point out his fake claims of genealogy, and the orthodox Muslims in general, who question the soundness of his beliefs and teachings. He also became concerned that his followers might assimilate into mainstream Islam once they learned about it or came in contact with other Muslims. He

began presenting himself as a teacher rather than a political leader, introducing
new doctrines that would give his community a distinct character, and thus
protect it from criticisms and eventual assimilation. He renamed it the Nubian
Islamic Hebrew Association. The Star of David, flanked by the crescent,
became the emblem of the community and the Bible became a source of
religious teachings as authoritative as the Qur'an. Women's dress was modified
and face veils were abolished. Communal life was stressed, with a body of rules
for conduct. Members are now regimentally organized and devote their life to
serving the community.

Other Organizations

The sixties and early seventies saw the emergence of many organizations that
vanished with the disappearance of the radical wave. The Islamic Party of
Muzafaruddin Hamid, the Hanafi Muslims of Hammas Khalifa Abdul Khalis,
and the Federation of American Muslims all faded for various reasons. In
some cases the enthusiasm and emotional appeal that led many to join such
revolutionary organizations was not coupled with adequate Islamic knowledge, which led to ideological crises. In other cases the economic basis of the
organization, which was often the backbone of such groups, ruptured causing
the group to fall apart. And in many cases the radical sentiments of the sixties
which inspired the formation of some organizations waned, rendering them
irrelevant.

Islamic organizations in America, like the Muslim presence in general, did not
develop steadily. Islam first came to America very early (before Columbus,
with the slave trade and in the last century), but its arrival was in staggered
waves, each time fading before it was solidly grounded. Whenever the second
Muslim generation assumed the leadership and it seemed possible for Muslims
to be integrated into American society, a new wave of fresh immigrants
overtook the older wave. The Islamic presence was again a foreign presence of
first-generation immigrant Muslims. Even when large numbers of indigenous
Americans embraced Islam, they were unable to assume leadership of the
Islamic movement and even failed to integrate into it. Nor could the immigrant
Muslim merge into the growing indigenous Muslim community.

It is interesting to compare the growth and development of both indigenous
and immigrant Muslim organizations in North America. It was during the
second decade of this century that the early immigrants organized their first
mosques in 1919 (See Table 1.1). This appears to parallel the attempts of Noble
Drew Ali to organize the Moorish Science Temple. A decade later, while the
immigrant community engaged in the second wave of mosque building (Cedar
Rapids, 1934; Michigan City, 1932), the Nation of Islam was founded and
started building its Muslim temples. The fifties saw the founding of the
national FIA and the spread of the Nation of Islam across the nation. (Both
organizations have been charged by other groups with Islamic immaturity.) In

Table 1.1 Development of Muslim Organizations

Period	Local Immigrant Muslims	Local Indigenous Muslims	National Organizations
1919–29	Early immigrants' mosques	Moorish Science Temple	
1930–50	Second wave of mosques	Nation of Islam	
1950–60			Federation of Islamic Associations Nation of Islam established itself as a national organization.
1960–75	Muslim Student Association formed (new immigrants build new mosques)	New Muslim (Sunni) groups formed	
1975–85			World community of Al-Islam formed Islamic Society of North America formed American Muslim Mission urged by its leader to integrate into the larger Muslim community
1985			ISNA tries to reach out to local community organizations

the sixties the Muslim students started to organize outside the FIA. At the
same time what was known as the "Sunni groups" started to organize parallel
to the Nation of Islam. In the midseventies Warith Deen Muhammad effected
the transition of the Nation of Islam to orthodoxy. About the same time ISNA
was emerging in the immigrant sector, replacing the FIA and building on the
new and more Islamically developed communities.

Many argue that those things that have kept various groupings within the
Islamic community separated were at least partially removed, and the associations of persons who consider themselves American Muslims are coming closer
to a position of cooperation and commonality.

Notes

1. I have relied mainly on my firsthand information accumulated during my long
involvement with the Muslim communities and organizations across the continent.
However, two references I found useful and did consult are Yvonne Y. Haddad, *A
Century of Islam in America*, an occasional paper published by the American Institute
for Islamic Affairs (Washington, D.C.: Middle East Institute, 1986), and M. Y. Shawarbi, *Al-Islam in America* (Cairo: Lajnat Al-Bayan Al-Arabi, 1960).

2. For further information, see Sameer Y. Abraham and Nabeel Abraham, *Arabs in
the New World: Studies on Arab-American Communities* (Detroit: Wayne State Univer-
sity, 1983); Baha Abu Laban, *An Olive Branch on the Family Tree: The Arabs in Canada*
(Toronto: McClelan and Steward, 1980); Barbara C. Aswad, ed., *Arabic-Speaking Com-
munities in American Cities* (New York: Center for Migration Studies of New York, 1974);
Abdo A. Elkholy, *The Arab Moslems in the United States* (New Haven: College and
University Press, 1966); and Alixa Neff, *Becoming Americans: The Early Arab Immigrant
Experience* (Carbondale: Southern Illinois University Press, 1985).

3. See Umhau C. Wolf, "Muslims in the American Midwest," *The Muslim World*
50 (1960), 39–48.

4. E. E. Calverly, "Negro Muslims in Hartford," *The Muslim World* 55 (1965), 340–
45; A. H. Fauset, *Black Gods of the Metropolis* (Philadelphia: University of Pennsylvania Press, 1944); Frank T. Simpson, "The Moorish Science Temple and Its 'Koran,'"
The Muslim World 37 (1947), 56–61.

5. For the teachings of Elijah Muhammad, see his *Fall of America* (Chicago:
Muhammad Temple of Islam No. 2, 1973); *Message to the Black Man* (Chicago:
Muhammad Mosque of Islam No. 2, 1965); *The Supreme Wisdom: Solution to the So-
Called Negroes Problem* (Chicago: University of Islam, 1957).

6. For studies on the Nation of Islam, see E. U. Essien-Udom, *Black Nationalism*
(New York: Dell, 1962) and Eric C. Lincoln, *The Black Muslims in America* (Boston:
Beacon Press, 1961).

7. For the teachings of Warith Deen Muhammad, see As the Light Shineth from
the East (Chicago: WDM Publications, 1980); *Lectures of W. D. Muhammad* (Chicago: WDM Publications, 1978).

8. For the teachings of Isa Muhammad, see *The Message of the Messenger Is Right
and Exact* (Brooklyn, N.Y.: Isa Muhammad, 1979); *Racism in Islam* (Brooklyn, N.Y.:
Isa Muhammad, 1982); *What and Where Is Hell?* (Brooklyn, N.Y.: Isa Muhammad,
1980).

2

Estimate of Muslims
Living in America

Carol L. Stone

Islam is believed to be the fastest growing religion in the United States today, yet it is still unclear how many Muslims currently reside in America. Estimates of 1.2 million[1] to 3 million[2] have been reported. To date, no systematic, statistically valid survey of Muslims in America has been conducted. This is largely because of a lack of reliable information about Muslims in this country.

The study reported in this chapter was conducted to obtain a verifiable and rigorous estimate of the Muslim population in America today. The geographical concentrations of several ethnic groups within the United States were also examined, as well as trends in immigration to America.

Method of Estimation

The number of immigrant Muslims living in the United States in 1980 was estimated from three sets of data: (1) 1980 census statistics, categorized by country of ancestry;[3] (2) 1980 immigration statistics, categorized by country of origin;[4] and (3) estimates of the percentage of Muslim population in countries around the world.[5] The mathematical products of (3) and (1) plus (3) and (2) were evaluated from each country or ancestral region around the world. These products represented a 1980 estimate of the number of Muslims in the United States from a given country or region of ancestry, and the number of Muslims who immigrated to the United States in 1980 from that country, respectively. The sum of these two figures produced the 1980 estimated American population of immigrant Muslims from a given country.

The Bureau of Census has established a format by which countries of ancestry are grouped into a subset of continental regions[6] (Table 2.1). These groupings were used to estimate Muslim population within geographical regions by cumulating individual estimates from each country within the region. The bureau has also broken down census data by ancestry into geographical regions within the United States.[7] These statistics, together with the percentage

25

Table 2.1   Grouping of Countries into Continental Regions

Geographical Region	Countries in Region
East Europe	Albania, Bulgaria, Romania, Russia,[1] Slavic, Slovak, Slovene, Ukraine, Yugoslavia, Other
Sub-Sahara	Africa, Cape Verde, Ethiopia, Ghana, Nigeria, South Africa, Other
Asia	India, Cambodia, China, Philippines, Indonesia, Japan, Korea, Laos, Pakistan, Taiwan, Thailand, Vietnam, Other
Middle East/North Africa	Arabia, Armenia, Assyria, Israel, Egypt, Iraq, Iran, Jordan, Lebanon, Morocco, Palestine,[2] Saudi Arabia, Syria, Turkey, Other
Caribbean	Bahamas, Barbados, Bermuda, Brazil, Dominican Republic, Dutch West Indies, Guyana, Haiti, Jamaica, Trinidad, Virgin Islands, British West Indies, Other

Source: *Ancestry of the Population by State: 1980*, pp. 12–32.

[1] Ancestral countries or regions not reported by the Zwemer Institute were provided percentage of Muslim populations by assuming an average percentage over the entire region. This was performed for the following reported ancestries: Slavic, Slovak, Slovene, Ukraine, and other within East Europe; Arabia, Armenia, Assyria, and other within the Middle East/North Africa; Africa, Cape Verda, and other within the sub-Sahara; Cambodia in South East, Japan in East, and other in South, South East, and East Asia combined, excluding Iran; Bahamas, Bermuda, Brazil, Dominican Republic, Dutch West Indies, Haiti, Virgin Islands, British West Indies, and other within the Caribbean.

[2] Immigration statistics from Palestine do not exist after 1976, and the proportion of Muslims in Palestine is also excluded from the Zwemer Institute. These values were therefore assumed to be identical to those of Israel.

of Muslim population in countries around the world,[8] were used to construct estimates of Muslim populations in California, New York, and Illinois. Immigration trends were evaluated by the same technique, using immigration statistics by country of origin from 1956 to 1986 at three-year intervals,[9] and estimates of the percentage of Muslim populations in each of those countries.[10]

The 1986 projected estimate of Muslims in the United States was constructed from the 1980 estimate, accounting for immigration and assuming a variable birth rate of 15.5–15.9/1000.[11] Deaths and emigration were not included in the projection because Muslims in the United States represent first- or second-generation immigrants, and the number of deaths and emigrations are therefore believed to be insignificant.

Regions of Western Europe, the Pacific, and South and Central America were not included in the study because the Muslim populations within these areas are believed to be primarily the result of recent immigration from other Muslim-populated countries. The population of Caucasian Muslims indigenous to this country was considered insignificant and therefore also excluded from the estimate.[12]

Sources of Error

This study assumes that the proportion of Muslims in a given country is equal to the proportion of Muslims currently residing in the United States with ancestry from that country. This assumption represents the largest potential source of error. The proportions may vary considerably due to economic, political, or social factors. Muslim immigration may be either exaggerated or minimized for the same reason. This is particularly true for those years in which a very large proportion of Muslims or non-Muslims immigrated to the United States from a given country relative to the proportion of Muslims reported in that country. The percentage of Muslims living in any given country is itself an estimate, assumed constant over time, and may further contribute to error. All potential errors reported by the Bureau of Census are relevant to this study as well.[13]

Number of Muslims in America

Using immigration and census statistics from 1980, as described earlier, and an estimate of indigenous African–American Muslims,[14] the number of Muslims living in the United States in 1980 was estimated at 3.3 million (Table 2.2). This estimate represented 1.5% of the 1980 U.S. population. The number of Jews, reported at 5.9 million, represented 3% of the United States population, while those who identified themselves as Christians represented 55% of the population.[15] Collectively, these data suggest that Islam is a significant minority among American religions, ranking close to Judaism.

Table 2.2   Estimate of Muslims in the United States, 1980

Ancestry	Estimate (thousands)
East Europe	880
Middle East/North Africa	940
Sub-Sahara	94
Asian	380
Caribbean	13
African–American	1,000[1]
TOTAL	3,000

Total U.S. population (thousands): 227,000[2]
Proportion of Muslims in U.S.: 1.5%

Projected estimate to 1986 (thousands):

1980 estimate	3,300
Immigration (1981–86)	350
Births (1981–86)	380
TOTAL	4,000

[1]*Muslim Journal*, 7801 S. Cottage Grove, Chicago, Ill.

[2]*Statistical Abstract of the United States* (Washington, D.C.: Bureau of Census, Department of Commerce, 1987), p. 8.

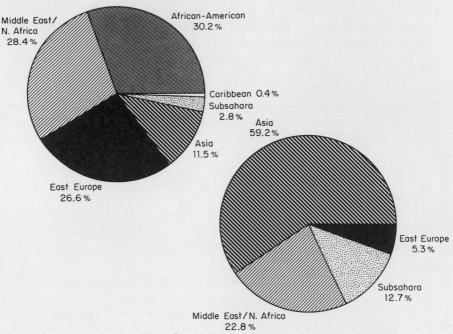

Note: Data calculated from "Muslim Population" (Report prepared for Zwemer Institute of Muslim Studies, Altadena, CA., 1987) p.1-14.

Fig. 2.1(a) Distribution of Muslims in America, 1980; (*b*) Distribution of world Muslims.

Indigenous African–American Muslims constituted over 30% of the Muslims living in America in 1980 (Fig. 2.1a). Another 28.4% were Muslims from the Middle East/North Africa, while East Europeans comprised 26.6% of Muslims in the United States. The remaining proportion of Muslims was composed predominantly of Asians (11.5%).

The proportion of Asian Muslims in the United States in 1980 (11.5%; see Fig. 1a) was relatively small compared to the number of Muslims recorded as living in Asia (59.2%; see Fig. 2.1b). Relative to the proportion of Muslims noted as residing in the Sub-Sahara and East Europe, a smaller proportion of Muslims from the Sub-Sahara and a larger proportion of Eastern Europeans lived in this country. More Middle East/North Africans and Asians immigrated to America in 1980 (Fig. 2.2), relative to the proportions residing in this country (Fig. 2.1a). Fewer East Europeans immigrated in 1980 (Figs. 2.1a and 2.2).

Starting with the 1980 estimate of Muslims in America, and cumulating Muslim immigrations and births from 1981 through 1986, the number of Muslims in 1986 was estimated at 4 million (Table 2.2). This represents an increase of 21% over the six-year period from 1981 to 1986. Assuming that this

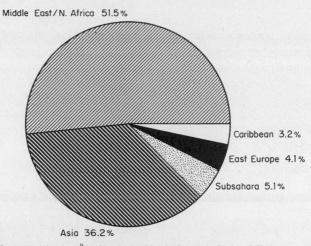

Middle East/N. Africa 51.5%

Caribbean 3.2%

East Europe 4.1%

Subsahara 5.1%

Asia 36.2%

Note: Data calculated from "Immigrants Admitted by Country or Region of Birth, 1954-1986" (report prepared for the Immigration and Naturalization Service, Department of Justice, Washington, D.C., 1987) p.1-14.

Fig. 2.2   Distribution of Muslim immigrants, 1980.

rate of increase remains constant for the next fourteen years, the number of Muslims in the United States by the year 2000 will have nearly doubled over the 1980 estimate.

Geographical Concentration of Muslims Within the United States

Census statistics from 1980 were used to estimate the regional concentrations of Muslims living in America in 1980. Three states with high immigrant populations were selected for the study: California, New York, and Illinois.[16]

The results of the study indicate that California contained the most Muslims in 1980, with more than half a million in its population of 24 million[17] (Table 2.3). This state contained the largest number of Middle East/North African Muslims of any state in the country, and Muslims from this continental region constituted the largest group of Muslims in the state. Nineteen percent of the Middle East/North African Muslims were Iranian, the largest concentration of Iranians in the United States.

Four hundred thousand Muslims resided in New York in 1980 (Table 2.3), comprising 2.3% of the state's total resident population.[18] A nearly equal proportion of East European and Middle East/North African Muslims resided in New York state, with African-American Muslims being the next largest group. Of the forty-five thousand Asian Muslims who lived in the state in 1980, 26% were from Pakistan or India. More than 56% of all Caribbean Muslims lived in New York.

The state of Illinois contained one hundred and seventy thousand Muslims in 1980 (Table 2.3). East European, Middle Eastern/North African, and African–American Muslims were equally represented in this state. A smaller number of Asian Muslims chose this state for residence, accounting for only 11% of the Muslim population in Illinois.

Thus, more than one-third of the population of Muslims living in the United States in 1980 was concentrated in California, New York, and Illinois combined (Table 2.3). Almost 62% of Asian Muslims resided in these three states, and almost 35% of East European Muslims. No other state in the country contained such large concentrations of Muslims.

Immigration from Muslim-Populated Areas

Immigration trends among Muslims were estimated as a function of time, to evaluate periodic concentration shifts in Muslim immigration. In some countries of Asia and the Middle East/North Africa concentrations of Muslims are

Table 2.3 Concentration of Muslims in Selected States, 1980

State	Ancestry	Number (thousands)
California	East Europe	95
	Middle East/North Africa	220
	Asia[a]	170
	Sub-Sahara	9.5
	African–American[b]	58
	Caribbean	0.5
	Total	550
New York	East Europe	160
	Middle East/North Africa	120
	Asia	45
	Sub-Sahara	14
	African–American	59
	Caribbean	6.7
	Total	400
Illinois	East Europe	50
	Middle East/North Africa	44
	Asia	18
	Sub-Sahara	4.4
	African–American	53
	Caribbean	0.2
	Total	170

[a]The large number of Chinese relative to other Asian countries may have exaggerated this value.

[b]An estimate of the African–American population within the United States was obtained from reported census values in *Ancestry of the Population: 1980*, pp. 31–33; the proportion of African–American Muslims among all African–Americans was calculated from the estimate of 26 million African–Americans, in *Statistical Abstracts*, p. 17.

relatively high while in others, such as India, Egypt, and Lebanon, the proportions of Muslims are smaller (12%, 82%, and 67%, respectively).[19] Evaluating the immigration trends of Muslims from those countries with a smaller concentration of Muslims may lead to misinterpretation, because the proportion of Muslim immigrants in relation to non-Muslims may vary significantly with time. Countries with predominantly Muslim populations may be examined, however, and the data viewed as immigration trends of Muslims from that country. This was done using statistics from Pakistani and Afghani immigrants within Asia (97% and 99% Muslim, respectively).[20] Turkish Muslims from the Middle East/North Africa (99.5% Muslims[21]) were also evaluated for periodic trends. North African Muslims were considered, with a collective Muslim population in Algeria, Egypt, Libya, Morocco, and Tunisia of 91%.[22] Iranian Muslim immigration trends were also evaluated (98% Muslim).[23,24]

Total Muslim Immigration

Relative to the total number of immigrants entering the United States, the number of Muslim immigrants has more than doubled over the last two decades, increasing from 4% of all immigrants in 1968 to 10.5% in 1986.[25] Whereas Asian and Middle Eastern/North African Muslims collectively represent 82% of the world Muslim population (Fig. 2.1B), Muslims immigrating from Asian and Middle Eastern/North African countries together now account for nearly all Muslim immigrants (Fig. 2.3). Only a very small number of Muslims from the Sub-Sahara, East Europe, and other continental regions are

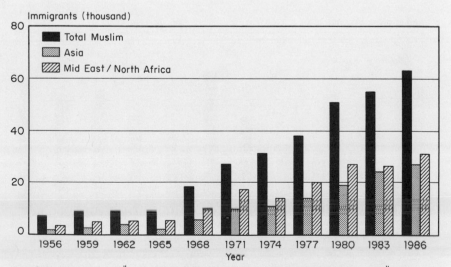

Note: Data calculated from "Immigrants Admitted by Country or Region of Birth, 1954-1986" 1-14.

Fig. 2.3   Muslim immigration trends to America.

now entering the United States. The numbers of Muslims immigrating to the United States from Asian and from Middle Eastern/North African regions (Fig. 2.3) are almost equal.

Asia: Pakistan and Afghanistan

Entrance of Pakistani immigrants to the United States has increased steadily over the last two decades, the number increasing almost ninefold since 1968 (Fig. 2.4). The steady increase in immigration from Pakistan began in the late 1960s. At present, nearly 6000 Pakistanis immigrate to this country annually. Immigration from Afghanistan has increased from 138 and 1977 to over 2800 in 1986. The dramatic increase in the number of Afghani immigrants in the 1980s coincides with the Soviet invasion of that country in 1979. While Pakistan and Afghanistan combined accounted for only 8% of Muslim immigrants from Asia in 1956 (Figs. 2.3 and 2.4), immigrants from these two countries now account for almost one-third of all Asian Muslim immigrants.

Middle East/North Africa: Turkey, North Africa, Iran

Although immigration from Turkey has fluctuated over the years, the number of immigrants has roughly doubled, reaching a peak in the early 1980s (Fig. 2.5). Immigrants from Turkey once accounted for nearly 24% of all those

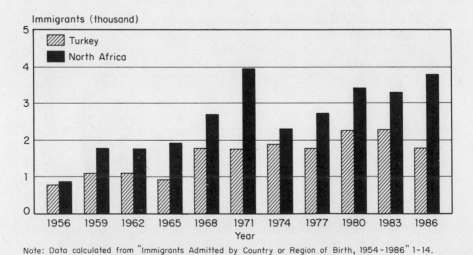

Note: Data calculated from "Immigrants Admitted by Country or Region of Birth, 1954-1986" 1-14.

Fig. 2.4 Middle East/North African Muslim immigration trends to America.

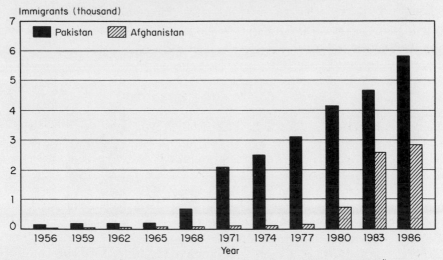

Note: Data calculated from "Immigrants Admitted by Country or Region of Birth, 1954-1986" 1-14.

Fig. 2.5 Asian Muslim immigration trends to the United States.

from the Middle East/North African region, but they now account for less than 6% of that group (Figs. 2.3 and 2.5).

From the North African countries, Muslim immigration increased strongly in the 1960s, peaked in numbers during the early 1970s, and then dropped suddenly in the mid 1970s (Fig. 2.5). The number of immigrants from this region rose thereafter to the current level of almost four thousand Muslim immigrants annually. Although Muslim immigrants from North Africa once accounted for more than 26% of Middle Eastern/North African immigrants (Figs. 2.3 and 2.5), the contribution has diminished over the years to 12%. The collective contribution of North Africa and Turkey to Muslim immigrants from Middle Eastern/North African nations has decreased from 50% in 1956 to under 18% in 1986 (Figs. 2.3 and 2.5), yet the number of Muslim immigrants from the entire Middle Eastern/North African region has increased, particularly in the last decade.

Of all the Middle Eastern/North African countries, only Iran has experienced a sharp and dramatic increase in immigration during this past decade (Fig. 2.6), and now alone accounts for 52% of Middle Eastern/North African Muslim immigrants (Figs. 2.3 and 2.6). One-fourth of all Muslim immigrants, from around the world, are Iranians (Figs. 2.3 and 2.6), outnumbering immigrants from all other Muslim-populated countries. Immigration from Turkey, North Africa, and Iran combined now accounts for 70% of all Muslim immigrants from the Middle Eastern/North African region (Figs. 2.3, 2.5, and 2.6).

Muslims living in the United States are entitled to the rights and privileges afforded all Americans. Given their increasing numbers within our country

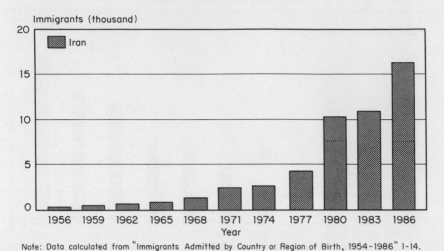

Fig. 2.6   Iranian Muslim immigration trends to America.

during the last three decades to a present population of perhaps 4 million, this religious and diverse ethnic minority has special needs that must be addressed. This is particularly true in the states of California, New York, and Illinois, where proportionately high numbers of Muslims reside.

The ethnic concentrations of Muslims vary considerably among the three states most populated with Muslims. Muslims in California are largely from the Middle East/North Africa and Asia, while Muslims in New York come predominantly from East Europe and Middle East/North Africa. Muslims in Illinois are equally East European, Middle Eastern/North African, and African-American. This variation in concentrations suggests that the potential base of political power among Muslims is also variable. Because ethnic groups are closely tied to distinct cultures and ways of thinking, Muslims are represented in radically different ways to the communities as well as to the politicians within their area.

Ethnic concentrations of Muslims vary from state to state, and the ethnic immigration patterns have also remained dynamic. In the past, Muslim immigrants from the Middle East/North Africa outnumbered those from all other geographical regions, but more recently the relative concentration has shifted, with more Muslims coming from Asia than any other region. Immigrant Muslims now come mainly from Iran and Pakistan.

The estimates reported in this study, as in any study of this kind, are subject to significant error. Because of the growing number of Muslims within our borders, it is important to obtain an estimate through other means, particularly census studies. With these studies, social and educational programs can be assured of reaching larger numbers of Muslims.

Notes

1. M. Arif Ghayur, "Muslims in the United States: Settlers and Visitors," *Annals AAPPS* 454 (March 1981): 153.

2. A figure of 3 million has been reported by the Zwemer Institute in Altadena, California, and Zaman in a report by Yvonne Haddad and Adair T. Lummis, "Islamic Values in the United States: A Comprehensive Study," unpublished paper, p. 1.

3. *Ancestry of the Population by the State*: 1980 (Washington, D.C.: Bureau of Census, Department of Commerce, 1983), pp. 12–32.

4. "Immigrants admitted by Country or Region of Birth, 1954–1986" (report prepared for the Immigration and Naturalization Service, Department of Justice, Washington, D.C., 1987), pp. 1–14.

5. "Muslim Population" (report prepared for Zwemer Institute of Muslim Studies, Altadena, Calif., 1987), pp. 1–4. Percentages reported here are similar to estimates reported in an independent publication, in Colin McEvedy and Richard Jones, *Atlas of World Population History* (New York: Facts on File, 1978). Data for China were a notable exception, where the Zwemer Institute reported 4%, and McEvedy and Jones reported 30% Muslim. An average value of 17.7% was chosen for the study, a value very similar to the average percentage of Muslim population in Asia.

6. *Ancestry of the Population by State*: 1980, pp. 12–32.

7. Ibid.

8. "Muslim Population," pp. 1–4.

9. "Immigrants admitted by Country or Region of Birth, 1954–1986," pp. 1–14.

10. "Muslim Population," pp. 1–14.

11. *Statistical Abstract of the United States* (Washington, D.C.: Bureau of Census, Department of Commerce, 1987), p. 59.

12. Ghayur provides an estimate of 40,000 Anglican–American Muslims in "Muslims in the United States: Settlers and Visitors," *Annals AAPPS* 454 (March 1981): p. 153.

13. *Ancestry of the Population by State*: 1980, pp. 77–78.

14. Muslim Journal, 7801 S. Cottage Grove, Chicago, Ill. (telephone interview, January 1989). Sr. Aisha Mustafa, editor of the journal, emphasizes that the estimate of one million represents an average of all African–American Muslims, both unaffiliated and affiliated.

15. *Statistical Abstract of the United States*, p. 52.

16. Estimates of geographical concentration may be exaggerated or minimized by large concentrations of Muslims or non-Muslims relative to the proportion of Muslims from that ancestral country.

17. *Statistical Abstract of the United States*, p. 20.

18. Ibid.

19. "Muslim Population," pp. 1–2.

20. Ibid., p. 2.

21. Ibid.

22. Ibid., p. 1. The relatively large number of Egyptian immigrants deflated the overall proportion of Muslim immigration to 87% in 1986 and may have led to exaggerated estimates during this time period.

23. Ibid., p. 2.

24. The proportion of Muslim immigrants from these countries may have deviated with time from the proportion of Muslims reported to reside in the countries. This would lead to exaggerated or diminished estimates.

25. The number of immigrants admitted to the United States was 454,448 in 1968 and 601,708 in 1986, as reported in "Immigrants Admitted by Country or Region of Birth: 1954–1986," pp. 6, 1, respectively.

References

Ancestry of the Population by State: 1980. Washington, D.C.: Bureau of Census, Department of Commerce, 1983.

McEvedy, Colin and Richard Jones. *Atlas of World Population History*. New York: Facts on File, 1978.

Ghayur, M. Arid. "Muslims in the United States: Settlers and Visitors." *Annals, AAPPS* 454 (1981): 150–163.

"Islamic Values in the United States: A Comprehensive Study." Report prepared by Yvonne Haddad and Adair T. Lummis. University of Massachusetts. Unpublished.

"Immigrants Admitted by Country or Region of Birth: 1954–1986." Report prepared for the Immigration and Naturalization Service, Department of Justice. Washington, D.C., 1987.

"Muslim Population." Report prepared for Zwemer Institute of Muslim Studies. Altadena, Calif., 1987.

Statistical Abstract of the United States. Washington D.C.: Bureau of Census, Department of Commerce, 1987.

II

PERCEPTIONS OF MUSLIMS
IN THE UNITED STATES

3

Perspectives of American Churches on Islam and the Muslim Community in North America: An Analysis of Some Official and Unofficial Statements

Byron L. Haines

The Palestinian–Israeli conflict, the oil crisis of 1973–1974, and Khomeini's Iran are situations that awakened the American people to the reality and importance of the Arab world and the religion of Islam. The perception of this reality has been enhanced by reports of events in our media, a force still shaping and informing the attitudes and opinions that most American people have about Arabs, Muslims, and Islam. The American Christian church and its members are no exception to this continuing process of attitude formation. However, there are portents of change in the stances of the American churches toward Islam, the Muslim world, and the American Muslim community. The aim of this chapter is to explore the nature of those changes and to suggest their impact on the kinds of relationships that develop between the American churches and the Muslim community in America. For this purpose, a number of documents published in recent years by American churches or by agencies representing a substantial number of Christians are analyzed.

A few initial observations are helpful in understanding this analysis. Although a substantial bibliography of writings on Christian–Muslim relations exists, very little has been done as yet on attitudes and interactions in the American context.[1] American church organizations, within their respective consultative processes, have only recently begun to reflect seriously on the interfaith character of the North American scene.

Further reflection by American churches on Islam and the Muslim community in America has not been self-generated. It has been forced on churches by changes taking place in the world, especially since World War II. In addition to the economic and political events mentioned here, the growing size of the Muslim community in North America has attracted the attention of American churches, especially given the importance of size in the American society as determinants of worth and value. As Yvonne Haddad has pointed out, the

American Muslim community—with approximately 3 million adherents—is now larger than the membership of the Episcopal Church. Representative of a much larger, worldwide community of 900 million members, it deserves increased attention from American churches.[2]

Finally, the interest of the American churches in the Muslim community is informed and shaped by their much longer association with other religious traditions through their overseas missions. The positions that have been taken, the manner in which issues are being discussed, and the programs and activities that are either in operation or being envisaged are all affected by the theological stances churches have taken in their claims for the truth of the Christian message and their understandings of their mission as Christian institutions. Therefore, even though the interest of the American Church in the American Muslim community is of rather late origin, how churches now are beginning to respond to its presence builds on the long history of theological reflection and praxis of churches engaged in mission or functioning in close association with people of other religious communities.

Categories of Response

The data on the responses to the presence of the Muslim community in America is sparse, but an analysis of what is available suggests at least three categories into which they can be grouped. For a given church the line between categories may not always be sharp, with the result that the character of the official statement is more tenuous than dogmatism generally allows. The categories, which will not surprise anyone familiar with movements within the American churches, are defined in terms of the general attitudes and emphases of more or less official and representative documents.

Our Common Life Together

The first category of responses is characterized by acceptance of the Muslim community as a legitimate part of the American religious scene. The religious beliefs and values of Islam are respected and the members of the church are called upon to associate with the Muslim community in the same way they associate with other religious communities and bodies, even other Christian bodies. Such a response does not ignore the significance of differences in religious beliefs and practices. Rather it seeks, through interfaith relations and the fostering of cooperative endeavors, to develop a common life in which all can share equally, where religious identity is not blurred by syncretism or a superficial romanticism about similarities, and within which all can be faithful to their particular religious calling. Central to this position is the role of dialogue as a means by which people of different religious traditions can live and work together.

The clearest and most recent articulation of this response is the policy statement of the Presbyterian Church (U.S.A.), enacted by its General Assembly in June of 1987.[3] This statement calls the attention of the Presbyterian Church to the presence of the Muslim community; it establishes policy that will lead local congregations and individual Presbyterians to a better understanding of Islam as a religion and of Muslims as a people who, like Christians (and the Christian church), are a witness to God's lordship over this world. The statement both encourages understanding and urges Christians to cooperate with Muslim organizations and peoples here in the United States, when appropriate, in seeking common solutions to issues of social justice and order within the American society and elsewhere. It calls on Christians to revise their understanding of the Church's mission by concentrating on an examination of their own efforts to be faithful to God and by working for full religious freedom and equality of all people. Though this Presbyterian statement does not speak directly to some significant theological issues, it does seek to move the Church in a radically different direction from its past ways of dealing with Islam and Muslim peoples. To implement this policy, an interfaith office has been established and a study book for church members was published.[4]

The Presbyterian Church was not the first church agency in the United States to recognize the importance of the Muslim community in America. In 1977 the National Council of the Churches of Christ in the U.S.A. (NCCC)[5] established its Office on Christian–Muslim Relations.[6] This office has the specific responsibility to represent the NCCC to the Muslim community in the United States and, conversely, to encourage Christian agencies and groups to include Muslim representation whenever their programs and activities impinge on the concerns and interests of the Muslim community.[7] The primary assumption in this effort is that Christians and Muslims need to develop a common life together rather than reproduce in America the historical tragedies of past associations. In this context Muslim leaders serve as observers to the meetings of the Governing Board of the NCCC and to the meetings of the NCCC Committee on Christian–Muslim Relations, the body that oversees the Office on Christian–Muslim Relations. (The rationale for this office is outlined in the Middle East Policy Statement approved by the Governing Board of the NCCC in November 1980.[8]) The emphasis is on the importance of dialogue to interfaith relations and the necessity for people of faith to work together for common solutions to the problems of injustice and inequality within our societies.

The positions of the two aforementioned church groups are deeply indebted to the work of the dialogue program of the World Council of Churches (WCC)[9] and to the Roman Catholic Vatican II statement which in 1965 defined the relationships between the Roman Catholic Church and people of other religious faiths, with specific reference to Islam and the Muslim community, in the section commonly referred to as "Nostra Aetate."[10] The document declared the Roman Catholic Church's esteem for Muslims because they worshiped the One God by seeking to submit completely to His will. The paragraph concludes with the following statement:

> Although in the course of the centuries many quarrels and hostilities have arisen between Christians and Muslims, this most sacred Synod urges all to

forget the past and to strive sincerely for mutual understanding. On behalf of all mankind, let them make common cause of safeguarding and fostering social justice, moral values, peace, and freedom.[11]

Though Nostra Aetate must be interpreted within the total context of Vatican II pronouncements, its position marked a major change in the attitudes and approaches of the Roman Catholic Church toward people of other faiths. Its openness as well as the recognition of the growing presence and importance of other religious communities in America, and in particular the Muslim community, led the National Conference of Catholic Bishops of America (NCCB) in 1987 to establish a Secretariat for Interreligious Affairs.[12] This Secretariat will provide a major source of leadership to the Roman Catholic Church in its relationships with the Muslim community in America by seeking to implement the insights of Vatican II.[13] Since this church probably represents the majority of Christians in the United States, the significance of this new direction by the NCCB must not be underestimated. Through this office, the Muslim community will be able to communicate its concerns directly to the highest levels of the Roman Catholic Church.

The United Methodist Church has also taken action that acknowledges the growing religious pluralism of the Western world, as it seeks to work with people of other faith traditions through dialogue. In a resolution called "Guidelines for Interreligious Relationships: Called to Be Neighbors and Witnesses,"[14] dialogue is advocated as a way for Christians to be both neighbors and witnesses to people of other faiths. Without ignoring the question of Christian witness, the document makes a very strong affirmation about the meaning of neighbor:

Today our Lord's call to neighborliness (cf. Luke 10:27), includes the "strangers" of other faith who have moved into our towns and cities. It is not just that historical events have forced us together. The Christian faith itself impels us to love our neighbors of other faiths and to seek to live in contact and mutually beneficial relationships, in community with them.

What does it mean to be a neighbor? It means to meet other persons, to know them, to relate to them, to respect them, and to learn about their ways which may be quite different from our own. It means to create a sense of community in our neighborhoods, towns and cities and to make them places in which the unique customs of each group of people can be expressed and their values protected. It means to create social structures in which there is justice for all and in which everyone can participate in shaping their life together "in community." Each race or group of people is not only allowed to be who they are, their way of life is valued and given full expression. . . .

The vision of a "worldwide community of communities" commends itself to many Christians as a way of being together with persons of different faiths in a pluralistic world. That suggests that we United Methodist Christians, not just individually, but corporately, are called to be neighbors with communities of other faiths (Buddhist, Jewish, Muslim, Hindu, and others), and to work with them to create a human community, a set of relationships between people at once interdependent and free, in which there is love, mutual respect, and justice.[15]

This stance is to be implemented by the United Methodist Church through its General Commission on Christian Unity and Interreligious Concerns.[16] Thus, the United Methodist Church has given its official support to programs and processes that will help its membership live and work constructively with their Muslim neighbors in the United States.

Other churches could be placed in this category, not because they have taken official action concerning the Muslim community in the United States but because they have directly supported dialogue programs with the Muslim community in an effort to promote human solidarity within our society, in the interests of justice and peace. These churches are the United Church of Christ, the former Lutheran Church of America, and the American Baptist Church. Given the number of churches in the United States, very few fully support the presence of its Muslim community. They exist, however, and among them they represent a dominant point of view within the Christian church in America.

Victory for Christ

The second category of responses to the presence of Muslims in America consists of those Christian groups who view Islam and the Muslim community as an opportunity for making converts. This view is guided by their particular interpretation of Matthew 28:19, which calls on Christians to "make disciples of all nations." The interpretation is further reinforced by the historic claim of the church that the only valid revelation of God is that which God gave in Christ. All other religions, by definition, are in error. Justice and peace in human terms are not a matter of cooperation and understanding between people of different religions, but rather the result of the gift of salvation, which comes through belief in Christ. The primary reason for Christians to associate with Muslims is to convert them and save the world.

In groups of this category, references to Islam and the Muslim community vary a great deal. Some have been extremely negative, such as that of the large mission organization called World Vision, whose former president, Stanley Mooneyham, saw Islam as a Satanic influence in the world.[17] Such a position articulated by the president indicates that he was speaking on behalf of the group as a whole, and certainly of a majority of its members. The literature of the well-known Zwemer Institute (now called the Zwemer Institute of Islamic Studies), designed to foster evangelistic programs, often implied that the Muslim community in the United States was a threat to the Christian church. Though later literature from these organizations has eliminated polemic, their basic understanding of the significance of the Muslim community as a potential source of converts has remained the same. This opportunity for making converts must be seized because the Muslim community is growing and undertaking conversion of America to Islam.[18] From this perspective, there is very little concern for the problems that confront American Muslims, for taking seriously the theological challenges presented by the claims of Islam (except insofar as these challenges must be answered by rebuttal or apologetics), or for cooperative action within local communities.[19]

Still within this "conversion" category, though considerably more moderate, are the attempts by the Department of Interfaith Witness of the Southern Baptist Convention to address interfaith issues. This department publishes a substantial journal entitled *Beliefs of Other Kinds: A Guide to Interfaith Witness in the United States*,[20] which seeks to guide Southern Baptists in their witness to the variety of religious communities on their doorsteps. Though the overall emphasis is on making the kind of witness to Christ that will encourage conversion, some of its statements about interfaith witness show a remarkable appreciation of other religious communities not found in the literature of similar groups.[21]

For this category of church people the most important issue in their relationships with people of other faiths remains conversion.[22] This goal has been a dominant one for almost all Western Christians over the past one hundred and fifty years. Thus, its continuation in a more refined form is not surprising, although it is interesting to note the absence of polemics or apologetics in the available documents.

The Difficult Middle Way

A third group of churches and church organizations falls somewhere between the preceeding two categories; that is, between those who are trying to develop a new understanding of how they should relate to Muslim communities and those adhering as closely as possible to the theological conviction that supports the older missiological stance. Groups in this third category seem, on the one hand, to appreciate and participate in dialogue and its emphasis on reconciliation; yet on the other hand, they have not developed any new way of working with the problem of pluralism other than to proclaim an understanding of the Gospel by means of the older, traditional missiology. Many argue for the legitimacy of this middle way insofar as it represents a serious struggle to deal both with the societal issues that religious pluralism engenders and with the exclusive claims that all religions and their communities make for themselves against competing claims. The churches and agencies in this middle way are clearly pulled in two directions, and the resulting tension is often left unresolved.

The best example of this is the work of the Reformed Church of America (RCA) on a preliminary statement of that denomination's position with respect to Muslims and Islam.[23] The following quotes demonstrate this church's concern to work cooperatively with the Muslim community as a part of its witness:

> The church must repent of its part in fostering causes of estrangement, confrontation and violence. . . . With honest confession and repentance as a first step . . . , the church must labor at opening avenues and creating structures of reconciliation. That is the substantial beginning to a genuine Christian witness. . . . The Muslim community cannot be viewed at a dis-

tance by Christians. The church and the Muslim community are related by history and by God as an expression and application of the covenant and promise with Abraham. Islam, therefore, has its place in God's purpose in election and creation. The church has a bond, a relationship to affirm with Muslims. . . . The church's witness must be taken up with a firm commitment to peace. One essential aspect of Christian peace-making is the opening of the heart's home to sharing the nourishment of love and friendship on all levels of human interaction. The church is wrong to burden the Christian conscience with agony over the small number of Muslims who respond to the invitation to accept Christ. The Muslim-as-friend and as partner in deep human concerns is both regarding and appropriate; this relationship need not necessarily pass over into Muslim-as-convert and Christian communicant in order to be legitimate and satisfying.[24]

To those familiar with the intricacies of Christian theological formulation, the significance of this carefully worded statement will not be missed. The ordering of peace and reconciliation between human communities is affirmed, not for the sake of making converts, but because such effort is at the heart of genuine Christian witness. Conversion is "not necessarily" the end to which all means must be subjected because Islam and the Muslim community already have their place in God's covenant. Most of those who identify themselves with the first category discussed could make the same statement.

Yet other statements in this document clearly emphasize that all faithful witness speaks to the authority of Christ within all human relations. It is this that redeems the Muslims, whether they recognize it or not. Thus their conversion is accomplished. The document ends with these statements:

It is the Christian's profound privilege to be Christ-in-the-flesh and to communicate that personality in whatever form befits the circumstances of any particular relationship. Christians must pursue with fear and trembling (Phil. 2:12) the opportunity of exercising this privilege.

It is a bold statement but true and compelling, that Muslims (and others) who avail themselves of the Christian offering and receive the Christian into their hearts as friend, receive Christ and avail themselves of him. They eat and drink of that friendship and, through the faithfulness of their Christian friends, Christ is remembered in them.[25]

It is the last paragraph of the document that moves this RCA statement toward the second category, because ultimately all witness leads to a "redemption" in Christ. The words used to speak of how Muslims receive this redemption are not, however, traditional. The point is that these statements, taken together with the first set of quotes, suggest a position with respect to the Muslim community that falls somewhere between the first and second categories. Because the RCA has been involved with dialogue programs within the conciliar movement, this document outlines a theological rationale that makes that involvement possible. More than that, it encourages Muslim and Christian cooperation without ulterior motives. But it does so within the framework of a more traditional stance, defined with untraditional words.

A second document that by inference advocates a middle way for its members is that produced by the Division of Theological Studies of the Lutheran Council in the United States, a cooperative agency of the major American Lutheran churches. Entitled "Counsel for Lutherans with Respect to Interfaith Worship,"[26] the statement is remarkable for its assumption of the possibility of worship between Christians and people of other faiths. Rather than condemning this, the report seeks to define the assumptions that underlie interfaith worship and to advise Lutherans as to the theological and practical implications of entering into interfaith worship. The thrust of this advice is a strong word of caution insofar as true Christian worship is understood as a proclamation of the Gospel. To compromise this position makes Christian worship less than what it ought to be or places persons of other faith in a position that reflects negatively on their faith tradition. The tensions created by this dilemma cannot be resolved easily. Therefore, the document advises the following:

> When in Christian conscience one cannot join in interfaith worship out of personal convictions of faith or out of concern for causing offense to the faith of others, one should decline to join.[27]

This advice, by implication carries over into all associations that Christians have with Muslims. The statement therefore does not endorse interfaith activity without serious reservations.

The real concern of this document, then, is less with interfaith worship per se than with a definition of the assumptions that lie behind interfaith worship. The assumptions treat the theological issues central to Christians' concerns for the substance of their relations with people of other faiths. If these assumptions are in any way normative for Lutherans, however, there is substantial hope for the relationships of that communion with the Muslim community in the United States. Briefly, the assumptions it identifies are as follows:

> a. First, our common humanity invites people of different faiths to consider joint worship, for there is a general human condition which is shared among all people which bridges our differences. . . .
>
> b. Second, as a practical matter we note that worship can be carried on by people who do not share exactly identical convictions of faith. . . .
>
> c. Third, we do not claim that Christians possess a monopoly on the holy. . . .
>
> d. Fourth, if Christians worship with others who do not share their faith, it must not be assumed that the act of common worship somehow causes all those present to be embraced in a Christian context. . . .[28]

These statements convey on openness to Islam and to Muslim people in the U.S.A. that moves the church beyond the parochial attitudes of the past and allows for association in all areas of human experience. Since interfaith worship is the most sensitive and difficult of all human associations, the allowance for its possibility creates room for cooperation between Christians and Muslims in all areas of human experience, despite the difficulties imposed by theological convictions.[29] For this reason this Lutheran document in fact represents a fairly positive assessment of the faith and practice of people of other religious communities.[30]

Based on associations with a number of church leaders from the wide spectrum of Protestant churches, this writer believes the majority of the Protestant churches associated with the NCCC fall into this third category with respect to the Muslim community in the United States. This assumes that church leadership, to some extent, represents the constituency to which it is responsible. This assessment does not speak against the possibility of these churches working closely with the Muslim community. Rather, the existence of a middle way indicates the seriousness these churches accord to Christian–Muslim relations even though they have not resolved all the problems involved.

As was noted at the beginning of this discussion, the analysis given here is based on statements, documents, and actions of official church groups or of people within those groups who can be considered representative in some measure of the position of most of the group's members. The limited number of such statements indicates that American churches, in general, have yet to take seriously the issues created by a religiously plural society. However, beginnings have been made, and that in itself is important to the concerns of America's Muslim community. Further, since official positions to some extent are always enacted after the fact, one can assume the number of people in all these organizations who are concerned with religious pluralism is far greater than the limited amount of official data suggests. The participation of Christians in a wide variety of interfaith activities and organizations supports this assumption.[31]

The three categories described here are fairly self-evident and do not represent a new contribution to interfaith discussions. However, the analysis is intended as both documentation of where churches are in the discussion at present and an articulation of the issues involved. The need for human reconciliation between people who differ is essential to the establishment of justice, equality, and peace. This need makes it imperative for religious people to cooperate with all other members of the human society to find ways of working together. Reconciliation, however, is achieved not only by a resolution of social, cultural, economic, and political forces, but also by a religious belief that makes an exclusive claim on behalf of God. How is this reconciliation possible when each religious tradition insists its own position and belief is exclusively valid?

This analysis shows that the American churches have answered this question in one of three ways:

1. By responding to the human need for reconciliation and peace, a need common to both Christians and Muslims. In the process of this reconciliation, churches are seeking to reformulate, if not eliminate, ideas and programs that teach superiority and claim an exclusive possession of the truth or of the way of salvation.

2. By emphasizing a particular interpretation of a religious teaching as an absolute that exists apart from human experience (and is therefore unaffected by what human beings do or say), but at the same time claims to have within it the only power to remedy human need and suffering.
3. By seeking to affirm both the obligations and necessities imposed on Christians and Muslims by our common life together and the validity of the Christian witness as the only solution to our human problem, accepting the tensions created by the dual affirmations.

The divisions between these three positions are not, of course, rigid. Any given church can have considerable overlapping of stances. In some cases it may be more a matter of emphasis than of substance. Even that emphasis, however, is significant because it determines how a church or church group will respond to the Muslim community in America.

In looking at church documents and statements from a historical perspective, one observes a major change in how the groups considered discuss Islam and the Muslim world. Leaving motivation aside for the moment, we observe that these groups no longer make use of the kind of prejudicial rhetoric that characterized earlier writing about Islam. On the contrary, all demonstrate a more objective understanding of Islam and encourage their people to seek the friendship of Muslims.[32] One supposes that a desire to avoid the accusations of bigotry and prejudice lies behind this change. To the extent this is the case, there is hope that a fair treatment of Islam will encourage Christians to be more balanced in their understanding of Islam and the Muslim world and more open to associations with Muslims than they would otherwise have been.

At the same time one cannot ignore the fact that in a number of Christian circles the old patterns of polemics and misunderstanding are still practiced. As we noted earlier, even with those groups that now seek to speak more objectively about Islam, the basic purpose of this understanding is to equip Christians with tools to make converts more successfully. This purpose is supported by the rhetoric that the growth of the Muslim community in America and the *da'wa* (missionary) activities of some Muslim organizations pose a threat to the church and to the country's Christian character. Further, since Muslim countries are denying entrance to Western Christian missionaries, some feel that Christians so denied should take advantage of the Muslim presence in the United States, where freedom of religion permits proselytizing activity. These "conversion" activities are reinforced by the U.S. political and social scene and unfortunately continue to generate enmity when practiced by either Christians or Muslims.

Finally, the fact that a number of denominations and church groups affirm the right of the Muslim community to freely practice their religion in this country, encourage religious organizations to include Muslims and Muslim organizations in their membership, and seek to cooperate with Muslims and the Muslim community in the United States gives hope for the future. Though generally bound by a common loyalty to God's revelation in Christ, the Christian church in America is not monolithic in its attitude and motivation with respect to the country's Muslim community. Christian groups differ, and Muslims need to take these differences into consideration. Many Christian churches are seeking to affirm the presence of the Muslim community in America and to explore with this community the meaning of their common life together. Presumably, if the Muslim response to these efforts is positive, the results may benefit both communities and serve their common concern to implement the values which their belief enshrines in the American life.

Notes

1. See, for example, Earle Waugh et al., eds., *The Muslim Community in North America* (Edmonton, Alberta: The University of Alberta Press, 1983); Yvonne Haddad and Adair Lummis, *Islamic Values in the United States* (New York: Oxford University Press, 1987; and the bibliographic materials these works contain.

2. In a discussion on Muslims in America, Yvonne Haddad made that observation at Hartford Seminary as early as 1983.

3. The full report is published in *Presbyterian Church (U.S.A.): 1987 Minutes of the 199th General Assembly*, Part I, Journal (New York: Office of the Presbyterian Church [U.S.A.], 1987), Full Report on pp. 492–94, para. 31.307–31.329; Amendment on p. 84, para. IV.A.1.a. The author has received seventeen letters of appreciation for this policy statement from leaders of prominent Muslim organizations located in the United States and the Middle East.

4. The Interfaith Office was established in the spring of 1987. The study book is that prepared by Byron L. Haines and Frank L. Cooley, eds., *Christians and Muslims Together: An Exploration by Presbyterians* (Philadelphia: The Geneva Press, 1987).

5. This organization represents thirty-five Protestant denominations in the United States that wish to identify themselves with the ecumenical or conciliar movement.

6. This office is guided and supported by fourteen major denominations and church organizations, three of which are not members of the NCCC itself.

7. See the *Newsletter of the Task Force on Christian–Muslim Relations*, No. 2 (March 1978), pp. 1–2, which outlines the purposes of the office.

8. See the second section of this statement entitled "Relations with People of Other Faith." This section is also the rationale for the NCCC's Office on Christian–Jewish Relations.

9. The literature related to the dialogue program of the WCC is extensive, covering a period of some forty or fifty years. As a summary of WCC programs, which deal with dialogue between Christians and Muslims, see *Christians Meeting Muslims: WCC Papers on 10 Years of Christian–Muslim Dialogue* (Geneva: World Council of Churches, 1977).

10. The full statement of this section in English is given by Walter M. Abbott and Joseph Gallagher, *The Documents of Vatican II: With Notes and Comments by Catholic, Protestant, and Orthodox Authorities* (New York: Guild Press, 1966), pp. 660–68. The formal title of the section is "Declaration on the Relationship of the Church to Non-Christian Religions." Of special importance was the publication by the Secretariat for Non-Christians of the *Guidelines for a Dialogue Between Muslims and Christians* (Rome: Libreria Editrice Ancora, 1969), the first book of its kind by any Christian organization.

11. Abbott and Gallagher, *The Documents of Vatican II*, p. 663.

12. The National Conference of Catholic Bishops set a precedent for this action when it established its Secretariat for Catholic–Jewish Relations in 1965, as a direct result of Nostra Aetate. According to Eugene Fisher, its present executive, for some twenty to thirty years before this a number of people within the Roman Catholic Church had been fostering Christian–Jewish relations. These efforts provided a base for the implementation Nostra Aetate in the American Roman Catholic scene. Also, Nostra Aetate had an immediate impact on the textbooks used in parochial schools as pejorative and biased statements about both Jews and Muslims were removed and attempts were made to present an objective history of Christian relationships with those communities.

13. In his recent visit to the United States, the Pope directly supported the initiatives of the NCCB and the concerns of Vatican II, when he met in Los Angeles on September 16, 1987, with representatives of four major religious groups. In his address he stated: "to the Islamic community [in America and elsewhere] I share your belief that mankind owes its existence to the one, compassionate God who created heaven and earth. In a world in which God is denied or disobeyed, in a world that experiences so much suffering and is in need of God's mercy, let us strive together to be courageous bearers of hope." He then stressed the need for religious communities to draw together "in a common concern for man's earthly welfare, especially world peace. . . ." (See the full text of the Pope's remarks as reported by the *NC News Service* on September 17, 1987. This meeting was also reported by the *Los Angeles Times*, September 17, 1987.) See also the Vatican's statement on dialogue and witness entitled "The Attitude of the Church Toward the Followers of Other Religions" (*Bulletin of the Secretariat for Non-Christians*, 56 [1984], 117–41), which was approved by Pope John Paul II and made public on Pentecost, 1984.

14. *The Book of Resolutions of the United Methodist Church: 1980*, ed. United Methodist Communications (Nashville: The United Methodist Publishing House, 1980), pp. 114–25. This resolution was drafted by the General Commission on Christian Unity and Interreligious Concerns of the Board of Global Ministries of the United Methodist Church.

15. Ibid., pp. 115–16.

16. This commission was established in 1964 and since that time has guided the UMC in interfaith endeavor.

17. See W. Stanley Mooneyham, "Keynote Address," in *The Gospel and Islam: A 1978 Compendium*, ed. Don M. McCurry (Monrovia, Calif.: Missions Advanced Research and Communications Center, 1979), pp. 23–24, in which Mooneyham states: "personally, I find much room for encouragement and optimism [about the evangelistic task]. If there were no reason other than the defensive reaction engineered by Satan as he sees his Islamic stronghold threatened, that is abundant evidence for me that God is about to do something and the enemy knows it."

18. A recent appeal from the Samuel Zwemer Institute for support, dated September 28, 1987, begins with this sentence: "Did you know that Muslims in this country are mobilizing to make converts to Islam throughout this country?" Robert Douglas, the institute's new director, goes on to say that these efforts should not be viewed with alarm because of the religious freedom guaranteed in this country. However, he then states, "Do you know what excites me right now? It is the opportunity we have to reach Muslims for Christ here in the United States."

19. Some organizations, with the support of Christians in America, focus their efforts specifically on Muslims overseas. See, for example, the group called Frontiers, which at present has one hundred seventy missionaries in thirteen countries with

Muslim majorities. Because it has difficulty in obtaining missionary visas, "Frontiers—whose specific aim is to reach Muslims for Christ, often in hostile settings—has to explore other methods of getting missionaries into the countries without its workers resorting to 'tentmaking' (obtaining a secular job and doing missionary work after hours). It all adds up to unorthodox 'entry strategies' for some countries." See the article by William Alnor, "Is it really God's time to reach the Muslims," *National and International Religion Report* 2: 5 (March 14, 1988) 8. For a Muslim response to this work and the work of the Zwemer Institute, see the article by Steve Johnson, *"Christian Evangelists Attack Al-Islam," the Muslim Journal* 2: 34 (June 19, 1987) 1 and 29.

20. This special journal was published in 1984 by the Interfaith Witness Department, Southern Baptist Convention, Home Mission Board in Atlanta, Georgia, for use in local churches. One section on world religions contains brief descriptions of Judaism, Islam, Buddhism, Hinduism, and Sikhism. The descriptions of "Islam" (pp. 121–25) and the "American Black Muslims" (pp. 126–27) are presented fairly, without prejudice or misunderstanding. Interestingly enough, the interfaith witness represented in this magazine also speaks of relations between Southern Baptists and other Christian groups.

21. Because many authors contributed to this magazine, their statements about interfaith witness vary in their openness and sensitivity. See the sections "The Interfaith Witness" (pp. 10–15) and "Lessons in Interfaith" (p. 11), on one hand, and the section "The New Arena" (p. 12) on the other.

22. Often the literature produced by those who support this goal use the euphemism for "making converts" of "sharing the Gospel with a friend," making friendship and understanding a means to an end. See, for example, Ray Register, *Dialogue and Interfaith Witness with Muslims* (Kingsport, Tenn.: Moody Books, 1979).

23. See "The Muslim Community in a Christian Perspective," in *Perspectives*, January 1987, pp. 8–11. This article was prepared by the Theological Commission of the Reformed Church in America. It is a shortened version of a major paper presented to the RCA's General Synod in 1986. It is not yet "official," but it reflects accurately where the RCA stands at this time.

24. Ibid., p. 11.

25. Ibid.

26. This document was published by the Division of Theological Studies of the Lutheran Council in the U.S.A. in New York. It was prepared and adopted by the standing committee of the division in October 1986, as a report for discussion within the Lutheran churches. Of the member churches, only the Lutheran Church Missouri Synod cast a negative vote because, for that denomination, doctrinal agreement is a preriquisite for joint worship.

27. Ibid., p. 4.

28. Ibid., pp. 1–2. Note that the theological implications of the position taken in the fourth assumption are the opposite of those of the RCA position in the preceding quote on p. 17.

29. The implications for sharing in the common life are reinforced by other statements made about interfaith worship. For example, "the consequence of joint public worship is a legitimation as well as an affirmation of the integrity and authenticity of the other person's faith" (ibid., p. 3), and "joint public interfaith worship communicates common assumptions about mutual acceptance and a willingness to cooperate to a certain degree not only socially and politically but also religiously and theologically" (ibid.).

30. The Division for World Mission and Inter-Church Cooperation of the American Lutheran Church, which is now a part of the Evangelical Lutheran Church in

America, convened a task force in 1984 to study the theological significance of Christian witness among Muslim peoples. This study resulted in the publication of a collection of seven papers called: "God and Jesus: Theological Reflections for Christian–Muslim Dialogue" (Minneapolis: Division of World Mission and Inter-Church Cooperation, 1986). Because this document was prepared for study only, it represents a contribution to the discussion by the individual members of the task force. The statements of the contributors parallel the stance already indicated with respect to the LCA document on joint worship.

31. Many ecumenical councils and agencies, without taking any official position, have incorporated interfaith concerns into their agendas and are seeking to include Muslims within their memberships. The Buffalo Area Metropolitan Ministries of Buffalo, New York, and the Interfaith Conference of Washington, D.C., are two examples of this kind of work. The National Association of Ecumenical Officers now has an interfaith committee and includes an interfaith component in the agenda of its annual convention. The role the academic community has played in fostering, by means of academic study, teaching, and seminars, a better understanding of Islam and the Muslim community is extremely valuable. When these academics participate in the life of the American churches, they bring their interests into the life and thought of the church, making an important contribution.

32. As a recent example of how Islam is being discussed in more conservative Christian arenas, see the article by Terry Muck, "The Mosque Next Door," *Christianity Today* Feb. 17, 1988, pp. 15–20. Muck, however, sees the zeal of Muslims to propagate Islam as a reason for Christians to propagate their own faith more forcefully in the struggle to attract converts. One notes also a recent news item in *U.S. News & World Report*, March 14, 1988, which says that many of the 3000 evangelicals who attended their annual prayer breakfast in Washington in February 1988 were "upset" when Prince Bandar, the ambassador from Saudi Arabia, an invited speaker, quoted from the Qur'an. A leader of the National Association of the Evangelicals said that "The inside word is that this will not happen again. . . . The focus of the National Prayer Breakfast has always been on the Bible, reflecting America's historic background. That is the way it should be."

4

The Muslim as the "Other": Representation and Self-Image of the Muslims in North America

Abubaker Y. Al-Shingiety

The politics of representing Islam and Muslims in American cultural and political discourse and the Muslims' reponse to it in how they interpret Islam and identify themselves, reveal a dialectical relationship between Western representations of Muslims and Muslims' self-image. In this dynamic process, the "otherness" of Islam and Muslims has two functions. It acts as a dynamic of identification, by default, for the American. At the same time, it is appropriated by the Muslim as a form of self-identification. Both functions are germane to a mode of representation characteristic to a particular and dominant political and cultural discourse in the United States: a mode that is essentially ethnocentric.

Instances in which Muslims have broken off or started to break off this ethnocentric mode of representation show the same signs: abandonment of absolutism and racism as an ideology; a move toward a more "orthodox" interpretation of Islam as a comprehensive way of life; demystification of social forms of organization, cultural symbols, institutions, and practices; identification with a broader Islamic political and social reality, which extends beyond the boundaries of the American experience geographically and historically; and finally, recognition of the American context as the ground for self-identification in a way that is more complex and sophisticated than earlier separatist beliefs and practices.

I have chosen to focus on the experience of the Nation of Islam to illustrate this thesis for two primary reasons: First, it is the largest organization to succeed in generating mass appeal based on its claims to Islam and black nationalism. Second, the kinds of ideological, political, organizational, and other forms of symbolic transformations the Nation of Islam has witnessed since it was founded in the 1930s provide a paradigmatic case for the study of the dialectic of representation and self-image.

Representation and Self-Image: The Case of the Nation of Islam

One of the most revealing illustrations of the dialectic of representation and self-image is the Nation of Islam, a separatist movement that emerged out of the Depression of the 1930s in the United States and generated a significant following among African–Americans between the late 1950s and the mid-1970s. The Nation of Islam based its political and ideological appeal on its claims to Islam, black supremacy, and the unity of black people against the white man, for the purpose of establishing an independent geopolitical entity—a separate state—where black people could live freely and develop their human potential in social, economic, and political terms.

Elijah Muhammad, founder of the Nation of Islam and its spiritual leader, focused on the message of freedom as a prerequisite to development:

> We the black people here in America, we never have been free to find out what we really can do! We have the knowledge and experience to pool to do for ourselves! All our lives we have farmed—we can grow our own food. We can set up factories to manufacture our own necessities! We can build other kinds of businesses, to establish trade and commerce—and become independent as other civilized people are.[1]

Here Elijah Muhammad seems to propose a notion of freedom as equal opportunity to produce and enjoy the fruits of production, a notion that strongly reflects the influence of the American libertarian tradition in its emphasis on economic parameters to define human values. This emphasis on "economic freedom" is characteristic of the Nation of Islam as a social movement. For poor American blacks in the big city ghettos during the Depression, the promise of economic freedom and prosperity was a strong appeal and a major attraction to the Nation of Islam. In other statements, however, Elijah Muhammad clarifies his notion of freedom and sets prerequisites for it:

> The white man, he has filled you with a fear of him from ever since you were little black babies. So, over you is the greatest enemy a man can have—and that is fear. I know some of you are afraid to listen to the truth—you have been raised on fear and lies. But I am going to preach to you the truth until you are free of that fear.[2]

Elijah Muhammad here focuses on the theme of fear as a tool for domination and as a precondition for a productive and effective slave–master relationship. He then sets himself to the mission of developing the consciousness of the utility and effectiveness of this tool and the will to challenge that fear as prerequisites for freedom. This statement, moreover, shows the awareness that challenging fear is an important element in the process of knowledge that mediates otherness—embodied in the white man—and self-understanding. It is at once a disarming and an empowering act. It disarms the white man of one of his most effective weapons in his war to establish ultimate supremacy. At the same time, it is a victory for the black people over an evil force imposed by the white man to distance them from his world and subjugate them to his will.

Hence, the elimination of fear is an important step in breaking the ethnocentric dominative mode.

However, Elijah Muhammad knew well that there is more to self-understanding than eliminating fear. He focused heavily on the knowledge of history, of "true" names and "true" language:

> Your slavemaster, he brought you over here, and of your true past everything was destroyed. Today, you do not know your true language. What tribe are you from? You would not recognize your tribe's name if you heard it. You do not know nothing about your true culture. You do not even know your family's real name. You are wearing a white man's name! The white slavemaster, who hates you.[3]

Here the themes of ethnicity and lost identity come to the forefront as Elijah Muhammad tries what one might call ethnic therapy: the shocking recognition of a lost identity, which is perceived as true and honorable, is sharply contrasted with a new identity, which is viewed as false and shameful, one determined and imposed by the white man to serve his own interests. In this direct attempt to break the cycle of false identity and self-hatred, we can see the interplay of the two constituents of the dialectic of representation and self-image at an early stage in its evolution. Then Elijah makes the strategic double move of negating false identification and proposing a new name and identity:

> And he [the white man] told you only that which will benefit himself, and his own kind. He has taught you for his benefit, that you are a neutral, shiftless, helpless so called "Negro." I say "so-called" because you are not a "Negro." There is no such thing as a race of "Negros." You are members of the Asiatic nation, from the tribe of Shabazz![4]

Here we see the confirmation of ethnic difference as a means for self-identification. The negation of negritude as an identity is a rejection of the Western domination at its highest level of signification: ethnicity. However, ethnic difference became the form for self-identification in Elijah Muhammad's philosophy. There is also the recognition—and the rejection—of the image of the Negro as neutral, shiftless, and helpless, indicating the strong awareness of social and economic injustices as products of ethnic difference. The choice, or the discovery, of a "true" identity for black people as members of "an Asiatic nation from the tribe of Shabazz" constitutes the second strategic move in self-identification, the effective use of renaming as a strategy for tapping the oppositional force of ethnic difference. As a matter of fact, renaming became a key element in the process of conversion from a "Negro" status and state of mind to a member of the Nation of Islam. A new member of the organization was required to write a letter to "The Honorable Elijah Muhammad" requesting "retaining" his "original" name and discarding the slave name given to him by the white man. He was then given the last name of "X," though he could retain the first name.

The consciousness and establishment of ethnic difference as a psychological base for political mobilization and organization became more concrete as the

Nation of Islam expanded in the black ghettos of major American cities, gained a reputation of militancy and radicalism, and found itself confronted with a particular representation in the American media as a racist cult based on hatred of American society and the American way of life. Mike Wallace and Louis Lomax produced a television documentary about "the rise of Black Racism in America" telecast by WNTA-TV, New York on July 10, 1959. The documentary was called "The Hate that Hate Produced." In his autobiography, Malcolm X describes his experience with the highly publicized program:

> The title—The Hate that Hate Produced—was edited tightly into a kaleido-
> scope of shocker images . . . Mr. Muhammad, me and others speaking . . .
> strong-looking, set-faced black men, our fruit of Islam . . . white-scarved,
> white-gowned Muslim sisters of all ages . . . Muslims in our restaurants, and
> other businesses . . . Muslims and other black people entering and leaving
> our mosques. . . . Every phrase was edited to increase the shock mood. . . . In
> a way, the public reaction was like what happened back in the 1930s when
> Orson Wells frightened America with a radio program describing, as though
> it was actually happening, an invasion by "men from Mars.". . . In New York
> City, there was an instant avalanche of public reaction. Hundreds of thou-
> sands of New Yorkers, black and white, were exclaiming "Did you hear it?
> Did you see it? Preaching hate of white people!"[5]

What Malcolm X is describing here is the process through which a particular interpretation of social reality becomes, through the production and distribution of mass-mediated messages, a conventionalized social reality with serious political, economic, and social consequences. As a matter of fact, that CBS documentary marked the beginning of a media crackdown on the Nation of Islam. Reporters, feature writers, and columnists started a campaign of outrage against the Nation of Islam with such descriptions as "alarming," "hate-messangers," "threat to the good relations between the races," "black segregationists," "black supremacists," and the like.[6]

This form of representation of the Nation of Islam in the media reflects and perpetuates the dominant ethnocentric ideology within which the "races" relate to each other. The term "black supermacists" is a projection of the inherent absolutism onto the other, an absolutism that manifests itself in movements such as the Ku Klux Klan and infuses the culture at large with the moral and economic value of ethnic difference. It is significant that perhaps, for the first time since the demise of the Nazis in World War II, America found an absolute other in the Nation of Islam, more so than the mysterious communism of McCarthyites or the Soviet Union of the cold war.

The Nation of Islam was a threat, not so much to the moral foundation of American society—it was, in the final analysis, a product of American values, aspirations, and history—but to the dominant culture within that society. And the threat it posed was not material destruction; it was striving for prosperity and economic opportunity for black people in America. The threat of the Nation of Islam was its challenge to American social consciousness: its unveiling and deliberate use of the fundamental Western axiom of ethnic difference as the basis for negotiating social reality at a time when race relations were perceived by many as improving. Moreover, there was the cultural shock, the unsettling effect of experiencing the elevation of an oppressed ethnicity to a new cultural space for positive identification, economic opportunity, and fuller social and political expression.

The response of the Nation of Islam to the media offense against them after the broadcast of the CBS documentary was symbolized by Malcolm X's reactions to reporters calling him on the phone:

> When we Muslims had talked about "the devil white man" he had been relatively abstract, someone we Muslims rarely actually came into contact with, but now here was that devil-in-the-flesh on the phone—with all of his calculating, cold-eyed, self-righteous tricks and nerve and gall. . . ,[7]

We see here the will to represent the Other (the white man) as he sees the black Muslims, as the devil. This strategy is what Warith Deen Muhammad calls "reverse psychology."[8] It reverses the metaphysical, existential, and moral claims of the white man and the black man as well, thus changing the psychological basis for self-identification. Such reversal was thought of as a prerequisite to the reconstruction of the social and economic realities of black people.

However, there was more to the assertions Malcolm X was making than reverse psychology. The concept of "the devil-in-the-flesh" as a rhetorical form is an appropriation of a popular cultural code—the devil as the embodiment of evil, on the one hand, and the possibility of materialization of absolute value (in-the-flesh), on the other. It was this form of appropriation and internalization of the cultural codes of representation that provided Malcolm X with the momentary power to return the reporters' fire:

> The white man so guilty of white supremacy can't hide his guilt by trying to accuse The Honorable Elijah Muhammad of teaching black supremacy and hate! All Mr. Muhammad is doing is trying to uplift the black man's mentality and the black man's social and economic conditions in this country.[9]

It is speaking the language of your enemy: denying the negative principle of racism while in effect practicing it, appealing to a Western rationality that makes claims to social and economic equality of all the races "in this country" while advocating a separatist ideology based on ethnic difference. It is the totality of human experience, the unity of shared assumptions and values that determines the dialectical nature of this process. It is this unity and this dialectic that make the Nation of Islam a truly American movement.

Another example of the appropriation and internalization of the cultural codes of representation is Elijah Muhammad's theory about the origin of the white man. The theory says that the black man grafted the white man out of himself, and before all people on earth were black. In the genes of the black man, the theory goes, are two germs, one dominant, which is black, and the other recessive, which lacks that original blackness. A black scientist succeeded in separating the recessive from the dominant and mating the recessive with the recessive, creating a number of races that are lighter, weaker, and genetically inferior to the black man. The lowest of this order of races is the Caucasian.[10]

The significance of this theory is not its ethnocentrism; many explanations are similar in this regard. Its significance lies in the fact that it stands as a strong example of the appropriation and internalization of the cultural codes of representation. As a rhetorical form, the theory is an appropriation of Western scientific rationality. Its content is a negation of one of the fundamental premises of that rationality, namely, white supremacy, and an endorsement (or a validation?) of the negative principle (black supremacy). Thus, it stands as an important element—in form and content—in the dialectical process of representation and self-identification. Moreover, it points clearly to the logical necessity of viewing human experience as a totality and the logical outcome of recovering the unity that is the essence and the telos of human society.

Now comes the fundamental questions: Where does Islam lie within these sets of parameters or identifiers? What function does it satisfy or not satisfy for the Nation of Islam as a movement, particularly in comparison with black nationalism and Christianity as two significant components of the social reality of black people in America? And finally, what kinds of changes occurred in the status of Islam as an identifier during the transformation period of the mid-1970s and into the 1980s?

To answer these questions it is important to note that the Nation of Islam appropriated not only certain cultural codes of representation, but also some important dynamics of identification. Among those was the mystification of the organization, its leaders, activities, codes of behavior, forms of talk, uniforms, names of persons and places of worship, and finally economic autonomy and political ambiguity.

Islam, among those elements of mystification, best represents absolute otherness within American culture. It is a mysterious religion that is absolutely alien to American experience and history and that "belongs" to an equally mysterious and alien culture. At the same time, Islam, for the African–American, is the symbolic word or world for emancipation from American culture and history. It is this symbolic function of a liberative force that was fulfilled by Islam and that provided a new form for self-identification absolutely other than the traditional ones imposed on black people by the white man. Black nationalism was necessary, but not sufficient in the struggle for freedom and economic progress. Black nationalism, in the final analysis, is an American outgrowth. It lacks the mystery and the appeal of foreign imports but, nevertheless, has been central to the ideological and political appeal of the Nation of Islam to the majority of its followers. No wonder, then, that Islam as ideology and practice or a means of negotiating social reality was almost absent in the Nation of Islam. The belief system, with its material concept of God (Elijah Muhammad promoted the belief that Fard Muhammad, the founder of the organization, was God-in-the-flesh), and its open-ended notion of prophethood (Elijah Muhammad claimed to be the Messenger of God), was distorted. The organization did not stress the fulfillment or the practice of any of the five pillars of Islam. The Quran was present only as a symbol in their temples and was rarely opened or read. Instead, the "Ministers of Islam," while dismissing Christianity as a white conspiracy, depended heavily on the Bible for negotiating social action and understanding.

This pattern reveals the logical necessity for mystification of a rationality of Islam as myth. Christianity, black nationalism, and the American values of freedom and economic opportunity constitute the positive elements or the contextual determinants in the process of knowledge that mediates otherness and self-identification, whereas Islam constitutes the negative principle, the absolute value that cannot be negotiated from within or from without the organization. Therein lies the logical necessity for mystification.

The closure of this episode, isolated historically by the death of Elijah Muhammad in 1975, is a paradox—the paradox of being an American black Muslim. The Nation of Islam, on one hand, did not develop sufficient coherence within itself to avoid fragmentation. Neither did it develop a degree of coordination with the social realities around it to facilitate the achievement of its goals. Warith Deen Muhammad, son of Elijah Muhammad and his successor in the leadership of the organization, was excommunicated several times before the death of his father. Malcolm X, the spokesman of the organization and its chief minister, was excommunicated after he made certain remarks following the assassination of President John F. Kennedy, soon after starting his own organization and abandoning fundamental doctrines of the Nation of Islam.

The death of Elijah Muhammed in 1975 marked the end of an era of confusion for the Nation of Islam, manifested in the paradox of identity, of being an American black Muslim. This paradoxical situation resulted from the movement's adoption of the ideology and logic of its opponents, its appropriation and use of ethnic difference as an absolute value for self-identification, and its failure up to that moment to tap the positive and universal values of Islam as a religion and a way of life.

From Myth to Reason: The American Muslim Mission

During Elijah Muhammad's funeral, the young black leader Reverend Jesse Jackson, referred to the "resurrection" of the Prophet (that is Elijah Muhammad), but he was wrong. With his death, the legacy of Elijah Muhammad came to an end, and a new era in the history of the Nation of Islam marked by a new rationality and a new self image began. The succession of the father (the Messenger) by his son (the leader) was, in a sense, the symbolic birth of reason out of myth. Warith Deen Muhammad embarked on a gradual process of reconstructing the Nation of Islam and its doctrines, orientation, organization, symbols, and practices, not only to conform with the basic doctrines of Islam, but also to be a more coherent social movement and more coordinated with the other agencies in its social environment. He still spoke highly of his father "The Honorable Elijah Muhammad," but he demystified him along with the organization and its beliefs, symbols, and practices. The name of the movement was changed from the Nation of Islam to the World Community of Islam in the

West. Their centers became mosques instead of temples. The ministers of Islam became imams and they were called into a rigorous training program in Islamic education supervised by Imam Warith Deen Muhammad himself. The University of Islam, the movement's alternative to elementary and junior education for children, was renamed the Sister Clara Muhammad Schools. The discontinuity was a tribute to tradition, the emancipation from a paradoxical mode of discourse dominated by the myth of black supremacy to an age of reason characterized by dialogue with the other, and a new sense of identity that is both Islamic and American. What the son embarked on was the fulfillment of the prophecy of the father through the negation of his fundamental premise.

The social realities surrounding this process of change were complex. First, the decline of black nationalism in the 1970s detracted from the radical Nation of Islam's strong appeal during the 1960s. Second, Islam as ideology and a way of life was becoming better known internationally after many Muslim countries gained independence during the 1960s and started the quest for national development. Third, the movement itself became large enough by the mid-1970s to attract international attention, and it became imperative to identify with a broader Islamic political and social reality extending beyond the American experience, geographically and historically. The experience of hajj (pilgrimage to Macca), with its cosmopolitan effect, travel to Muslim countries to visit or study, relations with other Muslim movements, leaders, and governments all contributed to this process of identification with a broader Islamic experience.

However, this emancipation beyond the boundaries of the American experience was parallel to—and actually coincided with—the recognition of the American parameters for self-identification. The implications of this recognition were many: ideological in the abandonment of the earlier separatist beliefs and practices, symbolic in their popular name, "The American Muslim Mission," and the name of their newspaper, *The American Muslim Journal*, as well as in the presence of the American flag in most of their functions and even their mosques, and political in relations with American institutions in government and business.

The consequence of this process of change was the reconstitution of the Muslim self-image in America, the development of a new sense of identity, which could best be described as "the American Muslim." This new sense of identity "elevated" Muslims from the position of the absolute Other to minority status, from which they could negotiate their social reality or even define the whole cultural space from their position as a Muslim minority. The inherent tension in this new sense of identity lies in its contradictory nature, the seemingly unbridgeable gap between the Islamic claim to universality and the ethnocentric frame of reference inherent in minority status. Another dimension of the same tension is the status of the United States as a superpower with huge resources and strong claims to global leadership in moral, political, and economic terms. Such claims are hard to reconcile with by the American Muslim particularly from a frame of reference that puts the Muslim Umma (global Muslim community) above all national affiliations. This process of reconciliation would be even harder if the interests of the Umma were at odds with the perceived interests of the United States.

The implications of this tension in the process of representation and self-identification of Muslims in North America are too important to be left unobserved and unstudied, particularly from an Islamic viewpoint. Moreover, such implications call for the development of a general Islamic theory of representation, if our observations and criticism are to be Islamic. Such remains the task for future researchers and theorists.

Notes

1. Malcolm X, *The Autobiography of Malcolm X as Told to Alex Haley* (New York: Ballantine Books, 1964), p. 256.
2. Ibid., p. 253.
3. Ibid.
4. Ibid., p. 254.
5. Ibid., p. 238.
6. Ibid., p. 239.
7. Ibid., p. 240.
8. Warith Deen Muhammad, *An African American Genesis* (Chicago: Progressive Publishing Company, 1982), p. 10.
9. Malcolm X, *The Autobiography of Malcolm X*, p. 241.
10. The theory was outlined by Warith Deen Muhammad in a speech delivered before the American Academy of Religion, November 19, 1978, in New Orleans. The full text of the speech entitled "Evolution of the Nation of Islam" was published in Warith Deen Muhammad's book, *An African American Genesis*.

III

ISLAMIC THOUGHT
IN THE UNITED STATES

5

Ismail R. al-Faruqi:
Muslim Scholar-Activist

John L. Esposito

On May 24, 1986, the Muslim world and the academic community lost one of its most energetic, engaging, and active colleagues—Ismail al-Faruqi. I think he would be pleased by the characterization of his life as that of a *mujahid*, one who struggled in the path of Allah. Such a designation might well be applied to all faithful believers, but it seems especially fitting for one who struggled from his early years both as a Palestinian refugee and later as an Islamic activist. Certainly it would be fair to say that he saw himself as a scholar–activist in the service of Islam. His Palestinian roots, Arab heritage, and Islamic faith made the man and informed the life and work of the scholar. Issues of identity, authenticity, acculturation, and Western political and cultural imperialism, which are so significant today, were continual themes in his writing, though he addressed them differently at different stages in his life. As we will see, his early emphasis on Arabism as the vehicle of Islam was tempered by a later centrality accorded to the doctrine of *tawhid* (divine unity) as the foundation for faith, knowledge, and society.

Ismail al-Faruqi was born into a well-established family in Jaffa in 1921. His education made him trilingual, at home in the language, music, literature, and other arts in Arabic, French, and English. He drew on these sources intellectually and aesthetically throughout his life. After an early traditional Islamic education at the mosque school, he attended a French Catholic school, College des Frères (Saint Joseph) in Palestine. This was followed by five years at the American University of Beirut, where he earned his bachelor's degree in 1941. Al-Faruqi entered government service and in 1945, at age twenty-four, became governor of Galilee; the future direction of his life seemed set. All came to an abrupt end with the creation of the State of Israel in 1948. Al-Faruqi became one of thousands of Palestinian refugees, emigrating with his family to Lebanon. Having jettisoned his career as an administrator, he turned with equal enthusiasm to academia. America became the training ground where he prepared himself by earning master's degrees at Indiana and Harvard universities and, in 1952, a doctorate in philosophy from the University of Indiana.

These were difficult years. Added to the trauma of exile from his homeland was the struggle to survive and support himself in his studies. Al-Faruqi even interrupted his studies after Harvard and turned to home construction. Although he prospered, his reminiscences in later years did not include much about this accomplishment. Instead, with a glint in his eyes, he would recount how he and a cousin survived on a diet of sardine sandwiches, adding the juice from a lemon when they could afford to splurge.

Although al-Faruqi successfully completed his degree in Western philosophy, both a scarcity of jobs and an inner drive brought him back to his Islamic intellectual heritage and roots. He left America for Cairo where, for the four years from 1954 to 1958, he immersed himself in the study of Islam at Cairo's famed al-Azhar University. Returning to North America, he became a Visiting Professor of Islamic Studies at the Institute of Islamic Studies and a Fellow at the Faculty of Divinity, McGill University from 1959 to 1961 where he studied Christianity and Judaism. He then began his professional career as Professor of Islamic Studies at the Central Institute of Islamic Research in Karachi, 1961 to 1963. During the following year, he was a Visiting Professor of History of Religions at the University of Chicago. In 1964, he joined the faculty of Syracuse University and then in 1968 became professor of Islamics and history of religions at Temple University, a post he retained until his death in 1986. During a professional life that spanned almost thirty years, he authored, edited, or translated twenty-five books, published more than one hundred articles, was a visiting professor at more than twenty-three universities in Africa, Europe, the Middle East, South and Southeast Asia, and served on the editorial boards of seven major journals.

Ismail al-Faruqi's Arab Muslim identity was at the center of the man and the scholar. For him, Arabism and Islam were intertwined. Yet it is possible to identify two phases or stages in his life. In the first, Arabism was the dominant theme of his discourse. In the second, Islam occupied center stage as he assumed the role more and more of an Islamic activist leader as well as of an academic. The first phase of Ismail al-Faruqi's thought is epitomized in his book *On Arabism: Urubah and Religion.* Here, Arabism is the central reality of Islamic history, faith, and culture. It is "as old as the Arab stream of being itself since it is the spirit which animates the stream and gives it momentum."[1] Indeed, it is the soul of the Arab stream of being, molded by the consciousness that God is and that He is one.

The borders of Arabism, for al-Faruqi, were indeed far-flung and inclusive, embracing the entire Islamic community (*umma*) and non-Muslim Arabs alike. Arabism is not simply an idea but a reality, an identity, and a set of values, integral to and inseparable from the identity of all Muslims and all non-Muslim Arabs. Arabism is the very spirit of the umma; it incorporates not only the Arabic-speaking members of the Arab world, but also the entire world community of Muslims since Arab language, consciousness, and values are at the core of their common Islamic faith. Al-Faruqi read the Qur'an through Arab eyes. As Arabic is the language of the Qur'an, so the content of revelation is regarded as a message to the Arabs. Thus, the Arabs are the referent for the

Qur'anic declaration, "Ye are the best people brought forth unto mankind." Regarding this reading as a judgment of faith, he formulated the following syllogism based on the Qur'anic mandate to enjoin good and prohibit evil: "To enjoin good, forbid evil and believe in God is to be ethically the best; the Arabs enjoin the good, forbid evil and believe in God; therefore, the Arabs are ethically the best."[2] The Arabs are an elite who ought to be expected to do better than those who are non-Arabic speaking.

The centrality of Arabism (*uruba*) to Islamic history and civilization in al-Faruqi's thought can be seen in the titles he selected for the four projected volumes in his series on Arabism: *Urubah and Religion*, *Urubah and Art*, *Urubah and Society*, and *Urubah and Man*. He regarded Arabness or Arab consciousness as the vehicle for the divine message and its immanence in faith, society, and culture. In this sense, Arabness is central to the history of religion, or more specifically, to the three prophetic faiths. Al-Faruqi could declare that it is cointensive with the values of Islam as well as with the message of the Hebrew prophets and Jesus.[3] He also maintained that Arabism is the heart of non-Muslim Arab identity, though often not recognized as such because of the influence of colonialism. They have "lived every value that Arabism recognized, including the Quranic values, but have regrettably maintained a pseudo-consciousness of a separate identity, under the indoctrination, encouragement and political instigation of foreigners in pursuit of imperialistic aims."[4] Al-Faruqi's thought here is rooted in his distinction between Arab Christians and Western Christians. The former have preserved the faith, original Christianity, in its pristine Semitic purity from what he regarded as the accretions and distortions of Jesus' message by the Pauline West. For this, they have been regarded as heretics and schismatics, persecuted by their coreligionists and driven from their lands, often more at home and able to function under the aegis of Islam.

Whether in his Arabist or his later Islamic period, Ismail al-Faruqi believed in and therefore sought to interpret reality as an integrated, interrelated whole. The center, Islam, provides the fullest expression of God's will for humankind and the value system to be followed. If Arabism is the spirit and best expression of Islamic values in a human community, then the pieces that do not seem to fit, such as non-Arab Muslims and non-Muslim Arabs, are to be understood as unconscious or uncultivated expressions of Arabism.[5] Though few would question Arab influence on non-Arab Muslim faith and culture or Arab Muslim influence on non-Muslim Arabs, the implication that they both find their ultimate expression and fulfillment in Al-Faruqi's interpretation of Arabism might be regarded by some as an attempt to establish the hegemony of Arab Islam or, more precisely, Arab Muslim culture. Such an attitude is reflected in al-Faruqi's observation that "This difference between a Muslim and a Christian Arab does not constitute a difference in culture or religion or ethics, but in personality."[6]

As we will see, Ismail al-Faruqi's later work and writing focused on a comprehensive vision of Islam and its relationship to all aspects of life and culture; however, he continued in later life to maintain the special place of

Arabism in Islam based on the integral relationship of Arabic to both the form and content of the Qur'an: "the Quran is inseparable from its Arabic form, and hence, . . . Islam is *ipso facto* inseparable from *urubah*."[7] Yet al-Faruqi was quick to distinguish uruba from any form of Arab nationalism or ethnocentrism. He regarded any emphasis on nationality or ethnicity as a modern phenomenon; thus, Arab nationalism of any sort was to be rejected as a Western import introduced by Arab Christians such as Constantin Zurayk and Michel Aflaq under the influence of modern European notions of nationalism. Such narrow ethnocentric nationalisms sharply contrast with al-Faruqi's understanding of an Arabism rooted in the universal revelation of the Qur'an, and therefore the common legacy to all Muslims. These Western-inspired nationalisms constitute a new tribalism (*shu'ubiyya*) aimed at undermining the unity and universal brotherhood of the umma.[8] During the period just prior to and after the writing of *On Arabism*, al-Faruqi was often described as a Muslim modernist. His approach in his teaching and interpretation bore this out. His course on modern Islam focused on the work and writings of Jamal al-Din al-Afghani, Muhammad Abduh, Sayyid Ahmad Khan, and Muhammad Iqbal rather than, for example, on Hasan al-Banna, Sayyid Qutb, or Mawlana Mawdudi. Living and working in the West, al-Faruqi tended to present Islam in Western categories to engage his audience as well as to make Islam more comprehensible and respected. In explaining Islam through his writing and lectures to an ignorant, ill-informed, or hostile Western audience, al-Faruqi emphasized the place of reason, science, progress, the work ethic, and private property. Like the fathers of Islamic modernism, he often presented Islam as the religion par excellence of reason, science, and progress.

Christian–Muslim Relations

A significant portion of Ismail al-Faruqi's life was spent in his tireless efforts for better understanding between Christians and Muslims. He did this through scholarship and participation in ecumenical dialogue. As *On Arabism* was the product of his study and lecturing in Cairo at al-Azhar and the Institute of Higher Arabic Studies at Cairo University, so too his experience at McGill University's Institute of Islamic Studies resulted in a major work, *Christian Ethics*. A Muslim study of Christianity, it was an ambitious two-year project during which he read widely in the history of Christian thought and Christian theology and had the opportunity to enter into extended conversation and debate with colleagues such as Wilfred Cantwell Smith, then director of the institute, Charles Adams, and Stanley Brice Frost, then dean of the faculty of divinity. For many, *Christian Ethics* was a ground-breaking exercise—a modern-trained Muslim's analysis of Christianity. Al-Faruqi combined an impressive breadth of scholarship with tireless energy, voracious intellect, and linguistic skills. Although some might take issue with his interpretation and conclusions, he could not be faulted for not doing his homework. Al-Faruqi's ecumenical intentions and his desire to proceed as an historian of religions were evident at the outset. The extended introduction to the volume attempts to outline the principles for what he called a metareligious approach, which set forth principles that transcended the boundaries of specific traditions. This was followed by an assessment of Muslim–Christian dialogue and a critical evaluation of several Christian comparativists (Stephen Neill, Hendrik Kraemer, A. C. Bousquet, and Albert Schweitzer).

Al-Faruqi advocated the need to transcend an apologetic or polemic approach to the study of comparative religions and to engage in what he regarded to be a more objective, scholarly study. He indicted much of past scholarship as proceeding from the biases of past confrontations and conflicts as well as missionary polemics and Orientalist distortions. In their place he proposed a methodology to transcend dogmatic theologies and return to a "theology-free metareligion" by basing the analysis of religions on a set of self-evident principles. The difficulties of this undertaking were clear from the outset. Al-Faruqi could speak of his desire to contribute to the task of identifying the spiritual principles of the future unity of humankind and, more specifically, to bring about a rapprochement between Christianity and Islam by uncovering their deeper common ground, the results of what he regarded as the "surgical knife" of criticism, however, were undeniably controversial. The claim that the unity of humankind gives all "a new citizenship," and with it the right to regard other traditions as their own legacy and therefore, as in al-Faruqi's case, to reconstruct Christianity and show Christians "where they have complacently allowed their ethical doctrine to run *ad absurdum*," is one that many find unacceptable. I doubt that most Muslims, including Ismail al-Faruqi, would be willing to accept a Christian's reconstruction of the Islamic tradition, especially when the principles or criteria for the understanding, as well as the conclusions, are highly controversial. Al-Faruqi maintained that the majority of books written on the religions of other peoples by nonbelievers were the products of the authors' subjecting a religion to standards taken from their own tradition. He concluded that "We do not know of any analytical book on Islam, for instance, written by a Christian, which does not reveal such judgment of Islam by Christian or Western standards."[9] Al-Faruqi's examination of Christianity provides a reverse case in point.

The foundation for Ismail al-Faruqi's study was the identification of "higher principles which are to serve as the basis for the comparison of various systems of meanings, of cultural patterns, of moralities, and of religions; the principles by reference to which the meanings of such systems and patterns may be understood, conceptualized, and systematized."[10] The first principle is internal coherence, that is, that "the elements of which [something] is constituted are not contradictory to one another."[11] Thus, in terms of the doctrine of the Trinity, Muslims maintain this is inherently contradictory. Similarly, when al-Faruqi states unequivocally that internal coherence excludes recourse to paradox as a theological principle, many Christians question the universal basis for this elevation of an assertion to the status of an inviolable or self-evident truth. While al-Faruqi's third principle maintains that God's commands cannot contradict one another, he does not adequately tell us by what criteria competing truth claims and contradictory statements are to be reconciled or resolved. He does state that, "after the rules of understanding religious systems [the theoretical and principles of internal and external coherence] have been scrupulously applied to a religion, we may expect that the internal contradictions of a religion have been removed."[12] Somehow, however, al-Faruqi never seems to acknowledge adequately the practical issues that such an approach raises such as who is to make this judgment and on whose authority, how others would regard this assumption of authority, or how one would counter the charge that one person's principles are another's presuppositions. What is the basis for assuming the validity of these principles? The answer to this question seems to be reason or rationality. Throughout the volume reason is employed to explain or critique Christian ethics. Jesus' resurrection from the dead is sympathetically but psychologically explained by an underlying assumption that this is the only "rational" explanation. Other Christian doctrines, such as the divinity of Christ, are denied or refuted because they do not make sense. Al-Faruqi characterized his methodology as based solely on reason: "the analysis is rational, critical; and the only argument that may be brought against its principles is an error of reasoning."[13] He maintained that this was an objective, indeed "absolute," critique, saying that "this work is neither a 'Muslim's' nor an 'Islamic' critique, but a human critique of Christian ethics."[14] He justified the seeming contradiction of this statement by asserting that his study embodied the Islamic spirit, which he identifies with rationality itself, maintaining that "in Islam faith (*iman*) means conviction based upon certainty of evidence . . . whatever is opposed to reason must *ipso facto* be repugnant to Allah."[15]

Some might be tempted simply to see the influence of the Mutazila's rationalist spirit here, but it is probably more accurate to note that this was a Muslim trained in Western philosophy writing for a Western audience. Thus, the canons of Western scholarship (reason and empiricism) were employed as the sole instruments for credible study. In the process, the historic tension between faith and reason in Islamic history and thought, as witnessed in the debates between the Asharites and the Mutazilites or the theologians and the philosophers, was bypassed or transcended. Long-standing theological positions and differences not only between Islam and other religions but within Islam itself were to be transcended to focus on what al-Faruqi regarded as primary—ethics: "Let us drop our old questions regarding the nature of God, which have brought nothing but deadlocks; and let us turn to man, to his duties and responsibilities which are, in fact, none other than God's will. Let God be whom He may; is it not possible—nay, necessary,—that all men agree to establish divine will first?"[16] Al-Faruqi believed that emphasis on the will of God, in terms of human responsibility and accountability, was the key to transcending theological differences and realizing the one brotherhood of humankind. Yet even this noble belief and intention had hidden presuppositions. The author presumed that believers would more or less agree on divinely revealed ethical principles, failing to acknowledge that though the three Abrahamic faiths have much in common, there are also important differences with regard to such issues as marriage (the permissability of polygamy), divorce, alcohol consumption, birth control, and abortion.

Al-Faruqi's analysis of Jewish and Christian ethics is remarkable for both its scholarship and its evaluative judgments. The text and its footnotes reveal the author's formidable preparation for this work. He indeed avoids the pitfall of those Christian comparativists whom he faulted for having relied on secondary and tertiary writings rather than working with primary sources. He demonstrates a broad knowledge of biblical texts and scholarship, Christian history, theology, and ethics. Yet, ironically, although he maintains that the world religious community for which he writes has little to gain from the work of missionaries and those who engage in the scientific study of religion, some of the conclusions following from his metareligious critique will strike many Jews and Christians as little different from those in the writings of a missionary or a religious historian. His section on "Hebrew Scripture as Record or Hebrew Racialism," and his conclusion that Genesis' priestly tradition or editing is more correctly a forgery, proceeds from Islamic beliefs and values about the nature of revelation and the community as well as metareligious principles grounded in reason.

Similarly, al-Faruqi's judgment that Jesus' revolution was betrayed by Christianity, and thus his distinction between Christianism and true Christianity, will strike many Christians as resulting from the use of reason to reach Muslim conclusions rooted in Islamic revelation and belief. The methodology may be different, missionary diatribe having been replaced by a sophisticated rationalist polemic, but the results are the same. One can see this merger, as it were, in al-Faruqi's characterization of Jews as falling into two categories. On the one hand are those who rejected understanding Hebrew scriptures in racial terms, whom he calls "unjewish" or truly Mosaic Jews who "stand fundamentally, in our camp from which that which is called Hebrew Scripture is regarded as a heavily edited, oft-changed version of that divine Torah which God had entrusted to Moses." And on the other hand are the Jews who "are regarded as those who gave up that divinely inspired pattern for the sake of tribalist self-seeking and assertion and preservation of their race."[17]

Christian Ethics ends with a moving call for Christians and Muslims to join together in producing a new theology, but many see it as a call to accept Islam's corrective vision of religious history. When al-Faruqi asserts that a second reformation is required which, though it does not reject all of the past, liberates itself from the authority and ambiguities of the cumulative tradition from the Gospels and Saint Paul to Barth and Tillich, many wonder what is left. The price seems too high for many Christians.[18] What then is the contribution of this work? First, it established Ismail al-Faruqi as a serious participant in the emerging fields of comparative religions and ecumenism. Here is a scholar who had demonstrated his knowledge of the Scriptures and scholarly tradition of the "other." This interest continued throughout his life, and is reflected in his publications and presentations at scholarly meetings and ecumenical dialogues. Second, al-Faruqi provided one of the earliest, perhaps the first, sustained critiques by modern Muslims of Christianity in general and Christian ethics in particular. It is an honest, clear, straightforward, informed analysis. He did not soften his criticisms to please or ingratiate, but pursued what he saw as the truth in the direct and bold manner that characterized both his writing and his conversation. Third, as in many other areas, al-Faruqi served as an example to other Muslim scholars of the importance of studying other faiths seriously. This belief was later institutionalized when al-Faruqi moved to Temple University, insisting that Muslim students seriously study other faiths and write dissertations in comparative religions. Fourth, *Christian Ethics* provides many observations and insights that force Christians not only to realize how an intelligent Muslim might perceive Christianity but also to acknowledge and reassess the past and see its implications in the present. Al-Faruqi's analysis of the two poles or "pulls" in Christianity—renunciation on the one hand and worldliness on the other—is useful in understanding the ambivalence in much of Christianity toward money and power. He argued that Christian tradition celebrated and emphasized the poverty and suffering of the crucified Christ and at the same time found it necessary to morally justify self-assertion and worldliness, the pursuit of power through conquest and colonialism, as sacrifice and altruism. This awareness is useful in understanding the role of imperial Christianity and the papacy in Christian history as well as modern Christian apologias for European colonialism, neocolonialism, and Western capitalism.

Stanley Brice Frost, Dean of Divinity during al-Faruqi's years at the Institute of Islamic Studies, McGill University, said of him: "He became a man of two worlds, intelligently at ease in both and at peace with neither."[19] His grappling with two worlds was no doubt responsible for his writing of *Urubah* and *Christian Ethics*. Arabism, Islam, and Western Christian culture were his religious, historical, and cultural baggage. If during the 1950s and 1960s he sounded like an Arab heir to Islamic modernism and Western empiricism, with his emphasis on Islam as the religion of reason par excellence, by the late 1960s and early 1970s Ismail al-Faruqi progressively resolved this struggle with his identity, assuming the role of an Islamic scholar–activist. Reflecting on this transitional period, he reminisced: "There was a time in my life . . . when all I cared about was proving to myself that I could win my physical and intellectual existence from the West. But, when I won it, it became meaningless. I asked myself: Who am I? A Palestinian, a philosopher, a liberal humanist? My answer was: I am a Muslim!"[20] This shift in orientation was evident in the recasting of his framework. Islam replaced Arabism as the primary reference point. The projected series of volumes on Arabism was replaced by books and articles on Islam. Instead of Arabism and culture or Arabism and society, it was now Islam and culture, Islam and society, Islam and art, Islamization of knowledge, Islam had always had an important place in al-Faruqi's writing, but now it became the organizing principle. Islam was indeed presented as an all-encompassing ideology, the primary identity of a worldwide community of believers and the guiding principle for society and culture. This holistic Islamic worldview was embodied in a new phase in his life and career as he continued to write extensively, to lecture and consult with Islamic movements and national governments, and to organize Muslims in America. Intellectually, it was epitomized in such works as *Tawhid: Its Implications for Thought and Life* and his last publication, *The Cultural Atlas of Islam*, which he coauthored with Lois Lamya al-Faruqi.

Al-Faruqi saw the world through the prism of his Islamic faith and commitment, focused on issues of identity, history, belief, culture, social mores, and international relations. Whatever the national and cultural differences across the Muslim world, for Ismail al-Faruqi analysis of the strengths and weaknesses (past, present, and future) of Muslim societies began with Islam—its presence in society and its necessary role in development. As we view the writings and activities of al-Faruqi during the 1970s and 1980s, we see old themes and new concerns, now brought together under the umbrella of Islam. His analysis of the plight of Muslim societies, its causes and cure, are cast in an Islamic mold. Spiritual malaise, the Westernization of society, education, poverty, economic dependence, political fragmentation, military impotence, the liberation of Jerusalem—all are addressed from an Islamic context. Islam, rather than Arabism or Palestinianism, was to be the starting point.

Al-Faruqi laid the failures of Muslim societies at the doorstep of the West and the Muslim community alike. He believed that the Crusades, European colonialism, Zionism, and superpower neocolonialism have been very much alive both as formative influences in the West's attitude and policies and as enduring political and cultural realities in the contemporary Muslim world. The Westernization of Muslim societies begun during the colonial era has continued to afflict modern Muslim states and societies. Nationalist governments spread this "despicable Western virus," a variation of the old disease of tribalism (*shuubiyya*) that divided and weakened the umma. Informed by secularism, Westernization has focused on material progress but neglected the integral place of the spiritual.[21] Religion has often been looked down on or marginalized by nationalist governments and modern elites. Modernization programs were uncritically adopted and transplanted from the West, alienating the Muslim from his past and making him a caricature of Western man. A debilitated community was further weakened by its political, economic, military, and cultural dependence on the West. But what of those Muslims and movements that have undertaken Islamic responses to revitalize the umma? Although al-Faruqi was a great admirer of the Salafiyya movements of the eighteenth and nineteenth centuries, he believed they were ill-prepared to face the challenges from the West. They enjoyed only limited success. Similarly, modern associations like Hasan al-Banna's Muslim Brotherhood failed to delineate in sufficient detail their Islamic blueprint for society. Whatever its accomplishments and gains, al-Faruqi found the condition of the Islamic community in a generally sorry state: divided, depressed, and dependent, an easy prey to its internal and external enemies. He believed that revival (*tajdid*) and reform (*islah*) were the order of the day.

An old Christian acquaintance of Ismail al-Faruqi once commented that al-Faruqi believed Islam needed a reformation, reflecting his impression that al-Faruqi aspired to be its Luther. Knowing him, I think he would have preferred the term *mujahid*, a true struggler for Islam. Or more simply, as I remember clearly from my days as his student, a *muslim*, one whose submission is a life-long struggle to realize or actualize God's will in personal life and in society. Whatever images we use, the writing and activities of the last decade of his life reveal a man driven by his desire and commitment to change the present and future condition of Muslims by rectifying the shortcomings of the past. Equipped with his knowledge of Islam and Western thought, he never ceased the struggle to provide the "ideational depth" and processes for the inculturation and implementation of Islam and Muslim societies. At the same time, he continued his efforts to present his vision of Islam to the West, convinced that the children of Abraham had to reach an accommodation on religious as well as political and cultural grounds.

Al-Faruqi combined the spirit of the Islamic modernism of men such as Muhammad Abduh and Muhammad Iqbal with the revivalist outlook of earlier leaders such as Muhammad ibn Abd al-Wahhab. Like Ibn Abd al-Wahhab, he was bitterly critical of the corrosive effects of Sufism and outside cultural influences on Islam and the need to see and understand all aspects of life as rooted in the doctrine of tawhid, God's unity or oneness.[22] Islam was to be the primary referent in all aspects of life. At the same time, al-Faruqi was an heir to the Islamic modernist legacy with its emphasis on Islam as the religion of reason. Reason and revelation are means to knowledge of the divine will: "knowledge of the divine will is possible by reason, certain by revelation."[23] We can see in al-Faruqi's writings this twofold influence of Muhammad ibn Abd al-Wahhab and Muhammad Abduh, both of whose works included a study of tawhid, in particular al-Faruqi's *Tawhid: Its Implications for Thought and Life*. Like them, al-Faruqi grounded his interpretation of Islam in the doctrine of tawhid, combining the classical affirmation of the centrality of God's oneness with a modernist interpretation (*ijtihad*) and application of Islam to modern life. Tawhid is presented as the essence of religious experience, the quintessence of Islam, the principle of history, knowledge, ethics, aesthetics, the umma, the family, and the political, social, economic, and world orders. Tawhid is the basis and heart of Islam's comprehensive worldview: "All the diversity, wealth and history, culture and learning, wisdom and civilization of Islam is compressed in this shortest of sentences—*La ilaha illa Allah* (There is no God but God)."[24]

The extent to which al-Faruqi was the product of and bridged two worlds is demonstrated by the ideas and language he employed in his writing and talks whether for non-Muslim, Western audiences or for his brothers and sisters in Islam. It is particularly striking in *Tawhid*, which was written as a "Muslim Training Manual." Here, despite his audience, al-Faruqi's presentation of Islam combines Islamic belief and values with Western philosophical/religious issues and language. Some might attribute this simply to the influence of his Western education and his living in the West. However, it is probably more correct to credit it to his desire to present Islam as the only viable response to modern issues that, in his estimation, Western culture has failed to address adequately. This approach meets a two-fold need. It offers a modern interpretation of Islam and takes into account the Western cultural tradition, which has increasingly penetrated the education and lives of Muslims. Thus, for example, Islam is presented as the religion of nature, true humanism, ethics, and society. *Tawhid* provides a unity of nature, personhood, and truth that subordinates them to God and, in turn, resolves any concern about a conflict between religion and science, affirms the ethical dimension of Islam, and legitimizes the need to rediscover the Islamic dimension of all knowledge through a process of Islamization. Al-Faruqi clearly affirms the integral or essential relationship of Islam to all of reality: "the Islamic mind knows no pair of contraries such as 'religious–secular,' 'sacred–profane,' 'church–state,' and Arabic, the religious language of Islam, has no words for them in its vocabulary."[25] His penchant for Western philosophical language can be seen in such statements as "hedonism, eudaemonism and all other theories which find moral value in the very process of natural life are [the Muslim's] *bete noire.*"[26] It is even more pronounced in his observation that "he [the Muslim] is therefore an axiologist in his religious disciplines of exegesis, but only to the end of reaching a sound denotology, as a jurist."[27]

It must be emphasized again that the use of Western categories and language did not betray an uncritical acceptance of and assimilation to Western culture. Indeed, it was to counter such dangers to Islam that al-Faruqi in his later years in particular focused on what he termed the Islamization of knowledge. A major focus of his work was the education of a new generation of Muslims, schooled in modern methods but Islamically oriented. Believing that many of the problems of the Muslim world are due to its elites and the bifurcation of education in Muslim societies, Ismail al-Faruqi addressed this problem in a variety of ways. Typically, he combined thought with action, ideology with institutionalization and implementation. He traveled extensively and regularly throughout the Muslim world, lecturing at universities and to Muslim youth groups. As he traveled, he took great care to recruit students for his program at Temple University. Their presence enhanced the learning experience of non-Muslim students, but more important, provided an opportunity for Muslims to obtain a modern university education combining the study of Islam and history of religions with other disciplines. He and his wife, Lois Lamya al-Faruqi, enjoyed a transnational extended family, often looking after the material needs as well as educational requirements of their students and providing for many a home away from home. Organizationally, al-Faruqi was a leader in the Muslim Student Association, a founder and president of associations of Muslim professionals such as the Association of Muslim Social Scientists, and chairman of the Board of Trustees of the North American Islamic Trust.

Throughout his scholarly life, Ismail al-Faruqi combined his commitment to Islam and Islamic Studies with his role as an historian of religion and an ecumenist. At the same time during the 1970s that he worked feverishly to establish Islamic Studies programs, recruit and train Muslim students, and organize Muslim professionals, he also established and chaired the Islamic Studies Steering Committee of the American Academy of Religion (1976–

1982). For the first time, Islamic Studies enjoyed a strong presence through a series of panels convened every year at the annual meeting. Several volumes issued from these proceedings.[28] One work in particular, *Trialogue of the Abrahamic Faiths*, reflected Ismail al-Faruqi's enduring interest in interfaith dialogue. As he traveled around the world in his capacity as an Islamic scholar–activist, so too he actively participated in international ecumenical meetings. From the publication of his *Christian Ethics* in 1967 until his death, he was a major force in Islam's dialogue with other world religions. During the 1970s, al-Faruqi established himself as a leading Muslim spokesperson for Islam. It would not be an exaggeration to say that al-Faruqi became one of a handful of Muslim scholars known and respected in both Western academic and ecumenical circles. His writings, speeches, participation, and leadership role in interreligious meetings and organizations sponsored by the World Council of Churches, the National Council of Churches, the Vatican, and the Inter-Religious Peace Colloquium, of which he was vice president from 1977 to 1982, made him the most visible and prolific Muslim contributor to the dialogue of world religions. In his writings, he set out the principles and bases for Muslim participation in interreligious dialogue and social action.[29] In addition to his specific concern for ecumenism, al-Faruqi's interest in other faiths as both an historian of religion and a Muslim led to the production of his *Historical Atlas of the Religions of the World* in 1975, in which he extended his earlier work on Judaism and Christianity into a more comprehensive study.[30]

By the late 1970s, Ismail al-Faruqi had become restless and frustrated with his situation at Temple University. Budget cuts and conflicting departmental priorities kept him from building the kind of program in Islamic Studies that had first attracted him to Temple. His own work was moving him more and more in the direction of what may be described as implementation and strategic planning for Islamic reform. As we have seen, al-Faruqi had increasingly devoted the bulk of his energies to sketching out his interpretation of the meaning of Islam and its implications for Muslim society and to organizing and educating Muslims. He realized that implementing new, non-Western models for the development of Muslim societies required the training of new generations of Muslims and the concerted efforts of those experts who were available. In his last years several projects in particular typified his "mission," consuming most of his time and energies. He established the American Islamic College in Chicago and served as its first president. For more than a decade he had talked about creating a major Islamic university in the United States where Islamic Studies and training could be done as he had envisioned them. His plans were grand, and on a number of occasions seemed close to realization. However, he had to settle for a more modest beginning with a small college in Chicago. At the same time, he realized a long-held dream when, in 1981, he created the International Institute for Islamic Thought in Virginia. Al-Faruqi realized that while one might object to the uncritical adoption of Western models of political, economic, social, and educational development, they are the established, entrenched models. Appeals and demands for more Islamically oriented states and societies must move beyond criticism of the status quo and ideological rhetoric regarding Islamic alternatives. Islamic activism must be prepared to move beyond opposition to implementation. It is no longer enough to decry what one is against and to proclaim what one is for. It is increasingly imperative to possess specific, concrete plans for the new Islamic order.

The growth of Islamic movements and of government appeals to Islam underscore the pressing need for think tanks of experts prepared to bridge the bifurcated world of modern secular elites and more traditional religious leaders. They can provide the studies and plans that address the question of what modern Islamic political, cultural, social, legal, and economic systems should look like. At the heart of his vision is what he called the Islamization of knowledge. He regarded the political, economic, and religiocultural malaise of the Islamic community as primarily due to the bifurcated state of education in the Muslim world and the resultant lack of vision. Al-Faruqi believed that the cure is two-fold: the compulsory study of Islamic civilization and the Islamization of modern knowledge. Here we find his familiar themes, a combination of the influences of the Islamic modernist and revivalist traditions. Weakness and failure are due to the abandonment of ijtihad, which is the source of creativity in Islam, the opposition of revelation (*wahy*) and reason (*aql*), the separation of thought and action, and cultural and religious dualism. In typical fashion, Ismail al-Faruqi combined thought and action. He published several pieces including *Islamization of Knowledge* and "Islamizing the Social Sciences,"[31] organized and participated in international conferences on the Islamization of knowledge in such countries as Malaysia and Pakistan, and served as an adviser to both Muslim governments and Islamic organizations and as a consultant to universities from Africa to Southcast Asia.

The twentieth century has made enormous demands on Muslims throughout the world, swept along by the realities of rapid political, economic, and social change. It has brought the rise of nationalist movements, the emergence of modern states, increased modernization and Westernization, the creation of the State of Israel and a series of Arab–Israeli wars, Arab socialist revolutions in the 1950s and early 1960s, civil and regional wars, and the resurgence of Islam in private and public life. Throughout this period, there has been a series of influential Muslims, such as Muhammad Abduh, Muhammad Iqbal, Hasan al-Banna, and Mawlana Mawdudi to name but a few, who have attempted to address critical issues of religious faith and identity. In recent decades, the world of Islam has had a number of prominent intellectuals who have combined the best of educations in Western universities with their Islamic heritage and attempted both to explain Islam to non-Muslim audiences and to contribute to the contemporary interpretation and understanding of Islam among Muslims. The growing importance of Muslim presence in America is reflected by the fact that the United States has also provided a context for this endeavor. Professor Ismail al-Faruqi was among its most prominent representatives. His belief that Islam combined faith and practice and that thought and intention must issue in action informed a life in which scholarship and activism were intertwined. Islamic thought for al-Faruqi was part of a process not simply of knowing but of doing. In his publications, scholarly colloquia, classroom teaching, ecumenical dialogues, and other activities, he wrote, spoke, and acted with the clarity and conviction of one who has a vision and mission. He was indeed a scholar–activist of Islam.

Notes

1. Ismail Ragi A. al-Faruqi, *On Arabism: Urubah and Religion* (Amsterdam: Djambatan, 1962), pp. 2–3.
2. Ibid., p. 5.
3. Ibid., p. 207.
4. Ibid., p. 211.
5. Ibid., p. 209.
6. Ibid.
7. Ismail R. al-Faruqi, *Islam and Culture* (Kuala Lumpur: ABIM, 1980), p. 7.
8. Ibid., p. 7.
9. Ibid., p. 21.
10. Ibid., p. 10.
11. Ibid., p. 11.
12. Ibid., p. 21.
13. Ibid., p. 32.
14. Ibid.
15. Ibid., p. 33.
16. Ibid.
17. Ibid., p. 54.
18. Ibid.
19. Stanley Brice Frost, "Foreward in Ismail Ragi al-Faruqi," *Christian Ethics*, (Montreal: McGill University Press, 1967), p. v.
20. As quoted in M. Tariq Quraishi, *Ismail al-Faruqi: An Enduring Legacy* (Plainfield, Ind.: The Muslim Student Association, 1987), p. 9.
21. Ismail Raji al-Faruqi, *Tawhid: Its Implications for Thought and Life* (Kuala Lumpur: The International Institute of Islamic Thought, 1982), p. ii
22. In later life, al-Faruqi translated and edited Ibn Abd al-Wahhab's writings on tawhid: *Sources of Islamic Thought: Three Epistles on Tawhid by Muhammad ibn Abd al-Wahhab* (Indianapolis: American Trust Publications, 1980); and *Sources of Islamic Thought: Kitab al-Tawhid* (London: I.I.F.S.O., 1980).
23. Ibid., p. 7.
24. Ibid., p. 7.
25. Ibid., p. 73.
26. Ibid., p. 16.
27. Ibid.
28. John L. Esposito, *Islam and Development: Religion and Sociopolitical Change* (Syracuse, N.Y.: Syracuse University Press, 1980), Ismail R. al-Faruqi, ed., *Essays in Islamic and Comparative Studies, Islamic Thought and Culture, Trialogue of the Abrahamic Faiths* (Herndon, Va.: International Institute of Islamic Thought, 1982).
29. In addition to *Christian Ethics*, see, for example, "Islam and Christianity: Diatribe or Dialogue," *Journal of Ecumenical Studies*, V, 1 (1968), 45–77; "Islam and Christianity: Problems and Perspectives," *The Word in the Third World*, ed. James P.

Cotter (Washingtion–Cleveland: Corpus Books, 1968), pp. 159–81; *"The Role of Islam in Global Interreligious Dependence", Towards a Global Congress of the World's Religions*, ed. Warren Lewis (Barrytown, N.Y.: Unification Theological Seminary, 1980), pp. 19–38; and "Islam and Other Faiths," *30th International Congress of Human Sciences in Asia and North Africa, Middle East 1*, ed. Graciela de la Lama (Mexico City: El Colegio de Mexico, 1982), pp. 153–79.

30. Ismail R. al-Faruqi, *Historical Atlas of the Religions of the World* (New York: The Macmillan Co., 1975).

31. Ismail al-Faruqi, *Islamization of Knowledge* (Herndon, Va: International Institute of Islamic Thought, 1982) and "Islamizing the Social Sciences," Vol. XVI, No. 2 *Studies in Islam*, (1979), 108–21.

6

Seyyed Hossein Nasr: Defender of the Sacred and Islamic Traditionalism

Jane I. Smith

I accepted the invitation to reflect on the scholarly contributions of Seyyed Hossein Nasr not only because he is a long-time colleague and friend, but because I greatly appreciate his perspective and the seriousness with which he analyzes the spiritual poverty of much of contemporary society. It is true that as a non-Muslim trained in the schools of modern Western academia I inevitably represent much of the orientation against which Hossein Nasr maintains vigilant defense. However, I find myself in real agreement with Nasr's obvious sense of alarm about the way modern man (to use his recurrent phrase) has wandered into very dangerous territory and seems to have lost, for the most part, the means for appropriation of the sacred. Thus, to the extent to which I can respond to and appreciate much of what Nasr describes, I may do some measure of justice to an analysis of the thoughts of one of the most articulate, influential, and prolific Muslims teaching and writing in this country today.

Perhaps a place to begin is with how Nasr sees his own task. His basic message is that modern man has lost sight of the essential, the eternal, in his quest for the trappings of modernity. One way to get quickly at his ideas is to note what it is that he most opposes and then what he consistently affirms. Among his targets, generally categorized as "-isms" (itself a recent formulation), are modernism, secularism, rationalism, evolutionism, humanism, materialism, and imperialism. Countering the "-isms" are the adjectives—sapiential, immutable, traditional, perennial, metaphysical, theomorphic—and nouns—permanence, gnosis, unicity—that make up the structure of Nasr's defense and the ground of his argument.

Nasr makes it clear that his writing is intended both for Westerners and for those Muslims who have come too much under the sway of the modern West.[1] On the most obvious level this means presenting the traditional Islamic perspective on questions that are presently being debated,[2] explaining traditional Islam to those who do not understand it or who have seemingly lost touch with it. Sometimes he says it is mostly for young Muslims who are the products of modern educational systems that he is concerned.[3] More specifically, in some of his writings his interest is to help explain little known aspects of Shi'ite intellectual life, often put in the context of his recurring efforts to counter the perception, most evident in Western scholarship, that Islam fell into decadence after the Mongol invasion. He calls it a dangerous illusion that modern Muslims are somehow separated from their tradition by an intellectual vacuum,[4] a "fantastic and abhorrent" theory that the Muslim world went into decay in the seventh/thirteenth century.[5]

This concern for a better understanding of Islam permeates Nasr's presentations. It is set, however, in the context of a somewhat more general discussion of the traditional perspective versus modernism, and in this sense Nasr views his task as exposing the illegitimacy of all of the "-isms" we mentioned. As he puts it, "What is illegitimate . . . is the secular perspective itself to which the analytical method is usually wed and the historicism which opposes metaphysics and the transcendent, and wishes to reduce reality itself to its reflection upon the surface of the flowing river of time."[6] In his most profound works—and I think especially of the brilliant 1981 Gifford Lectures published under the title *Knowledge and the Sacred*—he exposes his task as nothing less than reversing the process whereby secularized reason has been brought to bear on sacred traditions, of reviving the sacred quality of knowledge.

Nasr seems to have a kind of twin purpose in his writings, themes intertwined but nonetheless separable. On the one hand he gives a well-argued apologetic for the religion of Islam, and on the other he reveals his deeply held desire to talk about metaphysical realities. One might even imagine that Nasr consciously distinguishes in his own thinking between two types of audience—those capable of, or interested in, understanding on a more obvious level and those dedicated to dealing with matters of truth and reality on a more profound plane.

It is no surprise to discover that throughout Hossein Nasr's writings, even those written before Edward Said's popular volume attacking Western scholarship,[7] he consistently takes to task the Orientalist approach, especially in Western treatments of Islam. He sees that the entire structure of Islam has been attacked what he calls "an influential school of Western orientalists."[8] Among the sins committed by such scholars are reducing the distinction between the Sunni and Shi'i branches of Islam to a political one only, relying on the "so-called method of 'historical criticism,'" portraying Islam in a less than favorable light, especially compared with the treatment of Asian religions such as Hinduism and Buddhism, and studying Islam with no awareness of the reality of higher planes of consciousness.[9] He sees himself as an Oriental critic of the West who in some sense is reversing what Orientalists have been doing with all Eastern religions and cultures,[10] although he insists that such a reversal is not based on the kind of disdain for the West that would justify the claim of "occidentalism."[11]

One of the tasks of this assignment is to determine what changes have occurred in the development of Nasr's thought and presentation and to speculate on what may have been the causes of such changes. Perhaps it is testimony to the dominance of the concept of immutability in Nasr's orientation, but it is very difficult to point to significant new directions in his thinking; he is consistent with his own frequently stated and basic distrust of change, progress, and evolution. There are shifts in emphasis, of course, and one can detect the influence of certain major events such as the Iranian Revolution (though it must be acknowledged that his responses to the new rule in his native land are remarkably muted, considering the drastic consequences in his own life of that event).

Given the consistency with which Nasr articulated his arguments, it seems best first to look briefly at some of the changes in emphasis that can be noted, and then to turn to an overview of the themes he repeatedly develops. In his earlier writings he seems to have two primary, though clearly not unrelated, goals. The first is to offer scholarly presentations of aspects of Islamic thought and civilization for the general edification of the West. The tone of these writings is occasionally more anecdotal[12] than his later works. The second goal is to write a kind of Islamic *apologia*, describing the basics of Islam in their idealized form. The primary example of this, of course, is his 1967 *Ideals and Realities of Islam*. Here he talks about Islam without the consistent reference to "traditional" Islam that so pervades his later writing, interpreting it for a Western audience over against Christianity.

Perhaps the best way to express the shift in his emphasis, if shift there be, is to say that in the earlier period (before the 1970s) he wanted to explain Islam to a West that did (and generally still does) not understand it and to defend it against the attacks of Orientalists and others. Later, the emphasis changes slightly to an attack on Western secularism, which he seems to be increasingly aware could potentially destroy humankind. Even Islam cannot survive if young Muslims continue to be seduced by the false "-isms" of the modern West. A very subtle undertone to some of the later writings is that while traditional Islam clearly provides the structure for an appropriation of the sacred, that which is "traditional" in other religions also offers this access. To oversimplify the matter, we can say that whereas the earlier writings juxtapose Islam and Christianity, the dominant emphasis from the mid-1970s on is the traditional over against the modern, the necessity of recognizing the ephemeral nature of the secular so as to re-envision the permanence of the sacred. Underscoring all of his writings is the utter conviction that Islam, later prefaced by the adjective traditional, is the perfect means of achieving this.

From the time of the Iranian Revolution on, Nasr's writings have an increasing number of references to the dangers of those who falsely pose as traditionalists. "Not everything that is nontraditional is antitraditional," he says in *Knowledge and the Sacred*. "There is the third category of the counterfeit of tradition or countertradition which begins to play an ever greater role in the modern world."[13] It is in one of his most recent works, the 1987 *Traditional Islam in the Modern World*, that he begins to distinguish most clearly among what he sees as the dominant types of Islam, or orientations under the Islamic rubric, prevalent today.[14] First, and clearly a target for Nasr's attack, are the forces of fundamentalism. He locates these in various countries, and expresses his concern especially with fundamentalism in Iran "because of the presence of certain elements which are the veritable parody of traditional Islam. . . ."[15] Both traditionalists and fundamentalists may agree in accepting Qur'an and Hadith, but there are profound differences (here he cites the importance of the sapiential dimension for the traditionalists). Even more telling is the fact that while publicly denouncing modernism, fundamentalists accept some of the modernist's most basic principles. Two other contemporary strands of Islam he then identifies as modernism (a recurrent foe) and Islamic socialism or Marxism (a relatively new antagonist, which he also classifies as Mahdist).[16] These are pitted against traditional Islam, for which he is the persistent champion. He rues the fact that this interpretation has been virtually ignored in Western analyses of the Islamic world.

A recurrent theme for Nasr is the conviction that the Islamic world should learn from the mistakes of the West. He charges Muslims with a failure to critique what is wrong in the West, pleading that the West should be a case study in what to avoid.[17] Most insidious among Muslims, he observes, is the tendency not only to fall prey to what is alien but to adopt a Western ideology and preface it with the adjective "Islamic."[18]

A popular game in my area of the country these days is identifying oxymorons in the English language, those phrases whose components are in logical contrast such as "down escalator" or "jumbo shrimp." While Nasr does not use the term, it is clear that he considers such concepts as Islamic modernism or Islamic reformism to be essentially oxymoronic. Movements in the contemporary Islamic world are, in his opinion, completely anomalous on the premise that "it is the human that must conform to the Divine and not the Divine to the human." In fact, modern mentality in general (Western mentality) he calls an anomaly in history.[19] The only recourse is for Muslims to use what he calls the "sword of discrimination" and to embark on a kind of "intellectual iconoclasm" in an attempt to clear away the idols of the contemporary scene.[20]

One of the principal causes of modern Western man's problems is his excessive reliance on rationalism. This is not to deny the importance of human reason or to negate the Islamic understanding of man as an intelligent being or of knowledge as an immediate means of salvation. It is, however, to lament the fact that the intellect is commonly limited to its reflection.[21] Ultimately the danger of rationalism, evident in the fate of Western Christianity, is that it leads so directly to what he calls a fatal dichotomy between faith and reason. Western man's rational faculties have somehow become separated from what gives stability and permanence, what Nasr identifies as intellectual intuition and revelation.[22]

Stability and permanence—here, perhaps, is the real crux of Nasr's position, and it underscores his opposition to change, reform, or anything that would lead away from what he calls the "vision of the objective, transcendent and immutable Islamic principles which alone can enable one to judge from an Islamic point of view whether a particular form of activity or period of human society is decadent, deviated or resurgent with the characteristics of a true renaissance."[23] Thus, renewal (the task of the *mujaddid*) is different from reform. A reformer, he comments several times, is usually better categorized as a deformer.[24]

A 1981 *Parabola* article entitled "Progress and Evolution: A Reappraisal from the Traditional Perspective" summarizes many of his basic arguments on the matter. He challenges once again his old foes progress, rationalism, materialism, imperialism, modernism, and especially evolutionism. "Perhaps there is no modern ideology which has played as great a role in replacing religion and, as a pseudo-religion, attracting the ultimate adherence of human beings as the idea of progress, which later became wed to evolutionism."[25] This gives him another opportunity to take a shot at Marxism, which he calls the most dogmatic of Western ideologies, based on the inevitability of human progress. He presents the opposite case for Islam, saying that there perfection is associated with the Origin. The Prophet is thus identified as the most perfect man, Medina as the most perfect society.[26]

Nasr's strong interests in science and the importance of nature lead him to carry his crusade against the concept of evolution into the biological realm. Citing the failure of modern science to provide any laboratory cases of the changing of one species into another, he blames the modern appreciation for the evolutionist point of view on the failure to distinguish between scientific facts and the underlying philosophical assumptions. The structure of reality is unchanging, he insists; only human vision and perception of it change.[27] In other words, Western philosophy has lost a sense of the permanence of things. Reality has been reduced to a temporal process, which he identifies as a desacralization of knowledge and a loss of the sense of the sacred.[28]

It is this loss that has led modern man to feel the need to choose between creationism or the Darwinian theory of evolution. Caught between the alternatives of creation ex nihilo and a world in a state of constant change and becoming, he argues, modernity has lost touch with the metaphysical doctrine of man's being *in divinis*, having passed through multiple stages and levels of existence before his birth on this earth. Such a doctrine is not at odds with the world of scientific fact, as long as one accepts the idea of multiple levels of existence. As he insists, "the whole modern evolutionary theory is a desperate attempt to substitute a set of horizontal, material causes in a unidimensional world to explain effects whose causes belong to other levels of reality, to the vertical dimensions of existence."[29]

Much of contemporary Islamic thought tends to identify a renewed understanding of the notion of human freedom with the idea of continuing progress toward perfection.[30] Although Nasr rejects the ideal of progress insofar as it implicitly accepts evolution and change, he nonetheless insists on an understanding of human freedom. On one level he seems to be defending the reality of freedom of choice as a verification of human potential in the Islamic understanding and an apologetic for Islam as a religion not caught in the web of determinism or fatalism.[31] On another level it is clear that human freedom is essential to his metaphysical understanding of the nature of humanity.

Here again he distinguishes between the absolute and the relative. Although only God is absolute and thus alone has absolute freedom, man's freedom, while real, is relative. As Nasr puts it, "Man's freedom is as real as himself. He ceases to be free in the sense of independent of the Divine Will to the extent that he ceases to be separated ontologically from God. . . . Journeying from the relative toward the Absolute means at once losing the freedom of living in error and gaining freedom from the tyranny of all the psycho-material determinations which imprison and stifle the soul."[32] Or as he says in another context, "Pure freedom belongs to God alone; therefore the more we *are*, the more we are free."[33]

In a chapter devoted to the concept of freedom in *Islamic Life and Thought*, Nasr discusses the theme as understood in Islam by jurisprudents, theologians, philosophers, and Sufis, noting that Westerners perceive freedom in the context of action, but the traditionalist conceives of the freedom to *be*. He uses the discussion as an opportunity to affirm the *shari'a* as an institution that limits external freedoms but in return endows human life with the sacrality that ultimately makes possible a greater degree of inner freedom.[34] It is, however, the philosophical and Sufi schools of thought that he sees as having truly grasped the foundational meaning of freedom, as he develops in many of his other essays. Freedom, in that understanding, is the absolute opposite of individualism; the whole purpose of the Sufi path is to provide for or lead toward the integration of the individual into the universal. In that, the relative is lost in the absolute, which alone is complete freedom.

Nasr spends a good deal of time lamenting the fate of Christianity as it has lost touch with its traditional perspective. He tends to be more positive in his overall assessment of Catholicism than of Protestantism, doubtless in part because of his feeling that Catholicism has not moved as far from the original traditional perspective of Christianity. For most of its two thousand-year history Christianity managed to maintain its sapential dimension, which Nasr sees epitomized in the concept of the Logos, although that has been virtually lost with the secularization of knowledge.[35] When Christ was viewed as "the eternally present Logos" and not simply as an historical personage, he feels, the doctrine of incarnation was preserved intact. However, "as suprasensible levels of being began to lose their reality for Western man and Christianity became bound to an historical event, history itself became impregnated with ultimate significance affecting the Truth as such."[36] He particularly laments the virtual disappearance of the importance of Mary in the churches' rites and doctrines as a consequence of the promotion of the scientific worldview.[37]

Nasr finds little to defend in Protestantism, which to him embodies much of what he finds objectionable about the modern rational approach. Especially unfortunate is the Protestant ethic, which seems to identify work as a value in itself, something he assures his readers is not true in traditional Islam.[38] This association of economic activity with moral virtue he sees as being connected to the rise of capitalism and the notion of material progress.[39]

In a number of places in his writings Nasr displays his wide-ranging familiarity with and knowledge of Western philosophy, psychology, and theology. Frequently his critique targets those Christian theologians he feels have misunderstood or disregarded true Christian teachings about nature and man's relationship to it. *The Encounter of Man and Nature, the Spiritual Crisis of Modern Man* is devoted to an explication of his deep concerns about what he sees as the destruction of a basic equilibrium between humanity and nature through man's attempts to conquer and dominate nature. In another essay he refers to the "total alienation of man from his natural environment" as a result of "an aggressive externalization of human energy with the aim of indiscriminately raping and plundering nature."[40]

The sciences of nature have become secularized, and the resulting destruction of the equilibrium is a direct correlate to the destruction of the harmony between the human and the divine.[41] This again is linked to the reduction of metaphysics to a rationalist philosophy. Again focusing on Christianity, he comments that the spiritual vision of nature, based on metaphysical doctrines and long part of the traditional understanding of Christianity, must be revived in that tradition or the results will be disastrous. The blame for the current crisis he lays directly, though not exclusively, at the feet of Christian theologians and philosophers.[42]

The inevitable contrast between change and stability enters into this argument, too, when he accuses modern man of using his perception of the constantly changing aspects of nature as the excuse for wanting to change and adapt social, political, and religious institutions. Arguing for the regularity of nature, he insists that "It is because man's mentality has lost its anchor in the permanent and become itself a fleeting river of ever changing ideas and images that man sees only change in nature."[43] Nasr notes that modern man has actually become aware of his own deep spiritual crisis through an awakening of attention to the obvious crisis in the physical environment.[44] Modern science he sees as based on doubt and a philosophy of change and impermanence, thus deserving the name secular science. It lacks the crucial perspectives of a higher knowledge of the sacred.[45]

In contrast to this diagnosis of the sad state of modernity, he cites the Muslim view of man and nature, one which understands the perspective of time from the creation of the universe to its destruction on the last day, and the climactic, geographic, and other conditions that characterize natural history. The traditional Muslim knows the relationship of the world of plants and animals to his own life, and how the terrestrial and the celestial are intertwined to form a sacred history of which human history is but a part.[46] "This is why," he says, "while even in this world, man is able to move to the other shore of existence, to take his stance in the world of the sacred and to see nature herself as impregnated with grace."[47]

This perspective is in fact the view of *scientia sacra*, the opposite of modern secular science, the sacred knowledge that Nasr sees as being at the heart of every revelation from the divine. Revelation joins with intellectual intuition to induce the sapential or presential knowledge (*al-ilm al-huduri*), which is itself knowledge of ultimate reality. Here again he opposes this understanding of the role of the intellect to what he sees as the misguided emphasis on rationalism of the modern age. Man has knowledge through the combination of intuition and revelation not because he rationally imposes categories in which to understand what he perceives, but because consciousness is reality and knowledge is being.[48] There was a time when each man was a prophet and human intellect functioned so as to allow one direct knowledge of the sacred. Because we have become removed from that primordial state we need assistance in using our divine gifts, an assistance that comes in the form of revelation.[49]

We have noted on several occasions that, while Nasr at times seems to set Islam over against Christianity, the more pervasive comparison is between the traditional (exemplified for him most obviously in Islam) and the modern (characterized particularly in his writings by modern Christianity and especially Protestantism). How do these kinds of distinctions play themselves out when it comes to his views on Islam in the context of other world religions?

Clearly Nasr repeatedly applauds the works of Fritjhof Schuon and others who subscribe to a view of the transcendent unity of religions, and for him the very category "traditional" is an ultimately inclusive one; however, he has no use for what might be viewed as syncretism. Truth is perceived distinctly by each religion, but it is still the same truth (Nasr spells it with a capital T) and thus, he says, "to have lived any religion fully is to have lived all religions and there is nothing more meaningless and even pernicious than to create a syncretism from various religions with a claim to universality while in reality one is doing nothing less than destroying the revealed forms which alone make the attachment of the relative to the Absolute, of man to God, possible."[50]

The importance of particularity is a common theme in Nasr's writings. At a recent conference at Harvard Divinity School in which he was commenting on the remarks of Hans Kung concerning dialogue, Nasr cited the response of one of his Christian friends to the current ecumenical movement: "Let us get together and create the motto, 'O all antiecumenical forces of the world unite.'" No dialogue is worthy in the eyes of God, he concluded, that sacrifices for the sake of expediency what has been specifically revealed in each religion.[51] Sacred art, about which he has much to say in *Islamic Art and Spirituality*, is generated specifically in the context of a particular revelation and shares the genius of that particularity.[52] Even the perennial wisdom (*sophia perennis*) to an explication of which Nasr is ultimately dedicated, which is at the heart of every revelation, should not be used as an excuse to obviate the spiritual genius of each particularity. Each is an adaptation of the primordial tradition to a special segment of humanity, a means by which the divine is made manifest on the plane of the human.[53]

In a most interesting chapter in *Sufi Essays* entitled "Islam and the Encounter of Religions," Nasr argues that for traditional man other religions appear to be alien worlds. Because of the traditional orientation in earlier times, there was no need to move into these worlds. But because of the conditions of the modern world "where the bounds of both the astronomical and religious universe have been broken," one is suddenly faced with the dilemma of acknowledging the validity of one's own tradition while attempting to be open to the truths revealed by another.[54] Noting the modern argument that the plurality of religious forms negates the validity of all religions, he insists that, in order to preserve religion itself, it is urgent today to study other faiths.[55] Concluding as he so often does that it is the Sufis who are able to illuminate the metaphysical background against which particular forms can be understood, he points again to the inner unity of religions. As he disavows the superficiality of the eclectic, he affirms what he calls the core, the Center where "all the radii meet, the summit which all roads reach."[56] Only with such a vision of the Center can there be meaningful dialogue between religions.[57]

This, then, is a general overview of the various themes that blend together throughout the writings of Hossein Nasr. To do justice to the range of topics with which Nasr deals is, of course, impossible in a short presentation. His erudition allows him to range across a great breadth of materials. To read his books is to treat oneself in many ways to a rich classical education. Before concluding this brief examination of Nasr's thought I would like to highlight a few of the themes to which he has given particular attention throughout the course of his writings.

Art and architecture. As noted earlier, all of his recent work *Islamic Art and Spirituality* is devoted to examining classical art, under which he includes architecture, calligraphy, metaphysics, logic, poetry, music, and the plastic arts. The title suggests the orientation within which he makes these presentations. (On many occasions before he wrote this book he laid the groundwork to develop these themes.) Describing ours as a time of crisis brought on by secular modernism, he argues that if something drastic is not done immediately we are in grave danger of losing access to these various art forms as well as to the immutable attained through them.[58]

Several times he expands the theme of his concern for contemporary architecture in the Muslim world, which he considers a travesty and, despite its facades, not Islamic at all. Nostalgically describing the classical architecture of the Muslim *medina*, he reflects: "Something of the grace of the Quran and the soul of the Prophet spread over the whole ambience of the Islamic city, much as the call to prayers penetrates into every architectural space or the rain of mercy from Heaven falls upon the roof of every building. . . ."[59] Modern Muslims too often have lost touch with that ethos and, like the Westerners they wish to emulate, build their cities in defiance of nature, violating her rhythms and depleting her resources.

Gender Roles and the Family. In his 1967 *Ideals and Realities*, Nasr sounds some of the themes concerning this topic that have engaged many contemporary Muslim writers over the last several decades. Defending the institution of polygamy, he polemicizes that "the traditional family is also the unit of stability in society, and the four wives that a Muslim can marry, like the four-sided Ka'bah, symbolize this stability."[60] He identifies Islam as masculine and patriarchal, and indicates that the acts of rebellion by modern Muslim women against the structure of the traditional Muslim family are actually a rebellion against fourteen centuries of Islam itself.

In a section that Western feminists and some modern Muslims might find particularly difficult to accept, he identifies the role and duty of the Muslim woman as specified in the teachings of Islam to be "imposed upon her by the hands of destiny." For the woman to accept this role is not only for her to submit to the divine will but may actually lead to spiritual states of *faqr* (poverty) and *fana'* (annihilation of God) normally not available to women because of the active nature of their prescribed familial roles.[61]

Although his rhetoric is toned down slightly in some of his later writings, this position does not change perceptibly. In a chapter in *Traditional Islam* entitled "The Male and the Female in the Islamic Perspective" he stresses the complementary relationship of male and female, as determined by the metaphysical principles that govern human nature. Muslims must take special guard against the innovations that are destroying the perennial teachings of Islam. Making one of his very few concessions to gender-free language ("man, that is, the human being of whatever sex it might be")[62] he acknowledges that the question of relationship between men and women is not without complication. "The veil of cosmic manifestation, the *hijab* of Islamic metaphysics, makes the relation between the sexes an ambivalent one."[63]

Stressing a point that may be difficult for modern Westerners to understand, he says that from the Islamic perspective the goal is not to make everyone happy or satisfied, which in any case is an impossibility in the Qur'anic understanding of the world (*dunya*). The goal is rather to create the maximum degree of harmony and equilibrium, achieved by focusing not on the individual but on the group, society, and the family unit.[64]

Nasr's most significant point in this whole discussion, and it might be interpreted as the ultimate threat by those unwilling to accept his perspective, is that when distinctions between males and females become blurred, as by implication they do in the modern West, the resulting chaos of the social order virtually precludes the possibility of spiritual development by either sex. The only way men and women can approach the divine is by remaining true to the form and the destiny in and for which they have been created by God.[65] Although he does not say it specifically, however, the implication is that these reflections pertain to the exoteric realm, and on the ultimate esoteric plane gender distinctions—as distinctions in the particularities of different religious traditions—are obliterated. "To understand the nature of the male–female distinction in the human race and to appreciate the positive qualities which each sex displays," he says, "is to gain greater insight into the nature of that androgynic being whose reality both the male and female carry at the center of their being."[66]

Jihad. Responding to the ever-current questions, and general misinterpretations, by Western critics of Islam of the "holy war" concept, Nasr at several points makes great effort to present a correct interpretation. Noting that throughout history Christians have employed the sword as much as have Muslims, he says the difference is that by legislating war, Islam, in contrast to Christianity, actually limited it. War is part of the nature of things, he observes, and Islam simply acknowledged this and provided a means for controlling it through legislation.[67] (It is tempting to observe here that, despite his traditionalistic orientation, Nasr employs the very recent devise of reifying Islam, making it, and not God, the subject and initiator of such legislation.)

This theme deepens in *Traditional Islam*, in which, predictably, Nasr entitled the first chapter "The Spiritual Significance of *Jihad.*" Here he stresses the idea of equilibrium, the establishment of which in man is "the terrestrial reflection of Divine Justice and the necessary condition for peace in the human domain. . . ."[68] Preserving equilibrium requires the carrying out of *jihad* (exertion) at every point in individual and communal life. Like many others Nasr distinguishes between the external and internal aspects of this exertion or struggle, which on both levels serves as the "awakening to that Divine Reality which is the very source of our consciousness."[69]

Education. Both implicit and explicit throughout Nasr's works is the call for a re-education to the norms of traditionalism. He affirms repeatedly the values of a traditional Islamic education, stressing especially the importance of classical forms of philosophy and science. He rues the fact that today educational havoc exists in almost every part of the Islamic world. In a rare critical moment of the traditional, he notes some of the shortcomings of the *madrasa* system. Nonetheless he praises it not only as the repository of the traditional Islamic sciences but as the model for any system of education that claims integration with Islamic culture in any of its geographical manifestations.[70]

His concern for education is neither theoretical nor polemical only. In his contributions to volumes such as *Philosophy, Literature and Fine Arts*, part of an Islamic education series, he demonstrates his immediate concern for working at the grassroots level on issues of educational planning and developing teacher training curricula. It is a work clearly by and for Muslims, free of the necessity of defending the Islamic system to a Western audience, although also clearly aimed at those Muslims who, under the influence of secular Westernism, may have lost touch with the values of traditional education.

Sufism. In one way it is less than appropriate to add Sufism to a notation of special concerns such as this simply because attention to Sufism pervades Nasr's writings much more thoroughly than the other themes discussed here. I want to add it here, however, as a way of underlining the importance of the Sufi path for Hossein Nasr, both in its historic manifestation through the writings of the poets and philosophers who have adopted it and as a recognition of an esoteric expression of traditional Islam. In one way Sufism serves as a mirror, which reflects some of his many concerns in contrasting traditional Islam with modern rationalism and secularism.

A glance at a bibliography of Nasr's writings reveals the extent to which he has been deeply schooled in the teachings of the Sufi masters. He finds in the person of Jalal al-Din Rumi the ideal representation of his concern for the relation of the arts—poetry, dance, literature—to spirituality, calling Rumi "that unique orchestrator of the music of the heavens and revealer of the Divine Mysteries in the language of the angels. . . . "[71] And in his beloved Mulla Sadra, Nasr finds a synthesis of philosophy, Sufism, *kalam* (theology), and the sciences of *shari'a* reflected in his doctrine of the soul, which is basic to the issue of education.[72] Nasr points to the fact that at the same time that Sufism has served as a means of preserving the highest level metaphysics it has also been itself a source of criticism of modern secular thought.[73]

Finally it must be noted that Nasr rues the recent attempts on the part of many interpreters to see Sufism as a kind of transtraditional phenomenon, or an entity that is itself an independent tradition. If Sufism is not seen specifically within the Islamic context, he says, it simply cannot be understood.[74] Sufism is the soul of Islam, the integration of all that reveals the power of the traditional Islamic way, the means of moving from the periphery of existence toward the Center, a pathway on which one experiences the spiritual essence of Islam.

In sum, Seyyed Hossein Nasr persuasively makes the case for the absolute necessity of reappropriating the traditional Islamic perspective. In fairness it must be said that his work as a whole is somewhat repetitious, that in reading through his volumes one finds the same themes sounded, the same points repeated in a variety of forms. It could be argued that the very holistic nature of his presentation, the integratedness of his writing that reflects the integrity of the spiritual understanding and the spiritual path, necessitates a reiteration of the elements that contribute to this integratedness. Less elemental, but surely no less important in Nasr's presentation, is the assumption that, because he sees this message as crucial for the life and health of modern man, it bears repeating as often as possible.[75]

In many ways Hossein Nasr is the right person to make this presentation of the value of the traditional. He is a devoted Muslim, a Shi'ite,[76] a philosopher, a scientist, an artist, and one well acquainted with the Sufi path. In addition he has a broad classical education, cross-cultural experience, and obvious linguistic abilities, and he is well versed in Western physical and social sciences, history and philosophy, and classical and modern Christian doctrines and theologies. His Persian Shi'ite identity, while evident in some of his explications and in his pride of birth, does not unduly color his writings.[77] (His distaste for the contemporary religious regime in Iran is only implicit in his discussion of the dangers of contemporary Islamic fundamentalism, as well as in his presentation of Safavid Islam as representing the true essence of Shi'ite thought.)

In some ways, however, Hossein Nasr could be said to be in rather a bind. For example, one might question the nature of his real audience. That he has targeted certain specific audiences we noted earlier. But for whom is his message most persuasive? Non-Muslims will perhaps weary of his uncritical applause for traditional Islam. Secularized Muslims, those for whom Nasr has the greatest concern, most likely would not read him in any case, nor would the fundamentalists about whom he is alarmed. And traditional Muslims presumably are already persuaded, although there is no denying the power of reaffirmation in his words.

One might also ask whether Nasr's role as interpreter and defender of traditional Islam does not perhaps make it more difficult for him to explore the esoteric dimension of religious experience that cuts across discrete religious traditions (a question that he himself would probably not consider valid). Given the number of his works reiterating the same basic themes, one cannot help but wonder whether the time may have come for him to leave the apologetic to others. This is based not only on the grounds that he has said and said well what is important in this connection, but that the very resources he brings to the task of pursuing the transcendent dimension of interfaith conversation argue for his continued attention to such concerns. One hopes that the present situation of Islam in the world context, and perhaps especially of Muslims in America, does not dictate that a scholar of the capacity of Hossein Nasr remain unnecessarily locked into a cycle of defense, well-articulated as that position may be. Were he to be able to continue to apply his considerable skills, knowledge, and insight to further investigations of the esoteric and sapential dimensions of religion in general and Islam in particular, he would, in this writer's opinion, serve both traditional Islam and the cause of interfaith understanding.

A final word needs to be said, given the context of this presentation, about the ramifications of Hossein Nasr's analysis for those Muslims living in the West and particularly in America. To talk about the influence of secularism and rationalism is one thing, and a matter to which he certainly is not alone in having turned his attention. But a deeper concern comes out of Nasr's writings that I think must be addressed—his emphasis on context, atmosphere, and ambiance. What does it mean for Muslims to live in an environment that is not part of an ongoing tradition, in which there are not even remnants of Islamic civilization, art and architecture, history and philosophy? If the "totality" is wrong, is there hope that the remnant community can ever achieve that goal of movement from the periphery to the Center to which Nasr is so firmly committed and of whose validity he is so deeply persuaded?

I leave that important and potentially troubling matter—troubling at least to those who share Seyyed Hossein Nasr's convictions—to the Islamic community in America to ponder.

Notes

1. Seyyed Hossein Nasr, *Traditional Islam in the Modern World* (London: Routledge & Kegan Paul, 1981), p. viii; *Islam and the Flight of Modern Man* (London: Longman Group Ltd., 1975), p. xi. Unless otherwise noted, all works cited are those of Nasr.

2. *Traditional Islam*, p. viii.

3. *Islamic Life and Thought* (Albany: State University of New York Press, 1981), p. 2.

4. "The School of Ispahan," in M. M. Sharif, ed., *A History of Muslim Philosophy*, II (Karachi: Royal Book Co., 1983), p. 905.

5. *The Plight of Modern Man*, p. 123; see also *Traditional Islam*, p. 207.

6. *Islamic Life and Thought*, p. 2.

7. Edward Said, *Orientalism* (New York: Pantheon, 1978).

8. *Ideals and Realities of Islam* (New York: Frederick A. Praeger, 1967), p. 78.

9. Ibid., p. 250; *The Plight of Modern Man*, pp. 7–8, 125; *Islamic Life and Thought*, p. 33.

10. *The Encounter of Man and Nature: The Spiritual Crisis of Modern Man* (London: George Allen & Unwin, 1968), p. 15.

11. *Knowledge and the Sacred* (New York: Crossroad Publishing, 1981), p. viii.

12. See, e.g., "The School of Ispahan" (1966).

13. *Knowledge and the Sacred*, p. 120.

14. *Traditional Islam*, Introduction and Chapter 5.

15. Ibid., p. 87.

16. His identification of these "-isms" with Westernization is, of course, not new; see, e.g., the last chapter of *The Plight of Modern Man* in which he attacks Western Marxism, socialism, Darwinism, psychoanalysis, nihilism, and extentialism, among others.

17. *The Plight of Modern Man*, p. 13.

18. *Sufi Essays* (Albany: State University of New York Press, 1985; first pub. 1972), p. 52.

19. Ibid.

20. *Ideals and Realities*, pp. 96, 81.

21. "Who Is Man? The Perennial Answer of Islam," in J. Needleman, ed., *The Sword of Gnosis* (London: Arkana, 1986), pp. 213–14.

22. *Sufi Essays*, pp. 55–56, 85.

23. *The Plight of Modern Man*, p. 125.

24. Ibid., p. 126; cf. *Islamic Life and Thought*, p. 30.

25. "Progress and Evolution: A Reappraisal from the Traditional Perspective," *Parabola*, 4:2 (1981), 44–51.

26. Ibid., p. 45.

27. *The Encounter of Man and Nature*, pp. 127–29.

28. *Knowledge and the Sacred*, p. 43.

29. Ibid., pp. 169–70. The assumption that man is a creature in constant transition from one physical and mental condition to another, which he sees as the evolutionist position, is because of the "cloud of illusion" in which man lives, making it impossible for him to understand his environment, to discern the difference between the absolute (*mutlaq*) and the relative (*maqayyad*). Man's profound nature is essentially unchanging, attested to in the insistance of the Prophet that he would repeat to the end of time that the only answer to the question "What existed before Adam" is Adam. This is the person, this unchanging man, who is able to understand the message of tradition and who is able to be freed from the influences of theories of evolution and progress (*The Plight of Modern Man*, pp. 49–51; *Sufi Essays*, p. 86).

30. See, e.g., Jane I. Smith and Yvonne Y. Haddad, *The Islamic Understanding of Death and Resurrection* (Albany: State University of New York Press, 1981), pp. 28–29.

31. *Ideals and Realities*, pp. 20–28.

32. *Knowledge and the Sacred*, p. 146.

33. *Islamic Life and Thought*, p. 17.

34. Ibid., p. 18.

35. *Knowledge and the Sacred*, pp. 13–16; *Sufi Essays*, pp. 84–85.

36. "Progress and Evolution," 46.

37. *Knowledge and the Sacred*, p. 208.

38. *Traditional Islam*, pp. 38–39; cf. "Islamic Work Ethics," in J. Pelikan, J. Kitagawa, and S. H. Nasr, eds., *Comparative Work Ethics: Judeo-Christian, Islamic, and Eastern* (Washington, D.C.: Library of Congress, 1985), pp. 51–60.

39. "Progress and Evolution," 45.

40. *The Plight of Modern Man*, p. 75.

41. *The Encounter of Man and Nature*, pp. 13, 20.

42. Ibid., p. 105. Earlier (p. 95) he comments that if Christians spent less time trying to convert the followers of Oriental religions they would have a better chance of entering into intellectual dialogue, with them with the end result of restoring their lost spiritual vision of nature.

43. *Sufi Essays*, pp. 89–90.

44. *The Plight of Modern Man*, p. 12.

45. *The Encounter of Man and Nature*, p. 14; *Sufi Essays*, pp. 84–86; *Islamic Life and Thought*, p. 13; *Traditional Islam*, Chapter 8.

46. *Islamic Life and Thought*, p. 127.

47. *Knowledge and the Sacred*, p. 168. This entire volume is predicated on an understanding of the correct human perception of the world of nature. In a lovely passage on p. 214 he states: "The spiritual man . . . is always on nature's side for he sees in her the grand theophany which externalizes all that he is inwardly. He sees in the forms of nature the signatures of the celestial archetypes and in her movements and rhythms the exposition of a metaphysics of the highest order. . . . To contemplate the cosmos as theophany is to realize that all manifestations from the One is return to the One, that all separation is union, that all otherness is sameness, that all plenitude is the Void. It is to see God everywhere."

48. Ibid., pp. 130–31.

49. Ibid., p. 148.

50. *Ideals and Realities*, p. 16. See p. 25, where he refers to "the spiritually dangerous eclecticisms which have been showering mankind for the past century or two"; p. 75 where he affirms that "each religion emphasizes a certain aspect of the Truth."

51. "Response to Hans Küng's Paper on Christian Muslim Dialogue," *The Muslim World*, 77 (1987), 105. Cf. *Traditional Islam*, p. 263, in which he comments that "today it is too easy to be ecumenical, as this term is being currently understood in so many religious circles. When one does not have to believe in anything firmly, it is easy to open the doors to dialogue with other religions."

52. *Islamic Art and Spirituality*, p. 68. It is interesting to note that in this same volume he takes a more charitable approach to ecumenism in discussing the poetry of ʿAttar. "It is as if ʿAttar wanted to state in the classical language of Sufi poetry that veritable ecumenism is essentially of an esoteric nature and that it is only through the esoteric that man is able to penetrate into the meaning of other formal universes."

53. *Knowledge and the Sacred*, pp. 69–75.

54. *Sufi Essays*, pp. 124–25.

55. See *Islamic Life and Thought*, pp. 35–36, 70–72.

56. *Sufi Essays*, p. 150. Cf. "Self-Awareness and Ultimate Selfhood," *Religious Studies*, 13 (1977), 320–25.

57. For one of Nasr's most thought-provoking discussions of what this vision of the Center really means, the reader should see Chapter 9 of *Knowledge and the Sacred*, entitled "Principal Knowledge and the Multiplicity of Sacred Forms."

58. *The Plight of Modern Man*, p. 20.

59. *Traditional Islam*, p. 242.

60. *Ideals and Realities*, p. 111.

61. *The Plight of Modern Man*, p. 73.

62. *Traditional Islam*, p. 49; cf. *Islamic Life and Thought* in which he defines man "in both the male and female forms."

63. *Traditional Islam*, p. 49.

64. Ibid., p. 52.

65. *Islamic Life and Thought*, pp. 212–13.

66. *Knowledge and the Sacred*, p. 178. See *Islamic Art and Spirituality*, pp. 12 and 19 for his references to the gender identification of certain strands of Islamic art and symbolism.

67. *Ideals and Realities*, p. 31.

68. *Traditional Islam*, p. 28.

69. Ibid., p. 33; cf. *Islamic Life and Thought*, pp. 193–95.

70. *Traditional Islam*, pp. 178–79.

71. *Islamic Art and Spirituality*, p. 115.

72. *Traditional Islam*, p. 157; see *Sadr al-Din Shirazi and His Transcendent Theosophy* (Tehran: Imperial Iranian Academy of Philosophy, 1978), pp. 13–17.

73. "The Influence of Traditional Islamic Thought Upon Contemporary Muslim Intellectual Life," in R. Klibansky, ed., *Contemporary Philosophy* (Firanze: La Nuova Italia, 1968–71), p. 581.

74. See, e.g., *The Plight of Modern Man*, p. 49.

75. As early as 1974 he acknowledges that he has been forced to repeat certain arguments (see *The Plight of Modern Man*, Preface). It may seem excessive to some that these are still being repeated with little augmentation in 1988. See *Islamic Life and Thought* (1981), p. 3.

76. It can be argued that Shi'ites are better prepared in the traditional materials of both the Shi'ite and the Sunni traditions than are many others of their fellow Muslims.

77. In *Ideals and Realities* he mentions several times that it is "providential" that Islam contains both Sunnism and Shi'ism.

7

The Legacy of Fazlur Rahman

Frederick Mathewson Denny

Among the major Muslim thinkers of the second half of the twentieth century, Fazlur Rahman was one of the most learned in both classical Islamic and Western philosophical–theological discourse and had the widest scope in viewing and applying fundamental elements of the Islamic belief and action system. This essay is intended as a descriptive appreciation of his legacy through a selective sampling of his scholarly work, focusing on three main aspects: the philosophical–theological, the moral–ethical, and the religious–communal. Although the first aspect is the most purely "intellectual," in terms of following an argument to its logical conclusion (and Rahman was certainly one to do that), Rahman was in fact a Muslim intellectual who applied keen critical and analytical awareness to every serious topic, whether theoretical or practical, individual or communal, textual or contextual.

These three aspects of Rahman's legacy as a Muslim thinker should not be thought to be isolated from one another, whether in his numerous formal publications, in his role as a Muslim activist, or in his formative influences on the considerable community of students, Muslim and non-Muslim, he trained. Just as there was no disjunction between Rahman's thought, life, and works, so there is none among the three aspects of his legacy we examine here. For Fazlur Rahman, the scholarly, the moral–religious, and the legal–communal dimensions were all of a part. He considered religious belief without rational scrutiny both of motives and evidences to be not only foolish but immoral. Intellectualism devoid of spiritual insight and moral awareness he thought to be mere sophistry. And moral appeals and judgments without reasoned regard for their legal and communal ramifications he saw as wayward innovation, whether on the left or right of the religious–political spectrum.

A Biographical Sketch: Three Major Periods of Rahman's Work

Fazlur Rahman was born in 1919 in India's Punjab and educated there through the baccalaureate degree. He later studied at Oxford University under Professors S. Van den Bergh and H. A. R. Gibb, earning the Ph.D. in 1949 for a thesis on the medieval philosopher Ibn Sina.[1] In the 1950s, Rahman taught first at the

University of Durham in England, and later at McGill University in Montreal, Canada, where he was on the faculty of the recently established Institute of Islamic Studies. Soon after arriving at McGill, Rahman published the important *Prophecy in Islam*,[2] which drew on his Oxford philosophical and theological studies, in addition to classical Islamic texts and languages and major Western philosophical texts and commentaries in Greek, Latin, German, and French.[3]

In the early 1960s Fazlur Rahman was called to Pakistan to head the new Institute of Islamic Research in Karachi. He founded and for several years edited the journal *Islamic Studies* and was deeply engaged in Islamic affairs in Pakistan, both as a scholar and as an influential shaper of opinion and policy. When a new regime took over the country in the late 1960s, Rahman was placed in extreme personal danger by religious fanatics who rejected his modernist positions as inimical to Islam. Rahman was rescued, in effect, by an offer to teach at the University of California, Los Angeles; he moved there, with his family, in 1968. In 1969 he was appointed professor of Islamic thought at the University of Chicago, where he remained until his death in the summer of 1988. Although Fazlur Rahman's major contributions to scholarship included works published before his long Chicago tenure, it was at the University of Chicago that his position as the leading Muslim modernist scholar of his generation was solidified through publications, consultations, preaching, and religious leadership in the Muslim community, and especially through his training of younger scholars who came from various countries to study under him. Rahman was the first Muslim ever to be appointed to the faculty of the Divinity School of the University of Chicago and he was, ironically, the first (and to date only) Muslim to receive the prestigious Giorgio Levi Della Vida Medal for the study of Islamic civilization from the Gustave E. von Grunebaum Center for Near Eastern Studies of UCLA.[4]

Three Periods of Fazlur Rahman's Scholarship

Fazlur Rahman's earliest period of major scholarship, during his Oxford, Durham, and McGill years, focused mainly on philosophy and theology as known through classical Islamic sources. *Avicenna's Psychology* and *Prophecy in Islam* may be read as coolly objective studies by a professional philosopher with no apologetic agenda of his own, despite the fact that the latter work is a treatment of conflicts between philosophy and orthodoxy in Islam.

The Pakistan period saw continued foundational thinking, but with an agenda dictated by Rahman's leadership role in the development of a sound Islamic studies curriculum for the young country's religious leaders. Two works of fundamental importance were written in Pakistan: *Islamic Methodology in History* and *Islam*.[5] The first is an historical–critical analysis of the prophetic traditions, or *hadith*, and their role in the development of the idea of Muhammad's Sunnah as one of the two major sources of Muslim jurisprudence (the other being the Qur'an). The second is an advanced interpretive survey of Islam, with particular emphasis on normative legal and theological matters and their working out in history. Although *Islam* is often used as a university-level textbook, it is actually much more than that; it is an original, intellectually very demanding discussion of the main doctrines, developments, and institutions of Islam since its founding.[6]

Pakistan effectively ejected Fazlur Rahman for his controversial modernism but appeared to reverse itself when its most accomplished Muslim thinker gained much positive recognition at Chicago. Pakistan was, in any event, too small for Rahman, who needed and deserved the sophisticated and cosmopolitan environment of the University of Chicago with its splendidly abrasive intellectual style and wholesomely contentious atmosphere. A few years after his emigration, his *hijrah*, from Pakistan, Rahman was invited back for a visit, whereupon he was feted and honored by officialdom. Nevertheless, he did not change his opinion, which he was not afraid to express, that President Zia was a disaster for both religion and homeland. Rahman could not be bought by a conciliatory Pakistan any more than he could be silenced in the years when he had been a prominent figure going against the tide of what he experienced of fundamentalist obscurantism and threats.

During his Chicago years Rahman published a number of major articles[7] and four books, whose titles are a veritable memorandum of the complete range of his career. *The Philosophy of Mulla Sadra* is a good example of his continuing interest in purely academic scholarship. *Islam and Modernity: Transformation of an Intellectual Tradition* provides a critique of Islamic education and suggests remedies, and *Health and Medicine in the Islamic Tradition* offers a comprehensive discussion of how health and moral–ethical balance express Islam's ideal and empowering dynamic as integrality and wholeness. The fourth book, *Major Themes of the Qur'an*, marked a departure in Rahman's thought, bringing his other concerns more definitively than ever under the guidance of Islam's scripture and showing how that message can and should be directly applied in new and creative ways in the real world of today.[8]

Let us turn to the three foci of Rahman's thought suggested earlier and view their characteristic content and concerns and the ways in which he addressed them. We will draw on works from all periods of his career, but especially from the last, the Chicago years, when all three dimensions—the philosophical–theological, moral–ethical, and religious–communal—were fully integrated in Rahman's mature and vigorously Qur'anically based vision of authentic Islam for this age.

Philosophical–Theological Dimensions

The extent to which Fazlur Rahman's early period of scholarship was centered in a somewhat detached and chiefly philosophical pursuit of knowledge and understanding was brought out in comments that he once made to a group of graduate students at Chicago. The students wanted Rahman to meet with them on a regular basis to read in Arabic some works of the medieval theologian and legal scholar Ibn Taimiya (d. 1328). Today that great Sunni figure would be called a "fundamentalist," but that term does not do justice to Ibn Taimiya's truly radical posture with respect both to what in his time were considered traditional—and therefore acceptable—legal positions and to rational theology, which in spite of the hostility of Ibn Taimiya's own legal school (Hanbalite), was in his hands a deadly apologetic weapon. Ibn Taimiya claimed the right of independent legal decision-making (*ijtihad*), against the mainstream of orthodoxy, and he used the subtlest dialectic in his attacks on theological positions with which he disagreed—his *kalam* battered lesser *kalams*.[9] Rahman hesitated when the students, I among them, asked him to read Ibn Taimiya with them. Then he smiled and recalled that he had been obliged to read a great deal of Ibn Taimiya in the writing of *Prophecy in Islam* and in the process had been surprised at how much he came to admire his thought. We could tell, however, that it would take some persuading to get Rahman to spend several months in the company of a thinker who was not exactly his cup of tea—better Ibn Sina or Ibn Rushd (two medieval Muslim philosophers). But he assented, and we were treated to an extended dialogue between two very independent thinkers.

Most of *Prophecy in Islam* treats classical Muslim philosophers, especially al-Farabi and Avicenna (Ibn Sina), who were heavily influenced by the Greek traditions extending back to Plato and Aristotle. A much smaller portion of the book discusses the Muslim philosophical doctrines concerning prophecy in light of the orthodox theology of Ibn Hazm, al-Ghazali, al-Shahrastani, Ibn Taimiya, and Ibn Khaldun. Rahman's treatment of Ibn Taimiya, toward the close of the book, shows a shift, even a sea change toward a more self-consciously Islamic scholarship that in the ensuing years became more religiously and morally passionate without losing its philosophical penetration. His highly approving characterization of Ibn Taimiya's view of the goal of human life foreshadowed his own strong voice speaking through his later works written in Karachi.

> . . . Ibn Taimiya breaks through the scholastic formalism of Kalam and grapples with what are the basic issues between the intellectualist ethics of Hellenism and the moral dynamism of the Semitic tradition. He rejects the concept of the purely cognitive goal of human life because he thinks that despite the efforts of the Muslim philosophers to safeguard the transcendence of God and of truth, the intellectual approach to reality is essentially humanist and destroys the absolute character of the moral imperative.[10]

> According to the philosophers the goal of man in which his ultimate bliss consists is the contemplation of reality; in their thoroughly intellectualist-mystical attitude to life, life of religio–moral action is at best a ladder which is to be transcended. The orthodox impulse is activist; it does not reject intellectualism but subordinates it to the end of moral dynamism. The philosopher's reality is an immobile eternal truth; the orthodoxy's ultimate reality is also a certain eternal truth, but being primarily a moral truth, it must result in moral action. The orthodox conception of truth is therefore not of something which merely *is* but essentially of something which "commands." It is thus the evaluation of the shari'a that is at stake.[11]

Rahman had profound respect for Ibn Taimiya's moral earnestness, even though the two scholars' temperaments and styles could not have differed more. Ibn Taimiya was irascible, attacking people and positions without regard for prudence or his own safety. He spent considerable periods in prison for the forthright expression of his views. A high point of the graduate seminar at Chicago was the reading of Ibn Taimiya's essay on "The Divine Decree and Predestination,"[12] in which Ibn Taimiya refutes those who use God's foreknowledge and predistination as excuses for wrongdoing. On the contrary, God wishes and commands certain responses and attitudes from his creatures, but he does not force them.[13] If he did, religion and morals would be empty and meaningless. God wills certain unfortunate events, including human straying, but he does not necessarily either desire or approve them. Ibn Taimiya distinguished God's natural from his religiomoral will[14] and argued that the former entails the possibility of human wrongdoing. The point is that God desires a moral universe in which people make real choices, whether for good or evil. He does not like evil choices or deeds; rather, he permits them to occur. This in no way implies imperfection or weakness in God, according to Ibn Taimiya; on the contrary, it shows his deeply moral nature. God has created the world, as the Qur'an declares, for "just purposes,"[15] and this requires allowing the possibility of evil as well as good. It is up to human moral agency to respond to the conditions and challenges of life and to strive in the following of God's way as provided in the religion of Islam. Such freedom requires clear and precise thinking.

Rahman admired Ibn Taimiya's manner of arguing for free will in opposition to the prevailing predestinarianism that wanted to embrace God's inscrutable decree while insisting that humans somehow "acquire" their acts,[16] for which they are thus responsible. Neither Rahman nor Ibn Taimiya could agree with this classic Ash'ari position because it was contradictory in the formal logical sense and morally repugnant, as well, in that it encouraged fatalism. Other aspects of Ibn Taimiya's thought also appealed to Rahman, including his repudiation of popular saint veneration and other superstitions and any attempts at mystical interpretation of Islam in the direction of what he disparagingly labeled "theosophic intuitionism."[17]

Although Ibn Taimiya was severely critical of esoteric religion and folk superstitions, such as visiting saint shrines for blessings and intercession, he was not categorically anti-Sufi—in fact, he belonged to a Sufi order and was buried in the Sufi cemetery in Damascus.[18] Rahman included two chapters on Sufism in *Islam*. Although he offers a balanced and fair-minded account of the rise, development, and spread of Sufi ideas and organizations, there is an underlying tone of disapproval. Rahman insists that Sufism has never been able to provide an independent, supplemental knowledge of reality not already contained in the Qur'an and the Hadith. Nor has Sufism been helpful in focusing true Islamic beliefs and values; rather it has tended to adapt itself to numerous preexisting and varied cultural milieus. The monistic form of Sufi theosophy developed by the Andalusian genius Ibn 'Arabi was especially damaging to orthodoxy, Rahman argued, because it identified God with his creation. This doctrine of *wahdat al-wujud*, "unity of being," threatened a "*bouleversement* of the very concept of the Islamic Shari'a."[19] Al-Ghazali (d. 1111 C.E.) had Rahman's thanks for incorporating the admirable traits of Sufi insight and piety into orthodox Sunnism. Al-Ghazali demonstrated conclusively, through his experiential method, that Sufism

> has no *cognitive content or object but the verities of the Faith*. He [i.e., al-Ghazali], therefore, disallowed the pretensions of theosophic mysticism and castigated the men of ecstatic delirium. This was a remarkable lesson taught by a great mystic spirit, one of the most remarkable lessons, we venture to think, in the whole history of mysticism—viz., that mysticism is *not* a way of finding extra *facts* about Reality but is a meaningful way of looking at it, of looking at it as a unity. Further the unity of the mystic consciousness is *conditioned* by the factual content (however much it may try to transcend that content), which it tests and transforms by new *meanings*. This was an especially reassuring discovery for the position of the Shari'a, and it revolutionized the relationship of Sufism to the orthodox faith, producing in course of time men who worked out that relationship . . . and restated their faith in new terms.[20]

By the time Rahman had written this passage, he had been in Pakistan for several years, already directing the Central Institute for Islamic Research and editing its journal. The work on Ibn Sina that Rahman did for his doctorate provided the foundation for much of his later philosophical and theological work. Although Ibn Sina and other Muslim philosophers—al-Farbi, al-Kindi, and the last of the great Aristotelians, Ibn Rushd (Averroes)—were eventually rejected by the orthodoxyy, their intellectual contributions have been fundamental and enduring, as has been borne out in the history of philosophy in the West, in which Ibn Sina and Ibn Rushd, especially, have had a major impact on Christian scholastic theological methodology. It may be that Fazlur Rahman comes closer to such thinkers, all of whom by their own testimonies were sincere Muslims, than to the theologians of classical Islam, whether Mu'tazili "rationalists" or Ash'ari *mutakallims* of the Sunni mainstream.

Certainly Rahman was no Mu'tazili.[21] With all of his devotion to rational discourse in the discovery of knowledge and the proper adjudication of religious and legal matters, he considered the Mu'tazilis to have gone so far in their rationalism as to make human reason equal to revelation. Although they were trying in part to avoid extreme anthropomorphism (thus their metaphorical interpretations of the Qur'an), Rahman felt that they instead courted its opposite: anthroposophy, a rational cognition of spirit and divinity.[22]

One day during a major academic conference, after a particularly stimulating panel discussion on Christian–Muslim relations and controversies, several of the participants continued the conversation over lunch. Fazlur Rahman listened closely to a Muslim colleague, a prominent specialist in philosophy, who was expatiating on the relation between reason and revelation in medieval thought, both Muslim and Christian. Rahman politely but deftly questioned the scholar, forcing him to declare that, for him, God is ultimately not a person but a principle, whose nature and purposes can be known by philosophical reasoning. Rahman then snapped out, with flashing eyes and a dazzling smile: "Then, you are a Mu'tazilite!" There was no reply. Woe be to the person who challenged Fazlur Rahman in disputation. He never descended to ad hominem argument but always commanded the high ground of formal dialectic, without regard for personal likings or animosities.

Although Rahman was a great student of Ibn Sina, he did not resemble him in style or temperament. Ibn Sina apparently had a superior and self-sufficient attitude, declaring, for example, that he learned nothing new after his eighteenth year.[23] I compare Rahman more closely with Ibn Rushd, who unlike his great precursors al-Farabi and Ibn Sina was also a jurisconsult and judge and thus deeply involved in the concerns of the common people and sensitive to their convictions and needs. Al-Farabi's and Ibn Sina's lofty view that philosophy is superior to revelation is tempered in Ibn Rushd, who regarded them as being on the same plane. Ibn Rushd argued in favor of philosophical discourse within the Islamic sciences, not on purely intellectual grounds; rather, he argued on legal grounds that philosophy was not only permitted, but commanded as a sufficient duty (*fard kifaya*), though restricted to those fully qualified and not open to the generality of Muslims.

In the final phase of his career, at the University of Chicago, Fazlur Rahman published a major study of the great Persian philosophical theologian Sadr al-Din al-Shirazi, known as "Mulla Sadra."[24] Although by that time Rahman had abundant experience in practical Islamic affairs as well as in scholarship and teaching, he still pursued philosophic discourse as an occupation inherently desirable for a Muslim thinker. Most modern philosophy historians consider philosophy in Islam to have succumbed to al-Ghazali's famous attack in the eleventh century,[25] but only the classical Aristotelian and neo-Platonic forms were discontinued, or at least denied orthodox approval. Muslim scholars enthusiastic for theosophical forms of discourse in recent decades have reminded us that Islamic philosophic work flourished after al-Ghazali, although along lines more suitable to the religious experiences and convictions of Qur'anically based believers. Rahman argues in his study of Mulla Sadra that this scholarship has emphasized esoteric Sufi and thus "intuitionist" dimensions of post-Ghazalian Islamic theosophy, whether of the Illuminationist School of al-Suhrawardi (d. 1191 C.E.) or of the later Mulla Sadra. Characteristically, Rahman demonstrates the superior virtues in this literature of "its purely intellectual and philosophical hard core, which is of immense value and interest to the modern student of philosophy."[26]

Moral–Ethical Themes

Beginning especially with his work in Karachi, Fazlur Rahman's published scholarship was characterized by a sense of moral and ethical relevance if not urgency. Although he had long known the content of the Qur'anic message, a rereading when he was around fifty[27] seems to have moved him enough to write

a major intrepretative study of it. *Major Themes of the Qur'an* is not a traditional work of Qur'anic exegesis but rather an essay relating the text to both its
original context of seventh-century Arabia and the modern day. Rahman
discovered an underlying unity and cohesiveness in the message of the Qur'an
by centering on its ethical character. The details of social relations and understanding of the natural world may have changed since Muhammad's time, but
the deep moral dimension of Islam never alters. In *Major Themes* Rahman
sought to discover the principles by which God's "command," the essential
force of the Qur'an, should be understood and applied in every age. Rahman
sets himself free from traditional Qur'an interpretation in his effort to render
the Message accessible to his contemporaries. As Marcia Hermansen has put
it, Rahman "lamented the loss of this resource to most Muslims for whom it is
lost beneath benign neglect, taboolike reverence, or traditional commentary
which focuses on the intricacies of grammatical and rhetorical points and views
each verse atomistically."[28]

Major Themes treats God, Man as Individual, Man in Society, Nature,
Prophethood and Revelation, Eschatology, Satan and Evil, and the Emergence
of the Muslim Community. Rahman considered the Qur'an the major source
of Islamic law rather than the lawbook of Islam.[29] The difference is essential,
because regarding the Qur'an as lawbook limits its scope and application and
overlooks its flexibility and its dynamism for the development of a more truly
Islamic community.

> Generally speaking, each legal or quasi-legal pronouncement [i.e., in the
> Qur'an] is accompanied by a *ratio legis* explaining why a law is being
> enunciated. To understand a *ratio legis* fully, an understanding of the socio-
> historical background (what the Qur'anic commentators call "occasions of
> revelation") is necessary. The *ratio legis* is the essence of the matter, the actual
> legislation being its embodiment so long as it faithfully and correctly realizes
> the *ratio*; if it does not, the law must change. Traditional lawyers, however,
> while recognizing the *ratio legis*, generally stuck to the letter of the law and
> enunciated the principle that "Although a law is occasioned by a specific
> situation, its application nevertheless becomes universal."[30]

At the individual–personal level of moral accountability, Rahman discerned
taqwa, usually translated as "reverential fear" or "piety," as transcendentally
grounded "conscience."[31] He likened *taqwa* to an "inner torch" that guides one
through life's difficult choices. *Taqwa*, although it may operate at only the
minimal level of "naive self-righteousness," can reach a

> high point where one can almost completely X-ray one's state of mind and
> conscience. The kind of being "made public" of the inner self so poignantly
> portrayed as occurring on the Day of Judgment is what the Qur'an really
> desires to take place here in this life; for a man who can X-ray himself
> effectively and hence diagnose his inner state has nothing to be afraid of if his
> inner being goes public.[32]

Years before his rereading of the Qur'an as an essentially ethical message,
Rahman had criticized traditional Islamic philosophy for its avoidance of

ethical discourse. Although this may have been a product of philosophy's disinclination to become a rival system of "do's" and "don'ts," Rahman conjectured that it was a result of "the philosophers being too enamoured of their metaphysical heights to condescend to climb down to ethics."[33] One may question whether metaphysical preoccupations prevented Muslim philosophers (with few exceptions) from engaging in building a systematic ethics based on reason, arguing that it was the strong Qur'an- and Sunna-based piety of most Muslims that caused them to distrust value systems derived from human reasoning. In any case, Rahman called for the construction of a system of Islamic ethics growing out of the Qur'an.[34]

Religious–Communal Themes

Rahman insisted that Qur'anic ethics is both individual and communal. In fact, the Qur'an requires a strong communal bond among the Muslims to realize God's purposes on earth. The essential ingredient in relating the Word of God anew to the world in each generation is a sound educational system. In one of his late books, *Islam and Modernity: Transformation of an Intellectual Tradition*, Rahman surveyed and evaluated the history of Muslim intellectual life and education, with particular emphasis on modernism.

Already in Karachi during the 1960s, Rahman was beginning to envision new ways of training Islamic scholars, combining what is best in both traditional and modern sources and methods. In the 1970s, Rahman and his colleague at the University of Chicago, the political scientist Leonard Binder, codirected a Ford Foundation–funded project on "Islam and Social Change." *Islam and Modernity* was the product of Rahman's own scholarly involvement in the project in the form of a "general work on the medieval Islamic educational system, with its major features and deficiencies, and on the modernization efforts undertaken during the past century or so."[35]

Central to Rahman's book is a critique of how the Qur'an and Hadith were misconstrued by Muslim scholars in medieval times, made into rigid and inflexible guides—for all time, as it were—and not recognized as the products of their own times and circumstances. This is not to suggest that Rahman considered the Qur'an, particularly, to have been written by Muhammad. But he did feel that if it is not understood in relation to the times it originally addressed, Muslims will never really be able to apply it to changing times. This point is closely related to the one made previously, about the *ratio legis* of the Qur'an and the problem of its universal application.

In *Islam and Modernity*, Rahman shows how the Qur'an and Hadith became embedded in a rigid, static system of interpretation and jurisprudence. This led to the challenge for Muslims in modern times either to turn away from those sources if they would prosper and "catch up" in technology, science, and development, or to acquiesce to an essentially medieval worldview with an archaic, unworkable religious–legal system that thwarts progress and full participation in the modern world, with its benefits for human life. Briefly, Rahman argued that Muslims have a choice between secularism or an outmoded system, unless and until they return to the Qur'an and interpret it by understanding much of its content as general moral–ethical guidance and prescription and not rigid law. That is, the Qur'an can and must be liberated from its prison of commentary and law and applied in fresh ways and with flexible principles to new realities. Rahman was convinced that not only can the Qur'an withstand such employment, but only in this way can it prevail, leading Muslims to meet the challenges of the modern age and helping advance all modern life with renewed faith and dedication. Such an approach to the Qur'an can be likened to the Protestant reformers' conviction that the Bible is sole authority in doctrinal and communal matters. As the Bible was liberated from the medieval structures of Catholic tradition and interpretation, so also can the Qur'an be recovered as it was intended to be: the reliable, dynamic guidance that provides the principles for all imaginable circumstances, problems, developments, and opportunities that its faithful community will encounter.

We have surveyed three areas of Fazlur Rahman's thought as a way of discerning and appreciating his legacy. It is still too early to predict with certainty what his long-term influence will be. But it is safe to predict that there will be such influence and it will be significant, not simply because of the extent of his engagement with issues and persons over the past forty years, but even more because of the depth and quality of his engagement with the enduring sources and processes of both the Islamic and the Western intellectual heritage: namely, the Qur'an and Sunna, on the one side, and philosophy on the other. It would not be perverse, although it might surprise some, to suggest that Rahman considered the infinitely inventive human intellect to be, apart from the Revelation itself, the main "sign" (*aya*) of God's benevolent and just purposes in the created realm. The Qur'an certainly is the fundamental authority and its commands must be obeyed; but without the believers' intellectual exertion (*ijtihad*) to comprehend and apply it within the often confusing and contradictory circumstances of historical process, it will languish as a prisoner of dead tradition instead of being permitted to shed its full illumination and regenerating power in the Umma and the world. At bottom, Fazlur Rahman was fulfilled in his remarkable intellectual and activist Muslim odyssey through an eventful and productive life because he was both a keen student and a faithful servant of the Qur'an. His legacy is fundamentally intellectual and moral, as is suggested by the relative proportions dedicated to his thought in this essay. As for the religious–communal dimensions, it is up to Muslims to take Rahman's legacy and invigorate it through the actual structures and dynamics of corporate Muslim life.

Notes

1. The thesis was published as *Avicenna's Psychology* (London: Oxford University Press, 1952). It is a translation and commentary of Ibn Sina's *Kitab al-Najat*, Book II,

Chapter VI. Rahman published an edition of the Arabic text under the title *Avicenna's De Anima* (London: Oxford University Press, 1959).

2. *Prophecy in Islam: Philosophy and Orthodoxy* (London: Allen & Unwin, 1958).

3. Rahman had mastered German before he left India. He once told me that he had translated Ignaz Goldziher's fundamental study of classical Qur'an commentary, *Die Richtungen der islamischen Koranauslegung* (Leiden: E. J. Brill, 1920), into English but lost the manuscript in the confusion of India's partition in 1947. His labors at Oxford and afterwards prevented him from attempting to reconstitute the project.

4. On the occasion of the awarding of the Levi Della Vida Medal to Rahman in 1983, a conference was held at UCLA and the papers later published as *Ethics in Islam*, Richard G. Hovannisian, ed. (Malibu, CA: Undena Publications, 1985). Such recognition by an institution that has been dominated by Western, some would say Orientalist, approaches to scholarship, would probably not impress traditionalist Muslims, on the one hand, nor revisionist Western scholars, on the other. But Rahman was grateful for the award, which he knew symbolized genuine respect and admiration for his work. Others who have received the Levi Della Vida Medal are Robert Brunschvig, Joseph Schacht, Francesco Gabrieli, S. D. Goitein, G. E. von Grunebaum (posthumously), Franz Rosenthal, Albert Hourani, W. Montgomery Watt, and Annemarie Schimmel.

5. *Islamic Methodology in History* (Karachi: Central Institute of Islamic Research, 1965). The contents were first published in the Institute's journal *Islamic Studies*. *Islam* (London and New York: Holt, Rinehart and Winston, 1966; [paperback] New York: Anchor Books, 1968; [2nd ed.] Chicago: University of Chicago Press, 1979).

6. It is ironic that in Rahman's *Islam*, Islam, a system of religious symbols and action fully as centered in ortho*praxy* concerns as Judaism, is more focused on ortho*doxy* than it normally appears to be in surveys by Muslims. And it is strange that the book contains no description or analysis of Islam's ritual practices and only offers passing remarks on prayer, fasting, almsgiving, and pilgrimage when summarizing the contents of the Qur'an. *Islam*, 2nd ed. (Chicago: University of Chicago Press, 1979), pp. 36–37. It is possible that Rahman thought the Pillars of Islam and other devotional–ritual practices to be too obviously important, and thus not in need of elementary description and analysis in *Islam*, which otherwise includes much on practical legal and moral issues Muslims face. But Rahman was not a student of religion as much as he was a philosophical theologian with a strong legal bent. Religious experience and piety did not attract his attention nearly as much as did conceptual matters.

7. Among them are the following: (1) *philosophical–theological*: "The Eternity of the World and the Heavenly Bodies in Post-Avicennan Philosophy" and "The God-World Relationship in Mulla Sadra," in *Essays in Islamic Philosophy and Science*, ed. George F. Hourani (Albany: State University of New York Press, 1975), pp. 222–53; (2) *religious–communal*: "Islamic Studies and the Future of Islam," in *Islamic Studies: A Tradition and Its Problems*, ed. Malcolm H. Kerr (Malibu, Calif.: Undena Publications, 1980), pp. 125–33; "Some Islamic Issues in the Ayyub Khan Era," in *Essays on Islamic Civilization: Presented to Niyazi Berkes*, ed. Donald P. Little (Leiden: E. J. Brill, 1976), pp. 284–302; (3) *moral–ethical*: "Law and Ethics in Islam," in *Ethics in Islam*, pp. 3–16. Rahman chose the topic of ethics in Islam for the special conference that was held in his honor (see n. 4). He thought that the subject was too seldom treated by scholars, Muslim or otherwise. (Personal communication, autumn 1982.)

8. *The Philosophy of Mulla Sadra* (Sadr al-Din al-Shirazi) (Albany: State University of New York Press, 1975); *Islam and Modernity: Transformation of an Intellectual Tradition* (Chicago: University of Chicago Press, 1982); *Health and Medicine in the*

Islamic Tradition (New York: Crossroad, 1987); *Major Themes of the Qur'an* (Minneapolis and Chicago: Bibliotheca Islamica, 1980).

9. *Kalam* is an Arabic word meaning "words," "discourse," and is translated in this context as "dogmatic" or "dialectical theology." *Ilm al-kalam* is "the science of discourse," that is, "theology." A more religiously self-conscious term for the enterprise is '*ilm al-tawhid*, "the science of the Divine Unity."

10. *Prophecy in Islam*, pp. 104–105.

11. Ibid., 110. Rahman's emphasis.

12. "Fi 'l-qada' wa 'l-qadar," in *Majmu' at al-Rasa' il al-Kubra* (al-Qahira: Matba'a Muhammad 'Ali Sabih, 1386/1966), 2: 89–95.

13. On this related topic, see in the same collection of Ibn Taimiya's essays "*Al-'irada wa 'l-' amr*" ("The [sc. Divine] Desire and Command"), 1: 326–89.

14. Ibn Taimiya calls the first *al-'irada al-kauniya* ("universal [in the sense of 'natural'] desire") and the latter *al-'irada al-diniya* ("religiomoral desire"). '*Irada* does not quite mean "will" in the sense of *mashi'ah*; but it implies more than the English "desire," in the direction of "volition."

15. Sura 15, vs. 85. *wa ma khalaqna al samawati wa 'l-' arda wa ma baynahuma 'illa bi 'l-haqqi.*

16. This is known as the doctrine of *kasb* (also *iktisab*), "acquisition," formulated by the great Sunni theologian Abu al-Hasan al-Ash'ari (d. 935 c.e.). A perceptive and accessible discussion of the doctrine, with bibliography, is provided by George Makdisi, "Ethics in Islamic Traditionalist Doctrine," *Ethics in Islam*, ed. Hovannisian, ed., pp. 52–55.

17. "The Post-Formative Developments in Islam: I," *Islamic Studies*, I: 4 (December 1962), 21.

18. See Henri Laoust's article, "Ibn Taymiyya," *Encyclopaedia of Islam*, new edition, 3:953. See also George Makdisi's article, "Ibn Taymiyah," in *The Encyclopedia of Religion*, ed. Mircea Eliade (New York: Macmillan–Free Press, 1987). On Ibn Taimiya's Sufi connections, see George Makdisi, "Ibn Taimiya: A Sufi of the Qadiriya Order," *American Journal of Arabic Studies* 1 (1973), 118–29.

19. *Islam*, second ed., p. 147.

20. *Islam*, p. 144 (Rahman's emphasis).

21. A balanced introduction to "Mu'tazili thought is the article "al-Mu'tazila," by S. Nyberg, in *The Shorter Encyclopaedia of Islam*, ed. H. A. R. Gibb and K. H. Kramers (Leiden: E. J. Brill, 1953), pp. 421–27. Rahman discusses the school in *Islam*, pp. 87–92 and passim.

22. H. A. R. Gibb wrote that "the orthodox rightly rejected these pretensions, for in religion anthroposophy is a more insidious solvent than anthropomorphism." *Mohammedanism* (New York: Oxford University Press, 1962), p. 116. Quoted in Rahman, *Islam*, p. 90.

23. See William Gohlman, *The Life of Ibn Sina: A Critical Edition and Annotated Translation* (Albany: State University of New York Press, 1974), pp. 37–39.

24. *The Philosophy of Mulla Sadra* (Albany: State University of New York Press, 1975).

25. His *Tahafut al-falasifa* ("The Incoherence of the Philosophers") was very influential in bringing about the end of open philosophic discourse in the central Islamic lands. Ibn Rushd's brilliant and fair-minded counterrefutation, *Tahafut al-tahafut* ("The Incoherence of 'The Incoherence'"), written in the next century, although it carefully presented an entire Aristotelian philosophical system adapted to Islam, nevertheless had little influence on subsequent philosophy in Islam.

26. *The Philosophy of Mulla Sadra*, p. vii. Rahman argues that Mulla Sadra was not a Sufi, but a true philosopher who can be understood only through philosophic research. To approach post-Ghazalian Islamic philosophy with what Rahman considered inferior methods is to distort the literature's true intent with a misguided appeal to mystical intuition that some might consider safe from the scrutiny and criticism of guardians of orthodoxy. Rahman refutes "theosophic intuitionism" on both Islamic and philosophic grounds. See "The Post-Formative Developments in Islam-I," p. 21.

27. It is possible that this productive rereading took place around the time of Rahman's move to America in 1968, but perhaps it was later. In any event, while I was writing my dissertation on the Qur'an under Rahman's guidance in 1971–74, I was made keenly aware of his intense preoccupation with the Qur'an by his frequent remarks about its profoundly ethical nature. In phone conversations, he quoted long Qur'an passages to me from memory, providing both the original Arabic and his own always exemplary spontaneous English translation of the text. Although Fazlur Rahman was an extremely conscientious academic adviser—he returned fully annotated draft materials to me by return mail—his burning passion for the Qur'anic text during our conversations was, to my mind, prompted by something more fundamental than his concern to help a struggling dissertation writer (although that was also an almost sacred duty for him.)

28. Marcia K. Hermansen, "An Introduction to Fazlur Rahman," unpublished paper, p. 3. A perceptive and admiring but critical appreciation of Rahman's *Major Themes of the Qur'an* and *Islam and Modernity: Transformation of an Intellectual Tradition* is Kenneth Cragg's essay, "Fazlur Rahman of Karachi and Chicago," in his *The Pen and the Faith: Eight Modern Muslim Writers and the Qur'an* (London: George Allen & Unwin, 1985), pp. 91–108.

29. *Major Themes*, p. 47.

30. Ibid., p. 48.

31. Ibid., p. 29.

32. Ibid., p. 120.

33. "The Post-Formative Developments in Islam-II," *Islamic Studies* 2:3 (September 1963), 302. For a detailed discussion of Rahman's critique of both theological and philosophical, as well as mystical, reasoning patterns and processes in the formative Islamic periods, see Frederick M. Denny, "Fazlur Rahman: Muslim Intellectual," *Muslim World*, LXXIX (1989) 91–101.

34. "Law and Ethics in Islam," *Ethics in Islam*, p. 14.

35. *Islam and Modernity*, p. 1.

IV

ISLAMIC ACTIVITY
IN THE UNITED STATES

8

Political Activity of Muslims
in America

Steve A. Johnson

Islam has become an American religion. Recent estimates of the number of Muslims in America range from 2 million to 8 million, with the most reliable 1986 estimate being approximately 4.7 million.[1] The first major wave of Muslims emigrating from the Middle East to the United States began between 1875 and World War I. This was followed by second and third waves of immigration between the 1920s and World War II, and 1947 and the mid-1960s, respectively.[2] A recent study reports that "relative to the total number of all immigrants entering the U.S., the number of Muslim immigrants has nearly doubled over the last two decades. . . ."[3] However, despite the growing number of Muslim immigrants attaining U.S. citizenship, and the fact that nearly 30 percent of all Muslims in the United States are indigenous American citizens, as a group Muslims remain essentially a political nonentity.

This study is an initial investigation, albeit sketchy, into the political activity of Muslims in America. It describes two independent spheres of political activity, the political activity between Muslim groups in America and the current political activity of Muslims vis-à-vis the larger non-Muslim American society.

On December 6, 1986, the Planning Committee of the Islamic Society of North America (ISNA) held a public hearing in Plainfield, Indiana, in an attempt to identify what a broad cross-section of Muslims in America viewed as strategic priorities for Muslims in the next decade. The report submitted by that committee noted six priorities, including community development, which was further subdivided into political, legal, and social action. The section of the report on political action is brief but important:

> In order to exert influence on the political decision-making [*sic*] and legislation in North America, ISNA should launch a campaign to educate Muslim citizens about their voting rights and mobilize them to vote on issues affecting Islam and Muslims. On a longer term basis, ISNA should develop communication with and among politically active Muslims and establish a separate political organization in due course.[4]

This solitary paragraph is significant because it was the result of the growing criticism leveled by many ISNA members that no appreciable political activity was being undertaken by the organization. Thus ISNA, whose leadership rests primarily in the hands of individuals with Islamic movement backgrounds, that is, the Ikhwan al-Muslimun and Jamaati Islami, and who were generally more concerned with the Islamic movements in the countries from which they immigrated, was forced to begin considering political action inside America.

Although the debate on whether or not Muslims should enter the American political arena was raging, ISNA was confronted with the fact that local Islamic organizations were not waiting for a consensus opinion and were engaging in their own political activity. Should political action prove to be an ever more popular issue, ISNA, purportedly the leading Islamic organization in North America, needed either to take the lead or at some level to coordinate the local efforts.

Before considering the political activities either within or outside ISNA's domain, it is instructive to consider some of the Islamic groups opposed to the idea of political activity by Muslims in America. Three general groups are against any form of political activity, and a fourth group advocates caution with extended educational and spiritual preparation before engaging in politics. The opposition consists of the Tablighi Jamaat, the Salafis, and utopian separatist Afro–American Muslim groups.

The Tablighi Jamaat, composed largely of Indo–Pakistanis and Afro–Americans, boasts the single largest gathering of Muslims in North America. Their annual ijtima'at (literally "gatherings") draw in excess of 10,000 Muslims, all males. One author, contrasting the political involvement of the Tablighi Jamaat and ISNA, wrote the following:

> It is worthwhile to note here that the Tablighi Jama'at, unlike ISNA, is completely apolitical and will have nothing to do with politics in Canada or even with Islamic movements in the Muslim world, even if these be traditionalist movements like that in Afghanistan or Iran. The apolitical tendencies of the Tablighi Jama'at are not a reflection of traditionalism as such, because most revolutionary Islamic movements are traditionalist, in the manner of the Islamic Republic of Iran. Rather, the apolitical streak of the Tabligh appears to eminate [sic] from the background to traditionalism in India, which for various reasons has become apolitical for the last few centuries.[5]

The members of the Tablighi Jamaat confine themselves to the ritualistic elements of Islam with a special emphasis on calling lapsed Muslim males back to worship in the *masajid* (mosques). An example of the Tablighi view on political action was a criticism against ISNA's recommendation for Muslims to participate in that arena. The criticism occupied the pages of the newsletter of the Tablighi-controlled Cleveland, Ohio, masjid for several months in 1986. The essence of the criticism was that a *kufr* (unbelief) system (that is, the American government) cannot give rise to an Islamic state.

The Salafiyya, in recent years, have grown in number, visibility, and influence within America. This ultraorthodox interpretation of Islam, emphasizing purity of *aqida* (fundamental beliefs) and a return presumably to an understanding of the faith exemplified by the early Muslim generation (called the pious predecessors), is composed primarily of Gulf Arabs along with a handful of American converts, both African–American and Caucasian. The Salafis in America are only loosely organized under groups like the Qur'an and Sunnah Society (located in Vancouver, Los Angeles, and Washington, D.C.) and the Al-Hijra Society (New Jersey), both ideologically and financially supported through the Saudi Arabian Embassy, the Revival of Islamic Heritage Socity in Kuwait, and Dar al-Iftah in Saudi Arabia. Their activities are nearly exclusively confined to educational conferences on topics of aqida, the lecturers often denouncing what they take to be the heterodox Sufis, Shi'a or less frequently, the Ikhwan. They vehemently oppose Muslims becoming involved in any form of political activity in America.

Many pockets of utopian separatist Afro–American Muslims exist throughout the United States. Although this group does not constitute the largest body of African–American Muslims, their argument against political involvement is often repeated in less virulent forms among more mainstream Islamic organizations. One paradigm example of this group is Jamil Abdullah Amin (the former H. Rap Brown), the organizational and charismatic leader of a large Atlanta-based Afro–American Muslim community. In a presentation before ISNA's medium range planning committee in December 1986, Jamil advocated that the priorities of the Muslim community should be the pillars of faith, especially prayer, and the formation of an ideal Islamic community inside, but separate from, the larger American socicty. A similar extreme separatist view has also been expressed by Tariq Qureishi, the director of the North American Islamic Trust's (NAIT) American Trust Publications (ATP), also affiliated with ISNA. Qureishi is reported to have said,

> Those people who insist on entering U.S. politics say it on the presumption as if they are some kind of Jews who have to work for some state of Israel. . . . Some people think that one can distance himself or herself from the process, and then watch the process. But philosophically speaking it is not possible. The process will assimilate you, and then adopt you, and then change you to its own objective. . . . Even if you are ideologically very well indoctrinated, you will have to make compromises here and there.[6]

A fourth group advocates a somewhat more moderate position. It is not totally isolationist, but it does champion the notion that Muslims must not adapt to the American culture and that the best way to avoid such corruption is to develop themselves into an informed, cohesive, spiritually unified community. The most vocal proponents of this stance are Ahmad Zaki Hammad, current ISNA president, and his spiritual disciples Amer Haleem and Ibrahim Abusharif, both editors of ISNA's mouthpiece, the *Islamic Horizons*. In the conclusion of an article on contemporary *da'wa* (missionary) styles and views,

Amer Haleem describes Jamil Abdullah Amin's stance as countercultural, then writing, "but if Muslims want their da'wah here to succeed, a counter culture is what they must realize."[7] He also writes that "Muslims here are not going to vote Islam into the hearts of America, or convince people that it is the best of Western culture." He describes America as "a system organized by design to elevate the will of man above the will of God." Therefore, according to Haleem, the path to be taken by Muslims in America is clear. "We have no option but to pull ourselves into existence as a distinct, cohesive Community. . . . This means we must necessarily be free of the political, social, economic, and cultural leadership of the society we are offering our beliefs and values to. We owe it no loyalty."[8] Haleem concludes with a disclaimer that he is "not advocating disengagement and isolation"; however, he limits political involvement as follows: "we can be political simply in addressing political bodies, politicians, and more importantly the public directly on the issues."[9] Thus, political involvement is defined as Muslims educating non-Muslims about Islam while the Muslims maintain purity outside the American system.

In discussing the political activity of Muslims in America, one must distinguish the activity of Arab–Americans from the activity of Muslims per se. A number of Arab–American organizations are quite active politically; while Muslim participation has been minimal it is slowly growing.[10] Many, if not most Muslims, particularly those in organizations controlled by Islamic movement leadership, are dubious about entering politics in collaboration with Christian Arabs. One Muslim writer expresses this sentiment as follows:

> We are likely to be intensely engaged early on with the widening array of Arab political organizations, who have been actively wooing Muslims for years. As the Arab Christian minorities vanish in the American melting pot, the rush of Muslim–Arab immigrants becomes absolutely vital to these groups' lives.
>
> The early agenda for Muslim politicals [sic] makes this relationship with Arab American groups virtually inevitable. They'd like to begin by taking up the causes of Palestine and the Middle East, duck soup as far as building consensus among Muslims.[11]

Many Muslims fear that they will be "used" by Arab–American groups for the groups' goals, although those goals may not be in the best interests of Muslims. This was clearly the issue behind the hesitation of some ISNA leaders to supply information about Islamic activity, particularly political activity, for the "Focus on Arabs and Islam" column in *The Washington Report on Middle East Affairs*. Similarly, Michael Saba, the founder of the Attiyeh Foundation, which in recent years has been making overtures toward including Muslim participation in political concerns, was invited to speak at the 1987 Annual ISNA Convention only after very strong lobbying efforts by American Muslims inside ISNA. Even then he was included only in the Muslim youth program of the convention, although he was permitted to speak on political issues.

Despite Muslim criticism of the involvement of Muslims in the American political sphere and the fears of being coopted into Christian Arab–American political designs, there was ironically a general sense within the Muslim community that Muslims can safely support the Christian Democratic presidential candidate, Rev. Jesse Jackson. Jackson combined two features attractive to the Muslim community—that is, an Afro–American minority identity and a pro-Palestine platform.

Jackson received virtually unanimous support within the Afro–American Muslim community, despite rumblings from some quarters about his relationship with Louis Farrakhan, whose identity as a Muslim is still suspect by many within the Muslim community. Some Muslims have even called for a closer alliance with Jackson, combined with efforts to legitimize Jackson in the eyes of the more cautious Arab and Indo–Pakistani Muslim communities by blaming the larger Muslim community for the Jackson–Farrakhan friendship. Apparently this was part of the agenda in a speech delivered by Afro–American Muslim, Ihsan Bagby, director of the Department of Tarbiyyah at ISNA's Islamic Teaching Center (ITC). Bagby said,

> Ultimately we can never be full citizens of this country . . . because there is no way we can be fully committed to the institutions and ideologies of this country. . . . We can be citizens in the sense that we try to influence American policy. . . . For instance Jackson, who is running for President, he goes to Syria and he brings with him a person he calls his Muslim advisor—a man named Farrakhan. . . . Where are we in that picture? Why aren't we advising Jackson? Here is a person who is at least open-minded. But where are we? Do we talk to him? Have we sent him position papers? Have we called him and sat him down to give him the Islamic viewpoint?[12]

According to a March 22, 1988, *Wall Street Journal* article, Jackson is receiving the support of most factions within the Arab–Muslim community. "Lebanese, Palestinian, and Yemeni immigrants—the women a sea of white scarves—fill the hall of the Islamic Center with the chant 'Run Jesse Run, Win Jesse Win.'"[13] Two groups within the Arab–Muslim community are especially vocal Jackson supporters. One is the younger working-class Arabs who "have come from the Mideast in the past 20 years, and have more first-hand experience with the tensions in the region." The second, the smaller more politically radical Lebanese Shi'a community, naturally supports Jackson's challenges to American policy toward Israel. For example, Shi'ite leader Imam Mohamad Jawad Chirri in Dearborn, Michigan, is reported to have described Jackson as "a candidate who tells the truth, a candidate who believes the truth, a candidate for the people. . . . We've needed him for a long time."[14]

The same *Wall Street Journal* article noted that in Dearborn the older Arab Muslims, who have been associated with the United Auto Workers Union, supported Missouri Representative Richard Gephardt. Though most of them resonate sympathetically with Jackson's Middle East policy position, pragmatics win out and Gephardt's pro-union stance demanded their allegiance.

The Indo–Pakistani Muslim community has been less univocal in its political support at the presidential campaign level. In fact, the Pakistani community appears more interested in lobbying political candidates across party lines for

U.S. aid to Pakistan than in supporting any one candidate. For example, the Pakistani Federation of America in Chicago subtly supported Gary Hart's bid to be the Democratic presidential candidate by participating in a January 8, 1988, rally organized by the Illinois Executive Committee "to elect Gary Hart." The *Unity Times*, which describes itself as an independent Pakistani and Muslim newspaper, identified Hart's promise to increase aid and assistance to Pakistan to handle the Afghan refugee problem as the most significant point in Hart's speech.[15]

The Chicago-based Muslim League of Voters, U.S.A., which is dominated by Indo–Pakistanis, also lobbies for increased aid to Pakistan. In a letter advertising the "Candidates Forum '88" held on March 13, 1988, M. A. Rahman Khan, the League's chairperson, emphasized the group's efforts across party lines:

> The Muslim League-of-Voters was formed in 1983 to encourage this new block of citizens to take active part in the political and civic affairs of this great nation. We had very good response from all over the country; and we represented the Muslims in both the last National Conventions, Democratic in San Francisco, and Republican in Dallas.[16]

The Candidates Forum '88 issued invitations to Republican Robert Dole as well as Democrats Jesse Jackson, Michael Dukakis, Richard Gephardt, and Paul Simon.

Paul Findley's 1985 book *They Dare to Speak Out* has proven to be a timely incentive for Muslims to consider the possibility of forming political action committees. Findley confirmed Arab and Muslim fears about the pervasive influence of the more than seventy-five pro-Israel PACs.[17] Several Muslim PACs were developed since 1985.

Perhaps the first Muslim PAC formed was the Houston-based All American Muslim Political Action Committee (AAMPAC) established by the Islamic Society of Greater Houston. By November 1987 AAMPAC reported two thousand members residing primarily in Houston, but also from Dallas.[18] Aziz Siddiqui, the PAC's chairperson, says the PAC has a youth wing that has spurred young Muslim adults in political campaigns.[19]

At least three additional Muslim PACs have followed AAMPAC's lead. The very progressive Islamic Center of Southern California under the leadership of Maher Hathout, and more recently the charismatic leadership of former *Arabia* editor, Fathi Osman, has reportedly formed the Muslim Political Action Committee (MPAC). The Pakistan Muslim community in Michigan also formed the Pakistan–Political Action Committee (PPAC) under the auspices of the Pakistan American Friendship Society, whose goals are "to promote the ideology of Pakistan and to encourage the Pakistani Americans in the [*sic*] local politics."[20]

ISNA announced in November 1987 that it had just formed its own PAC, called ISNA–PAC. The PAC is still searching for active representatives. The leading force of the PAC has been SAAR employee, Abd ar-Rahman al-Amoudi (SAAR is the financial wing of the Washington, D.C.-based multimillion–dollar organization, the International Institute of Islamic Thought [IIIT]).[21] ISNA Secretary General Iqbal Unus has said that he expects the ISNA–PAC to hold think tanks and seminars to crystallize the specific political agenda to be adopted by Muslims in America. Unus envisions ISNA–PAC as the umbrella PAC for the grassroots-level "mini" PACs.[22] However, given ISNA President Ahmad Zaki Hammad's misgivings about the appropriateness of Muslim political action at what he apparently views to be the current low level of Islamic awareness among Muslims, it is doubtful that ISNA–PAC will grow appreciably under Zaki's leadership.

The politically oriented bodies formed by Muslims were not PACs. Although Muslims have an inordinately small number of political organizations in contrast to other ethnic and religious groups of comparable size, at least two types have arisen. First are Islamic and ethnic Muslim associations of which political action is only one activity. Second are groups of Muslims organized specifically for political action. An example of the first type is the National Council on Islamic Affairs (NCIA) located in New York. NCIA, under the dynamic supervision of Mohammad Mehdi, has been more successful than most Islamic organizations in cutting across ethnic lines for membership, particularly in bringing together Arabs and Indo–Pakistanis. The organization has effectively used the media to publicize Middle East issues and political issues inside the United States that bear on the Middle East. Mehdi has appeared on numerous television and radio programs, including Ted Koppel's program "Nightline," and has championed interfaith work perhaps more than most Muslim leaders in America. NCIA's most notable contribution has been heightening the political consciousness of Muslims through its modest monthly one-page newsletter; however, it has sold nearly 20 percent of the shares necessary to begin publishing *Islam in America*, described as a "weekly organ of America's 8 million Muslim population."[23]

Other examples of the first type of organization include Muslim ethnic associations, which the Indo–Pakistanis seem particularly inclined to form. Two Pakistani organizations that lobby in Washington, D.C., for U.S.–Pakistan relations are the New York–based Pakistan Forum of the U.S.A. and the Friends of Pakistan Committee. In March 1987 both groups met with a number of congressmen from the House Foreign Affairs Committee's Subcommittee on Asian and Pacific Affairs, White House Associate Director of Public Relations, and Representative Stephen J. Solarz (D–NY), when the Pakistani community became concerned that Reagan's administration would lower aid to Pakistan in fiscal year 1988. Both organizations have sponsored dinners honoring politicians who support aid to Pakistan, for example, Representative Charles Wilson (D–TX) and Representative Walter Jones (D–NC).[24]

Perhaps the best example of the second type of organization—that is, one designed specifically for political action—is the San Francisco–based United Muslims of America. Founded in 1982 with forty members, by the end of 1987 its membership had risen to four hundred, with chapters in Los Angeles and Sacramento. The president, Abdul-Ghafoor Serang, reports that its activities include "registering Muslim citizens to vote, publishing a newsletter focusing on political issues, and holding lectures."[25]

The bulk of organizations of the second type are the numerous Muslim Leagues of Voters mushrooming across the United States. Leagues can be found in cities such as Chicago, Los Angeles, Cleveland, Houston, New York, and Atlanta. Their activities, however, appear to be sporadic and plagued by lack of participation and poor organization. Serang complains that "complacency describes the whole thing. Most Muslims aren't used to participating in politics. So with rein in hand we have to bring the horse to water, and make it drink."[26]

The February 15, 1988, NCIA newsletter contains the following statement: "NCIA has been active in support of several Muslim candidates for the U.S. Congress. Please do your utmost participating in the election process and supporting our candidates."[27]

Two of the more prominent Muslim congressional candidates are Riaz Hussain of New York and Bill Quraishi of California. Although both men have courted the Muslim vote by appearing in Muslim gatherings such as ISNA Zonal Conferences, the Muslim World Day Banquet, and the Muslim World Day Parade in New York, the more conservative Islamic organizations have been critical of what they perceive to be the candidates' overly Western appearance.[28] Individuals in ISNA as well as some of those in the Jamaati Islami-controlled Islamic Circle of North America (ICNA) who have recently entered the political waters have failed to endorse the candidates, most likely because of their perceived accommodations to American culture, such as lack of a beard, in one case a Western name, and failure to use traditional Islamic argot. The candidates have not encountered such problems with more liberal organizations such as NCIA.

Muslims are also running for lower-level political positions. For example, the March 1988 issue of *Unity Times* covered the campaign of Atiq A. Jilani for precinct committeeman on the Republican ticket in York township, DuPage County, Illinois. Jilani's campaign appears to be supported by members of the Indo–Pakistani community who do not come from an Islamic movement background.[29]

One factor severely vitiating Islamic political action in America is the growing fragmentation that has occurred over the past few years within the Muslim community. Three divisions that have become noticeably more intense are Sunni–Shi'a, Salafi–Ikhwan, and intra-Ikhwan. The most obvious of these has been the Sunni–Shi'a division. Prior to the early 1980s both these historically important divisions were deemphasized within America. For example, according to Ilyas Ba-Yunus, former ISNA president, four early Muslim Student Association (MSA) presidents were Shi'i, and during that time Sunnis and Shi'a worshipped together. However, with the escalation of the Iran–Iraq war, relations between the groups deteriorated. Thus the Muslim Students' Association–Persian Speaking Group (MSA–PSG), often paralleling the MSA groups, have appeared on university campuses. Organizations such as ISNA, MSA, and MAYA, all purportedly funded largely with Gulf Arab country money, began to distribute anti-Shi'a literature such as, *Up from Shiism*, *Khutoot al-Areedah*, and *The Devil's Deception of the Sheeah*. The Salafi publications produced by Al-Hijra in New Jersey, the Majliss of Al-Haq Publication Society in Vancouver, and Salafi-oriented newsletters such as *Al-Basheer* from Boulder, Colorado, and *As-Salaf as-Salih* and *Naseeha*, produced by the Association of American Muslims in Bloomington, Indiana, are also predictably critical of Shi'a beliefs.

Of course, the Shi'a and pro-Khomeini groups responded with pro-Shi'a and pro-Iranian literature that often emphasized the corruption of Islamic organizations such as ISNA, MSA, IIIT, and MAYA because of their alleged financial alliance with the governments of Saudi Arabia, Kuwait, Qatar, Bahrain, and the United Arab Emirates. Publications such as the Canada-based *Crescent International* and *Islamic Forum*, as well as the Maryland-based publication, *New Trend*, edited by former MSA *Islamic Horizons* editor Kaukab Siddiq, and other books distributed through the Iranian Interest Section of the Algerian Embassy and the Mostazafan Foundation in New York are almost universally condemned by theologically conservative Muslim Arab students along with the Ikhwan and Jamaat Islami–dominated groups.

Some ISNA officials have used the fact that more than three hundred masajid and Islamic centers are affiliated with, and are held in trust through, the North American Islamic Trust (NAIT) to prepare for the possibility that the Shi'a could mobilize enough Muslims to win local masjid elections. Theoretically, in such a case NAIT could intervene and assume control of the property.

The confrontations that have typified Salafi–Ikhwan interactions in countries such as Kuwait, Egypt, and the Sudan, have emerged recently in America. While the Ikhwan preceded the Salafis in developing Islamic organizations in North America, over approximately the past three years the Salafis have taken significant steps toward organizing. Two main centers of Salafi organization have developed in New Jersey and in Canada. The Canada-based Majliss of Al-Haq Publication Society (Qur'an and Sunnah Society) has, through the efforts of Mahmoud Murad, helped form strong Salafi centers in Los Angeles and Washington, D.C. One of the Saudi princes at the Saudi Arabian Embassy in Washington, D.C., as well as Abdur Rahman Abdul Khaliq, a former Ikhwan member but now a leading force in the Revival of Islamic Heritage Society in Kuwait, has shown keen interest in supporting the organizing efforts of the Salafis, particularly those of the Qur'an and Sunnah Society.

Several incidents have occurred between Salafis and the Ikhwan over the past year. Salafi observers have reported that at the summer 1987 Intensive Summer Arabic Program in Washington, D.C., sponsored by the Saudi Arabian Embassy and conducted by a large number of Salafi instructors, Salafi and Ikhwan students actually engaged in physical fights, resulting in several Ikhwan students completing the program early. Salafi leaders in America have been acutely unhappy about what they perceive to be a campaign led by Ahkmad Zaki Hammad, ISNA president, against Salafi-controlled Islamic centers and Salafi teachings. The Salafi leaders were initially upset with Zaki when an article he wrote was published in *Islamic Horizons* shortly after he was elected president. In the article he mentioned the Salafis in a manner the Salafis took as derogatory.

In the months following the article's appearance Salafis in Angola, Indiana, Syracuse, New York, and College Station, Texas, blamed Zaki for mobilizing the Ikhwan in those areas to maneuver the Salafis out of political power. How to respond to these alleged political maneuverings was an informal topic of conversation at the first national Salafi conference held at the American Islamic College during the 1987 Thanksgiving holiday. One possible response raised at the conference was to inform wealthy Salafis in the Gulf countries about the Ikhwan "conspiracy," so that the donors would no longer finance ISNA and its constituent organizations.

Although organizations such as ISNA have courted indigenous Muslims to curb a growing trend toward the more educated and active members of that group adopting a Salafi interpretation of Islam, Salafis have capitalized on some of ISNA's blunders with American Muslims. For example, in ISNA's 1986 "Guidelines for Medium Range Planning," under a section explicating ISNA's view of Islamic movement, the following statement was rather poorly received by indigenous Muslims: "Recognizing that in 10 to 15 years the leadership of ISNA should rest in the hand [*sic*] of Muslims born in this land; ISNA should continue to involve such Muslims at the level of committees and field structure with the purpose of training and preparation for leadership."[30]

Another example was an article appearing in *Islamic Horizons* entitled, "Life After Shahada." The article enraged a number of indigenous readers with remarks such as the following:

A few [American Muslims] are calling for American Muslims to form their own support groups, to come together to discuss issues significant to American Muslims, and to come up with solutions for themselves by themselves. . . .

American Muslims, who, as Americans, may subconsciously see themselves as superior to "third worlders". . . .

Calling for them [American Muslims] to come together and figure things out on their own isn't really as much a solution as it is a platform.[31]

Such statements were considered to reveal a condescending attitude of ISNA toward converts. Consequently, in August 1987 ISNA's indigenous membership was only approximately four hundred. Salafis, on the other hand, have recruited as converts editors, leaders, and students of Arabic and Islam in Medina, Saudi Arabia. Thus, the Salafis have had so many converts that they have begun to hold more conference lectures in English and are publishing one of their newsletters exlusively in English that was formerly only in Arabic. In the last two years the number of their English publications in America went from one to four.

The Religious Affairs section of the Saudi Arabian Embassy has also been quite successful in developing good relations with the Afro–American Muslim community. Khalil al-Khalil, allegedly a member of the Saudi Ikhwan, was transferred from California to the Saudi Embassy in part as a result of his ability to be trusted within the California American Muslim community. Khalil supposedly helped the Embassy, which sponsored an intensive summer Arabic program primarily for the Afro–American Muslims. The participants were given free room, board, and a scholarship of at least five hundred dollars. ISNA, which also conducted an intensive Arabic program at the same time, lost students who withdrew to join the Saudi program, despite the fact that Afro–American Muslim Ihsan Bagby was the prime mover behind the ISNA program. Bagby had designed the program specifically with American Muslims in mind.

It is still too early to determine whether the Ikhwan-controlled organizations will be able to overcome their negative image among American Muslims or whether the Salafis' initial positive achievements can be maintained. Past Saudi efforts among American Muslims have frequently failed because American Muslims felt they were being "bought off." American students studying in Saudi Arabia have not been particularly successful in adapting to the environment. The students have become disillusioned and the Saudi universities, in turn, have become somewhat cautious about accepting American students.

The Ikhwan can be credited with forming several of the Islamic organizations in America. MSA, formed in 1963, has often been a collaborative effort of Ikhwan members from Egypt, Iraq, Syria, and the Sudan. However, a number of Jamaat Islami MSA members became discontented with what they believed was a lack of movement within ISNA. Thus, during one of the ISNA conventions those members formed the Islamic Circle of North America (ICNA). ICNA is still primarily an Indo–Pakistani member organization, but recently the organization has considered including more indigenous leadership and entering the political arena. In Chicago ICNA has surpassed ISNA in grassroots mobilization of Muslims on the issues of Palestine, Afghanistan, and in responding to the "misrepresentation" of Islam in the media, despite the fact that the ISNA president resides in Chicago.

Splits among Ikhwan factions constituting ISNA became apparent during the 1986 ISNA elections. It is alleged by some ISNA members that the nomination process was postponed several times until IIIT was able to rally enough support to ensure Ahmad Zaki's (supposedly a member of the Egyptian Ikhwan) election. Evidently, some of the old guards in the more "orthodox" Ikhwan supported Shawki Zahran over Ahmad Zaki. The Sudanese, Tunisian, and more liberal factions of the Ikhwan supported past-ISNA president, Qutbi Mehdi. The Malaysian students were split, with the Ikhwan-modeled Malaysian Islamic Study Group (MISG) naturally supporting their champion, Ahmad Zaki. The members of the Muslim Youth Movement of Malaysia (ABIM), still bitter about what they took to be Ahmad Zaki's involvement in splitting the Malaysian students in America, supported Qutbi Mehdi. The Sudanese attempted to rally several groups, including the American Muslims, behind Mehdi, but they had waited too long and the other factions of the Ikhwan had already launched a telephone and letter campaign to inform fellow Muslim Brotherhood members how to vote.

Upon Zaki's election as ISNA president, some obvious changes in representation within the ISNA committee structure and participation in events occurred. Following are some examples of actions attributed to Zaki.

1. Muhammad Nour, reportedly a member of the Islamic National Front (INF) of the Sudan under Hassan el-Turabi, was replaced as chairman of the ISNA Fiqh Committee by Taha Jabir, the Iraqi director of IIIT.
2. Abdulaziz O. Abdulaziz, also allegedly an INF member, was relieved of his responsibilities in the ISNA Headquarters.
3. Talat Sultan, the director of ISNA Department of Education and a member of the Jamaat Islami was relieved of his responsibilities inside ISNA. He went to Mecca, Saudi Arabia, to teach.
4. Invited speakers at the 1987 ISNA Annual Convention included many more overseas members of the Ikhwan than in conventions in the recent past.
5. Divergent opinions within the *Islamic Horizons* were virtually eliminated, with more emphasis placed on the ISNA president's articles and opinions than had occurred in the past.
6. An American Muslim close to the INF resigned from an ISNA Headquarters position in protest of the manner in which the ISNA elections were held and the direction Zaki was leading ISNA.
7. It was reported that the Muslim Arab Youth Association (MAYA) membership was automatically made a part of the ISNA membership with the right to vote in ISNA elections. This move alone would help guarantee the Ikhwan's control over the organization for many years to come. MAYA's president at the time of the decision was Ahmad el-Hattab, allegedly a member of the Egyptian Ikhwan and a close personal friend of Ahmad Zaki.

These changes did not occur without response. A March 1988 *Crescent International* article, also reproduced in the April 1988 issue of the *Islamic Forum*, attempted to attack Zaki's character by alleging that in 1978 and 1979 Zaki and other Ikhwan members of MSA received the money for their salaries through the Libyan Embassy.[32]

The political infighting among Muslim groups has had several effects that could potentially influence the participation of Muslims in the American political arena:

1. A number of Muslim converts have grown disillusioned with the discrepancy between rhetoric and reality about Islamic brotherhood. Some Muslim leaders have become alarmed at the number of apostates and are trying to develop programs to address the problem.
2. No single Islamic organization appears capable of addressing the diversity of views about Islam and Islamic work among Muslims in America. Strong local organizations, such as the Islamic Center of Southern California and the Muslim Community Center located in Chicago are being elevated to national status offering alternatives to the existing

national organizations. It is likely that a number of similar organizations will serve as rallying points for like-minded Muslims if the polarization within the established organizations continues.

3. With dwindling funds coming from the oil-producing countries, along with a growing number of Islamic organizations, money for political action will be more difficult to raise. Budgets will be strained just to meet maintenance costs. Already ISNA is hampered by a nearly one million–dollar deficit.

It remains to be seen how Muslims and Islamic organizations will deal with the serious problems of increasing fragmentation, growing indigenous–immigrant rifts, financial problems, discontent among a growing number of Muslim women toward the traditional Islamic roles for women, increased pastoral demands on an unprepared Islamic clergy, and so on. It is highly likely that the large congregational splits typifying Christian groups in America will become the rule for Islam in America, with each group politically lobbying for its own concerns.

Notes

1. Yvonne Y. Haddad, *A Century of Islam in America* [The Muslim World Today, no. 4] (Washington, D.C.: Islamic Affairs Program, The Middle East Institute, 1986), p. 1; and Carol L. Stone, "Census of Muslims Living in America," February 1988, p. 6 (photocopied).

2. Haddad, *A Century of Islam*, pp. 1–2.

3. Stone, "Census of Muslims," p. 13.

4. "Islamic Society of North America, Guidelines for Medium Range Planning, Report of the Planning Committee," December 22, 1986, p. 6 (photocopied).

5. S. H. Azmi, "An Analysis of Religious Divisions in the Muslim Community of Toronto," December 27, 1987, p. 26 (photocopied).

6. Amer Haleem, "Path to Peace: Calling to Allah in America," *Islamic Horizons*, 16 (December 1987), 29.

7. Ibid., 30.

8. Ibid.

9. Ibid., 31.

10. On university campuses: The Organization of Arab Students in the United States and Canada (OAS), General Union of Palestinian Students (GUPS), Arab Student Association (University of Wisconsin, Madison), Arab Student Society (Harvard University), Palestinian Student Association (University of Maryland), Palestinian Solidarity Committee (State University of New York at Binghamton), Committee in Solidarity with the People of Palestine (UCLA), Coalition for the Defense of Palestinian Human Rights (University of Kansas), and Palestine Human Rights Committee (Cornell University). See Jonathan S. Kessler and Jeff Schwaber, *The AIPAC College Guide: Exposing the Anti-Israel Campaign on Campus* [AIPAC Papers on U.S.–Israel Relations, no. 7] (Washington, D.C.: America Israel Public Affairs Committee, 1984), pp. 7, 13. Nonuniversity: Association of Arab-American University Graduates (AAUG), National Association of Arab Americans (NAAA). Palestine Human Rights

Campaign (PHRC), American–Arab Anti-Discrimination Committee (ADC), and Attiyeh Foundation.

11. Haleem, "Path to Peace," 29.

12. Videotape of speech given by Ihsan Bagby, n.d.

13. *Wall Street Journal*, 22 March 1988.

14. Ibid.

15. *Unity Times*, January/February 1988, pp. 1, 12.

16. Flyer announcing Muslim League of Voters, U.S.A., "Candidates' Forum '88," February 19, 1988.

17. Paul Findley, *They Dare to Speak Out* (Westport, Conn.: Lawrence Hill and Company, 1985), pp. 41–47.

18. Nahid Khan, "Start PACing," *Islamic Horizons*, 16 (November 1987), 14.

19. "Islamic Society of Greater Houston," *Islamic Horizons*, 16 (December 1987), 44.

20. Pakistan Association of America (Detroit, Mich.), *Newsletter*, February 1988.

21. Khan, "Start PACing," p. 13.

22. Ibid., p. 14.

23. National Council on Islamic Affairs (New York), *Bulletin*, No. 38, February 15, 1988.

24. Samir El-Sayed, "Focus on Arabs and Islam," *The Washington Report on Middle East Affairs*, 5 (April 1987), 14.

25. Khan, "Start PACing," p. 14.

26. Ibid.

27. National Council on Islamic Affairs, *Bulletin*, No. 38.

28. *Unity Times*, January/February 1988, p. 4.

29. *Unity Times*, March 1988, p. 1.

30. "Islamic Society of North America, Guidelines for Medium Range Planning," p. 3.

31. Nahid Khan, "Life After Shahada," *Islamic Horizons*, 16 (December 1987), 16.

32. *Crescent International*, March 1–15, 1988, p. 10.

9

Da'wa in the West

Larry A. Poston

Da'wa in America: From East to West

The concept of missions in Islam is essentially subsumed under the Arabic word *da'wa*. This term comes from the root meaning "to call" or "to invite"; da'wa thus means "a call" or "an invitation" and, in specialized usage, "missionary activity" in the sense that the Muslim invites someone he considers a nonbeliever to submit to Allah.[1] In the Qur'an this idea appears in such passages as Sura 16:125: "Call unto the way of thy Lord with wisdom and fair exhortation, and reason with them in the better way." But the revelation suggests no specific methodological or strategic model, and consequently the actual working out of this command to "call" has taken a number of forms through Islamic history.

The Prophet, for instance, invited the population of Mecca to join him in worshipping the One God by means of a verbal proclamation of *tawhid* in the environs of the Ka'ba. Upon his death, knowledge concerning the *din Allah* was spread by the *mujahidun* (those who conquered the Middle East and North Africa), by emigrants from Arabia to the new Muslim lands, and by traders. Subtle changes in the concept of da'wa were introduced by the Sufis, who called men and women to a direct experience of God in addition to knowledge of His attributes. For the Isma'ilis the term took on political overtones and their *da'is* ("callers" or "missionaries") sought to spread a particular form of Islam by what some would consider highly suspect means. During the Middle Ages the Sufi *tariqas* became the chief agencies through which Islam was spread and Muslim populations were extended deep into Africa and Asia and eastward as far as Indonesia.

Not until the nineteenth century was the *da'wah ilalislam* heard in North America. In this chapter we seek to classify the missionary philosophies of the roughly 4 million Muslims currently residing in the United States and Canada. One way to do this is to suggest two generally distinguishable approaches that can be called, respectively, the defensive–pacifist and the offensive–activist. The first characterizes the attitude of introversionist Muslims, in the sense that they are concerned solely or primarily with retaining and maintaining their own Islamicity, and not with the extension of that Islamicity through da'wa to the non-Muslim environment that surrounds them. The second applies to those who want to transform non-Muslim society, at both the individual and communal levels, to reflect Islamic values and beliefs.

The defensive–pacifist orientation is a consequence of the factors that spurred the early waves of Muslim immigration to the United States and Canada. The ideological and theological impediments to the residence of a Muslim in the *dar al-kufr* ("the abode of unbelief") were mitigated by pragmatic considerations, that is, the need to escape the increasingly chaotic conditions in Eastern Europe and the Middle East. The settlers quickly adopted the spirit of individualism so characteristic of other Americans, and this enabled them to blend easily into society. Religious considerations were limited to the establishment of organizations that reflected the various ethnic backgrounds and concomitant religious convictions of the different Muslim populations.

The adherents of the activist group consist primarily of a minority of Muslim immigrants to North America who resisted the melting-pot syndrome and became only minimally assimilated. These individuals are convinced that the assimilated Muslim is incapable of bearing a credible witness to the society around him. He is unable to offer an alternative to prevailing social conditions because identification with and acceptance of those conditions are implied in his own life-style. The activist therefore wishes to separate himself in certain ways from American society and so allow his life to present a contrast to the life-styles that surround him.

A second element in the activist category is composed of new immigrants who are being injected into North American communities at the rate of 25,000 to 35,000 per year. Although many of these would have been considered passive or even nominal Muslims in their home countries, an interesting psychological phenomenon occurs when they enter a non-Muslim country, as observed by Haddad and Lummis: "many have found their consciousness about religious identity enhanced in the American context as people question them about the basic tenets of their religion."[2] A considerable number of Muslims, then, become activists as the result of a specific reaction to a cultural or environmental situation. But these reactions are often not grounded in a clearly defined Islamic ethos, and thus lack coherence. This occasionally results in confusion between partisan, ethnic, and nationalistic considerations and what may be considered truly Islamic matters. Only a few have been able to think in terms of a supracultural form of Islam not identified with any specific ethnic background.

For a number of reasons, including those just cited, Muslim missionary activism in North America must be characterized as being yet in its infancy. But a slow maturation can be seen in the increasing awareness of the need for an Islamic form of what might be called an internal/personal as opposed to an external/institutional approach to missionary activity. What do these terms signify? Generally speaking, strategies for propagating religious tenets can be divided into two categories. These are determined by the societal level at which entry of a missionary agent is made into a target culture and by the view held concerning religious conversion. Entry may take place initially at either the upper, controlling levels of a society (at the level occupied by executive, legislative, judicial, economic, and other bureaucratic structures) or at the lower, subject levels (among the masses). The former approach is mainly concerned with transforming political, social, and economic institutions into religiously based structures and bringing about the outward conformity of individuals to the precepts of those structures—hence the label external/ institutional. The internal/personal approach, on the other hand, seeks first to bring about an inner religious transformation in as many individuals as possible, based on the belief that, in time, the influence of such persons will change the structures of society. In the history of Christianity these concepts are associated with varieties of church polity and liturgy and provide a paradigm according to which specific denominations or sects are classified. External/ institutional groups subscribe to the eschatological doctrine of amillennialism and view the Kingdom of God as a realm in which the religious and political spheres of life are inextricably bound together. Thus, expansion of the political hegemony of a Christian country is tantamount to expansion of the Kingdom of God.

Early Islamic missiology was predicated on just such an external/institutional approach, subsumed under the concept of *jihad*. The political conquests of the seventh and eighth centuries A.D. created an environment in which the Muslim faith could be planted, tended, and harvested. Nehemia Levtzion notes that even modern Muslim historians stress "the role of temporal power in creating a total Islamic environment as a precondition of the fostering of the right attitude and state of mind in individuals."[3] This environment was formed by the Muslim institutions created by the mujahidun and those who followed them. These structures included the *masjid* (mosque), the *madrasa* (school), a legislative system based on the law or Shari'a, a court system, and a system of economics. The environment created by these institutions particularly influenced the younger inhabitants of the conquered lands, since it replaced the culture to which older persons were bound by the process of enculturation. For the young, in whom this process was not complete, the change of allegiance to new political, social, economic, and religious forms was not a difficult adjustment. With each succeeding generation, enculturation became more and more to an Islamic environment, since the former culture was usually either forgotten or only inaccurately retained in folklore.

Turning to the subject of our study—the North American continent—the question arises as to whether such a missionary strategy could be implemented in the United States and Canada. It is difficult to imagine that a minority that represents less than 2 percent of a total population can hope to create a truly Islamic ambience within that population through an external/institutional approach. An alternative strategy is thus necessary.

In Christianity such an alternative appeared in the century following the Protestant Reformation when the German Lutheran Philipp Jakob Spener proposed that the focus of the religious life of Christians be changed from external considerations (including political affairs) to internal matters at the level of the individual. This emphasis, known as Pietism, is significant for missiology not because it is concerned with acquiring control over societal structures to produce an environment within which individual conversions can occur, but because it aims first at converting individuals at the level of the masses. It is assumed that the gradually increasing number of converted and reformed individuals will have a leavening effect on society in general.[4] This is the essence of the internal/personal approach.

In the history of Islam we find that the phenomenon known as Sufism is similar in many respects to Christian Pietism. In Sufism the external/institutional concept of jihad was spiritualized and used as a description of the struggle to purify one's inner self. The famous Jalal al-Din Rumi describes how prophets and saints participate in the greater jihad of killing the ego and abandoning personal wishes and sensual desires.[5] Just as Pietist Christians were able to bypass the external/institutional missiology of their time by focusing attention on the masses, Sufism has also exhibited an internal/personal missiology that aims at the conversion of individuals followed by training in Islamic precepts, the application of which potentially enables each convert to exercise an influence on society. Sufi missiology, then, is readily adaptable to the situation in which Muslims find themselves in America.

Sufism, however, apparently has not played a major role in establishing a direct Muslim witness in America. This writer has found few allusions to any of the major Sufi orders in the dozens of conversion testimonies he examined. Nor have either discussions with Muslims or the literature of various Muslim organizations engaged in da'wa activity yielded such references. And yet many of these same organizations have adopted an internal/personal missionary philosophy. From where have they acquired such an approach? I contend that an *indirect* Sufi influence has occurred, traceable to two movements in the Muslim world that, although they originated and evolved in separate countries, display notable similarities in ideology and praxis.

The first of these movements was institutionalized in the organization known as al-Ikhwan al-Muslimun (the Muslim Brotherhood), founded by the Egyptian Hasan al-Banna (1906–1949). From his earliest days al-Banna was subjected to multiple influences, including the teachings of a Sufi merchant named Abu Muhammad Shousha. In developing his program of outreach, al-Banna recognized in true Sufi fashion that "the essential step in the renaissance, and more important than 'practical reform,' is a vast 'spiritual awakening' among *individuals*. . . . A people cannot be saved until *individuals* are [emphasis mine]."[6] The long-range objective of his Muslim Brotherhood became the establishment of an Islamic Order. This concept referred to "a set of legal (not political) principles which were regarded as fundamental to Muslim society whatever the particular form of political order [emphasis mine]."[7] Thus, the Islamic Order is seen in some circles as nearly synonymous with Levtzion's "ambience." The only difference between the two is context rather than substance. Levtzion's ambience was the result of the traditional external/institutional approach, whereas the logical order of the Muslim Brotherhood's four main objectives represents a reversal of this strategy: (1) make every individual a true Muslim; (2) develop the Muslim family on Islamic lines; (3) establish a Muslim 'umma; (4) establish an Islamic state in Egypt.[8] Placing individuals at the top of the list of priorities allowed for participation by the masses in reformatory activity and offered the people an obtainable goal.

The second organization that has exercised an indirect Sufi influence on American Islam by emphasizing an internal/personal approach is the Jamaat-i Islami, the creation of the Indian Abul A'la Mawdudi (1903–1979). Like al-Banna he was subjected from an early age to Sufi influences, being a direct descendent of Abul A'la, the first member of the Chishti order to settle permanently in India. Mawdudi spoke of an Islamic movement, and, like al-Banna, sought to provide the masses with interim goals and activities in the absence of an established Muslim community, state, or caliphate. According to his thinking it was not necessary to await the establishment or renewal of these institutions to create an Islamic milieu. Such an environment could be created by the people themselves, and this would eventually result in revolutionary changes at the upper levels of society.

The concept of the Islamic Movement has had great significance for Muslims in the West. It is appealing because of its holistic emphasis; the idea that Islam affects every aspect of an individual's life transforms the religion from a mere appendage of particular ethnic backgrounds to an aspect of daily life requiring personal commitment and action. The internal/personal emphasis on the masses, specifically as composed of individuals, contributes to dissipation of the helpless feeling that the determination of the circumstances of life is completely out of the hands of the common person.

The missionary philosophies of al-Banna and Mawdudi have entered the North American continent by at least three different routes. The first route is the influx of immigrants from the countries of Egypt and Pakistan during periods of repression characteristic of the more recent histories of these two countries. The influence of these immigrants has been diffuse, however, since it is not generally characteristic of Muslims in America to live in geographical proximity to each other. But this phenomenon has been significant in that organized attempts at da'wa have had a sympathetic group of persons to draw from.

The second avenue has been the Muslim Student Association, undoubtedly the most activistic of the da'wa organizations in America. Many of the founding members of this agency were members of or had connections to one or the other of the two organizations in question and it was through these persons that the ideologies of al-Banna and Mawdudi were integrated into the goals and philosophies of the organization.

The third significant avenue by which the ideas represented here have entered the West is the speeches and writings of Khurram Murad, a disciple of Mawdudi. Murad has taken what were essentially Eastern ideas and applied them to Western contexts; in so doing he gave a philosophical and strategic coherence to the concept of da'wa in America. For him the Islamic Movement is "an organized struggle to change the existing society into an Islamic Society based on the Qur'an and the Sunna and make Islam . . . supreme and dominant, especially in the socio-political spheres."[9] Although this has the appearance of an external/institutional philosophy, in other writings he makes it clear that the "socio-political sphere" includes the masses and "the ultimate objective of the Islamic movement shall not be realized unless the struggle is made by the Locals. For it is only they who have the power to change the society into an Islamic Society." Murad's immediate goal is to "communicate the basic message of Islam to every non-Muslim to gain their true understanding of Islam, leading to genuine sympathy for and then to acceptance of the values and concepts which Islam teaches."[10]

The strategy for accomplishing this involves inviting non-Muslims "to their own religion—'the oldest religion'—and not to something new."[11] The idea is presented that Judaism and Christianity, in their original forms, were precisely the same as the Muslim faith is today. North Americans are thus to be invited to what their forefathers actually believed and propagated.

Murad believes that the Muslim should begin his witness not with a repudiation of what is wrong with others, but rather with an invitation to reflect on commonalities. What is advocated is a change in approach that would place initial emphasis on the concepts and values rather than the forms of Islam. These are the human values that are universally agreed upon by Muslim and non-Muslim alike. Only after such commonalities are established should the invitation (the da'wa) be extended to submit to distinctively Islamic teachings.

A final aspect of Murad's strategy involves the mastering of fundamental aspects of communications theory and the contextualization of the teachings of Islam. The religion must be shown to be relevant to contemporary issues, such as nuclear disarmament, unemployment, care for the elderly, and the like. Murad recognizes the value of imbuing youth with a respect and appreciation for Islamic principles and believes that an appeal to relevance is the only way the imaginations of young people can be captured.

Murad's thinking is becoming increasingly influential in North America; at the 1987 Annual Convention of the Islamic Society of North America he was billed as the keynote speaker, and his address ended with a ringing challenge to the listeners to both maintain and refine their Islamicity in the midst of a secular environment. If this is done, he stated, America will eventually become a Muslim continent.

The Institutionalization of Da'wa in the Western Context

The Christian Pietist patriarch Jakob Spener gathered his followers in homes on weekdays and formed an educational institution at Halle in Denmark as an alternative to European universities, which for the most part were controlled by state churches. Direct outgrowths of Halle University included the Danish–Halle Mission and the Moravian Missionary Society as the first of what have recently been termed "parachurch" agencies. Such groups today justify their existence by accusing traditional church structures of excessive internecine competition, duplication of effort, a distorted focus on architectural structures, espousal of a clergy–laity dichotomy, conservatism, and lack of relevance to modern culture. Nearly all of these criticisms have been applied to American masjids as well, and this dissatisfaction has contributed to the establishment of what might be termed "paramosque" agencies.

With regard to the paramosque phenomenon per se, one cannot make a radical distinction between offensive–activist and defensive–pacifist Muslims, for both have established organizations that operate parallel to the traditional mosque structure. Nor should it be assumed that Muslims who are deeply committed to and heavily involved in paramosque institutions have forsaken the masjid, for this is not the case. The majority either continue regular attendance at a local mosque or form their organizations so that they assume such functions at appropriate times, that is, Fridays and Muslim holidays.

There is, however, a qualitative difference between the goals and philosophies of defensive–pacifist organizations and those of the offensive–activists. Many agencies evince a distinctly introverted orientation,[12] but classification of these organizations as defensive–pacifist in no way implies that they are inferior; on the contrary, they perform functions vital to the Islamic community. The main focus of their activity, however, is directed toward Muslims, and this allows a distinction to be made between them and those organizations that seek to reach out to others.

Activist paramosque agencies are as yet comparatively few, but their numbers are increasing. Some have drawn their internal/personal approach directly from Christian Pietism through imitation of Christian missionary methodologies, and some have adopted the Islamic Pietism of al-Banna and Mawdudi.

Representative of organizations at the local level is the Islamic Information Center of America, an independent grassroots Muslim organization. It was founded and is now directed by Musa Qutub, a professor of geography at Northeastern Illinois University, and uses as its headquarters a condominium located in the Chicago suburb of Prospect Heights. The objectives of the organization are indisputably da'wa-oriented: "to deliver the Message of Islam in its totality and purity to the American people, to inform non-Muslims about Islam and to aid Americans who embrace Islam in delivering the Message to others."[13] These goals are fulfilled by means of personal contacts with individuals and families; giving lectures to schools, colleges, and universities; conducting seminars and workshops; writing, publishing, and distributing pamphlets, booklets, and flyers; distributing copies of the Qur'an; using radio, television, and newspapers and arranging dialogues between Muslims and adherents of other faiths.

The Muslim Student Association, headquartered in the vicinity of Indianapolis, was formed on January 1, 1963, on the Urbana campus of the University of Illinois. The growth this agency has experienced is nothing less than phenomenal; as of 1983 the organization boasted 310 student chapters with more than 45,000 members.[14] The Association makes it clear that it considers its chief task to be that of da'wa:

The most important task which only the MSA can do efficiently is da'wah among non-Muslims. Of all the places in North America, the campus is the only area where the most curious, the most inquisitive and the most open-minded audience for Islam . . . may be found. . . . This, according to the recommendation of the Majlis ash-Shura of the ISNA 1983, must be the first priority of the MSA in the future, insha'Allah.[15]

From the very beginning the MSA was joined by nonstudent Muslims; by 1983 the number of local community groups affiliated with the organization was nearly the same as that of the campus chapters. In keeping with the needs and interests of these groups, organizations such as the Association of Muslim Social Scientists, the Association of Muslim Scientists and Engineers, and the Islamic Medical Association were formed. Such a diversity became increasingly difficult to manage and the very name "Muslim Student Association" became a misnomer; consequently in the summer of 1983 the Islamic Society of North America was founded to act as an "umbrella" organization overseeing the activities of the various agencies mentioned here. This has allowed the MSA to concentrate on the purposes for which it was originally founded.

The association is divided functionally. The Islamic Book Service (now known as the North American Islamic Trust) is responsible for the dissemination of Muslim literature in the United States and Canada; the catalogs of this agency list hundreds of titles in both English and Arabic. The Islamic Teaching Center is another branch that has recently attained high visibility among offensive–activist Muslims in North America. This center is responsible for the training of young people in the principles of the Islamic faith and for preparing "Islamic workers"—individuals who will be effective in communicating the message of Islam to non-Muslims. The center arranges lectures and study groups concerning da'wa, prepares correspondence courses, and organizes training camps for aspiring da'is. It also contains a Department of Correctional Facilities, which in 1981 contacted four thousand inmates in three hundred and ten prisons, enrolling more than five hundred individuals in an Islamic Correspondence Course.[16]

The Muslim World League is an international organization founded by the Saudi Arabian government in 1962. This agency seeks to strengthen and expand Muslim communities wherever they are found but recognizes that adherents of the Islamic faith residing in the non-Muslim West have special needs. The League assists Islamic Centers with youth camps, summer schools, and other such programs; it has also provided teachers and imams for these centers, developed prison ministries, provided fellowships and grants for Muslim university professors, contributed to the production of television and radio programs on a small scale, and aided in the establishment of Muslim newspapers and journals.[17]

The Shi'ites in North America are represented by the Islamic Societies of Georgia and Virginia, both founded by Yasin al-Jibouri. The former organization was established in 1973 and grew rapidly by means of proselytization.

Literature for distribution to both black and white Americans was sent from Iran by the World Organization for Islamic Services, from East Africa by the Bilal Muslim Missions of Tanzania and Kenya, from India, and from Pakistan. By 1977, 55,770 copies of books and booklets had been mailed out, free of charge, mostly to African–Americans who could not afford to buy such literature.[18] In the late 1970s al-Jibouri relocated to northern Virginia and in 1982 established the International Islamic Society of Virginia. Two of the seven objectives of this organization are "to promote Islam through the provision of reading materials for interested non-Muslims" and "to serve as a liaison between Muslim and non-Muslim communities." Toward this end computer and word-processing equipment has been purchased to produce literature centered on the fundamental tenets of Islam and the central doctrines of Shi'ism, with exposés of the American media's distorted presentation of Islam and Muslims.

The International Institute of Islamic Thought, also located in northern Virginia, was organized in 1981 "to promote and serve research in Islamic Studies throughout the world. Its objective is to stimulate Islamic scholars to think out the problems of thought and life pertinent to Muslims in the modern world and to articulate the relevance of Islam to these problems."[19] This group concentrates on the writing and publication of college-level textbooks that present the Muslim perspective of each academic discipline. It also conducts seminars, workshops, and regional conventions and solicits funds to be used for fellowships allowing Islamic scholars to conduct research in various fields. Particularly interesting is the recent focus on development of "a science of Tawhid Cybernetics," which involves the creation of a "computerized data-bank, assembling all human knowledge in a form suitable for the introduction of purpose in artificial intelligence."[20] Upon completion of such a databank one would in effect have a computerized majlis al-shura or a supranational, supracultural ulama capable of providing solutions to problems faced by modern Muslims.

Representative of Canadian organizations is the Islamic Circle of North America, headquartered in Montreal. This agency was established in 1971 "to call Muslims and non-Muslims alike to the path of Allah."[21] One of its chief contributions to the cause of da'wa in the West has been its publication of *A Manual of Da'wah for Islamic Workers*, containing sections dealing with the concepts and techniques of missionary activity from a Muslim perspective. Although some of its suggestions are outmoded and impractical, it is probably the only publication of its kind as yet available to the American Muslim community.

The Ahmadiyya Movement is considered by some to be modern Islamic history's prototypical da'wa organization. This group entered the United States in 1920 and in that year founded a mission in Chicago. The missionaries of this agency receive their education from the Missionary Training College in Pakistan; the seven-year program includes studies in linguistics, world religions, contextualization of the Ahmadiyya message, apologetics, use of the mass media, and the doctrines of the sect. In recent years American Ahmadis have shown a tendency to adopt specifically American strategies of outreach, many of which have been borrowed from methods used by evangelical Christians.[22]

No account of daʿwa would be complete without reference to the American Muslim Mission (formerly known as the Black Muslim Movement). Although long the focus of controversy and debate, this indigenous group was nevertheless for a long while "the prevailing Islamic presence in America."[23] It has been estimated that some 2 million blacks in the United States are either members of or are in some way connected with this movement, and it is significant that in 1978 the Gulf States of Saudi Arabia, Abu Dhabi, and Qatar named Warith al-Din Muhammad, the head of the main body of Black Muslims, "sole consultant and trustee for the recommendation and distribution of funds to all Muslim organizations engaged in the propagation of the faith in the U.S."[24]

This list of organizations is by no means exhaustive; dozens of other groupings could be mentioned, and their very number is indicative of an increasing awareness on the part of North American Muslims of their responsibility to perform daʿwa among their neighbors. These organizations were severely criticized, however, in an article that appeared in the December 1986 issue of *Arabia: The Islamic World Review*.[25] They were castigated for their failure to contextualize their message, for having given cultural interests a higher priority than the interests of the Muslim community as a whole, for having failed to evolve a "daʿwa language," for failing to engage in meaningful dialogue with Western institutions, for failing to engage in critical self-evaluation, and for the general incompetence of their leadership. These are serious charges, but research by this writer indicates that they are exaggerated. Problems do indeed exist, but it appears that the Muslim community is aware of them and is taking steps toward their resolution. Generally speaking, the health of offensive–activist organizations in North America appears to be good and my prediction is that if Muslims in America continue to gain confidence in themselves as the bearers of a viable religious alternative and to increase their commitment to a internal/personal strategy of missions, their daʿwa activity will increase substantially in the years to come.

Notes

1. Hans Wehr, *A Dictionary of Modern Written Arabic*, 3rd ed., ed. J. Milton Cowan (New York: Spoken Language Services, Inc., 1976), pp. 282–83.

2. Yvonne Haddad and Adair Lummis, *Islamic Values in the United States* (New York: Oxford University Press, 1987), p. 22.

3. Nehemia Levtzion, "Toward a Comparative Study of Islamization," in Nehemia Levtzion, ed., *Conversion to Islam* (New York: Holmes and Meier Publishers, Inc., 1979), p. 11.

4. For a detailed analysis of these concepts see J. H. Bavinck, *An Introduction to the Science of Missions*, trans. David Freeman (New Brunswick, N.J.: Presbyterian and Reformed Publishing Co., 1960), pp. 287–97.

5. See William C. Chittick, *The Sufi Path of Love: The Spiritual Teachings of Rumi* (Albany: State University of New York Press, 1983), p. 154.

6. Richard P. Mitchell, *The Society of the Muslim Brothers* (London: Oxford University Press, 1969), p. 234.

7. Ibid., p. 235.

8. *Memoirs of Hasan al-Banna Shaheed*, trans. M. N. Shaikh (Karachi: International Islamic Publishers, 1981), p. 41.

9. Murad in Abul A'la Mawdudi, *The Islamic Movement: Dynamics of Values, Power and Change* trans. Khurram Murad (Leicester: The Islamic Foundation, 1984), p. 36.

10. Khurram Murad, *Islamic Movement in the West* (Leicester: The Islamic Foundation, 1984), p. 36.

11. Khurram Murad, *Da'wah Among Non-Muslims in the West* (Leicester: The Islamic Foundation, 1986). p. 18.

12. Shawarbi notes that "this Federation goes out of its way in working for the advancement of the religious, cultural and social aspects of all Muslims on the American continent. . . . In our opinion this Federation will be a powerful agent in spreading Islamic culture to the widest possible boundaries among American *Muslims* [emphasis mine]," Mahmud Yusuf al-Shawarbi, *Al-Islam w'al-Muslimun fi'l-Qara al-Amrikiyya* (Cairo: Dar al-Qalam, 1963), p. 14. Haddad also remarks that "the Federation is less militant in its efforts at propagating the faith than the MSA, and generally more social in orientation," Yvonne Haddad, "Muslims in the U.S.," in Marjorie Kelley, ed., *Islam: The Religious and Political Life of a World Community* (New York: Praeger, 1984), p. 272.

13. "The Islamic Information Center of America," brochure, n.d.

14. "MSA and Family Builds in the U.S.," *Arabia: The Islamic World Review*, May 1983, p. 63.

15. "Know Your MSA," brochure, n.d.

16. Ibid., p. 63.

17. For more on the activities of the Muslim World League, see S. Mazhar Hussain, *Proceedings of the First Islamic Conference of North America* (New York: Muslim World League, 1977).

18. Yasin T. al-Jibouri, "A Brief History of the Islamic Society of Georgia, Inc." (Atlanta: Islamic Society of Georgia, n.d.), p. 2.

19. Isma'il al Faruqi, *Islamization of Knowledge: General Principles and Workplan* (Washington, D.C.: International Institute of Islamic Thought, 1982), p. 61.

20. Robert D. Crane, "Premise and Process in the Islamization of Knowledge: A Contribution Toward Unity in Diversity," in Robert D. Crane, ed., *Preparing to Islamize America* (Reston, Va.: International Institute of Islamic Thought, 1987), p. 10.

21. *Manual of Da'wah for Islamic Workers* (Montreal: Islamic Circle of North America, 1983), p. vi.

22. See Tony Poon-Chiang Chi, "A Case Study of the Missionary Stance of the Ahmadiyya Movement in North America," Ph.D. Dissertation, Northwestern University, 1973.

23. C. Eric Lincoln, "The American Muslim Mission in the Context of American Social History," in Earle H. Waugh et al., eds., *The Muslim Community in North America* (Alberta, Canada: The University of Alberta Press, 1983), p. 224.

24. Ibid., p. 231.

25. See "Muslim Organizations in the West: An Overview," *Arabia: The Islamic World Review*, December 1986, pp. 24–25.

10

Muslims in Prison:
Claims to Constitutional Protection
of Religious Liberty

Kathleen Moore

In *The Myth of the Judeo-Christian Tradition*, Arthur A. Cohen questions the notion that a Judeo-Christian tradition even exists, suggesting that it is an invention of twentieth-century American politics spawned by efforts to promote interfaith harmony. The conception of such a tradition is, in Cohen's words, "mythological or, rather, not precisely mythological but ideological and hence, as in all ideologies, shot through with falsification, distortion, and untruth."[1]

A political use of the term has gained particular currency in the 1980s as reliance on certain religious values and rhetoric in public discourse has gained acceptance, notwithstanding the ideal of separation of church and state. However, what is meant by the Judeo-Christian tradition remains ambiguous.[2] Rather than promoting interfaith harmony, the current use of the concept excludes those judged to be "deviationists" or nonbelievers, that is, persons conceived to be a threat to the bedrock values of America.[3] Public figures appeal to our sense of patriotism by talking about the United States as a Judeo-Christian nation, which, in effect, serves to exclude other religious groups (such as Muslims) and nonreligious groups from the mainstream of American society.[4] Observers of the American political scene have noted that the adjective "Judeo-Christian" is often used as a code word by those who actually mean to promote an exclusively Christian America.[5] In the late twentieth century, support for this tradition has become a test of true Americanism.

The most controversial use of this emotionally charged term is in legal debates. Within the American judicial tradition, the courts have struggled to construct a broad, "functional"[6] definition of religion that does not reflect any a priori judgment of the content of the beliefs in question. As a result, the courts have variously interpreted the meaning of "religion" to bring under the protection of the First Amendment[7] a variety of religious belief systems, many of which range far beyond any common understanding of a Judeo-Christian norm. From the "anti-Mormon" cases of the late nineteenth century[8] to cases involving the Amish,[9] Jehovah's Witnesses,[10] Seventh Day Adventists,[11] and Native Americans,[12] and most recently the Rastafarians,[13] the Krishna Consciousness,[14] MOVE,[15] and others,[16] the courts have consented to review the adherents' claims to constitutional protection. Although not all claims have been accommodated, the courts by and large have been most willing to protect the "preferred" freedom of religious exercise when presented in cases involving minority religious groups.

The fact that Islam is not popularly considered to be part of the dominant Judeo-Christian tradition in America, is viewed as a foreign creed, and is often maligned by its association in the media with terrorist activity abroad, makes it one of the religions most vulnerable to attack and in need of constitutional protection. Society in general, including public servants such as court officials as well as those who run our prisons, armed services, hospitals, and schools, are unfamiliar with Islamic beliefs and practices and, being subject to reflexive but human prejudice, may be prone to treat Muslims unjustly.

The issue whether Islam is a religion worthy of constitutional protection has arisen in the courts most often in cases brought by African-American Muslim inmates confined in correctional facilities. Records indicate that African-American Muslims, compared with any of the Muslim immigrant groups, have been most active in pursuing legal claims to obtain equal rights and access to the resources of the larger society. The realm of prisoners' rights to free exercise of religion is no exception. The responsiveness of the courts to Muslim inmates' claims for religious liberty has turned on a number of factors: the issue of equality of treatment of religious groups in prisons; the courts' reticence to reverse the decisions of prison officials; the degree to which the inmates' challenges would undermine the fundamental interests of the state (for example, prison security, administrative efficiency); and the showing that Islam is similar to the conventional Protestant, Catholic, and Jewish faiths.

The purpose of this study is to examine the treatment of Islam and Muslims by the courts. More specifically, the focus here is on religious liberty claims raised in the prison setting. To what extent are the courts willing to grant Muslim inmates exemptions from otherwise valid prison regulations when those regulations impinge on Islamic practices? An examination of the courts' willingness to extend First Amendment guarantees of free exercise of religion to Muslims in the particular institutional setting of prisons will reveal the extent to which the American judicial system succeeds in protecting religious liberty. After a brief review of the development of a judicial definition of religion, we will see how Islam has fared as a religion in the courts, and similarly, when Muslim practices have been protected by the First Amendment.

Definitions of Religion

Early judicial definitions of religion, developed for the purpose of determining when to extend First Amendment protection, were theistic. That is, the courts contemplated belief in a Supreme Being as an indispensable characteristic of religion. The view was that the term *religion* applies to any belief system based on the recognition of a divine being and a relation to that being that involves obligations that take precedence over those arising from any human relation.[17] By the middle of this century, the Supreme Court began to shift its position, abandoning theism as a requisite feature and embracing a less normative definition of religion.[18] The Court adopted the position that religious freedom includes "the right to maintain theories of life and of death and of the hereafter which are rank heresy to followers of the orthodox faiths."[19] Later, the Court asserted that "it is no business of courts to say that what is a religious practice or activity for one group is not religion under the protection of the First Amendment."[20]

The judicial conception of religion expanded to include doctrines that do not necessarily teach a belief in the existence of God. The Supreme Court moved away from a "theistic" position in favor of another, which scrutinized not the doctrine at issue but the nature of the adherent's beliefs. In a major draft-exemption case, *United States* v. *Seeger*, the Court proposed a test for determining when a belief constitutes a religious belief, for purposes of constitutional protection:

> The test . . . is whether a given belief that is sincere and meaningful occupies a place in the life of its possessor parallel to that filled by the orthodox belief in God of one who clearly qualifies for the [conscientious objector] exemption.[21]

With this test, called the "ultimate concern" test, there is no inquiry into the content of an individual's beliefs; rather, the courts are asked to focus on the importance and place of the beliefs in the individual's life.[22] Several lower courts have adopted this test.[23]

Constitutional Protection of Islam

Islam has been recognized by the courts as a religion deserving First Amendment protection according to both the theistic and the "ultimate concern" definitions. In *Fulwood* v. *Clemmer*, the U.S. District Court for the District of Columbia held that it is not

> the function of the court to consider the merits or fallacies of a religion or to praise or condemn it. . . . It is sufficient here to say that one concept of religion calls for a belief in the existence of a supreme being controlling the destiny of man. That concept of religion is met by the Muslims in that they believe in Allah, as a supreme being and as the one true god. It follows, therefore, that the Muslim faith is a religion.[24]

In this case, the court found that Islam is a theistic belief system, and thus worthy of constitutional protection. In other instances, the courts have refused to base their decisions on a review of Islamic tenets, but have recognized Islam to be a religion because of the function it serves in the lives of Muslims.

Constitutional protection, however, has not been automatic. Muslim organizations such as the Nation of Islam have been treated as cults, or suspect and dangerous groups, partly because of the perception that Muslims teach racial hatred. It has been argued before the courts that Muslim doctrine contains political aspirations and economic goals as well as racial prejudice, and should be suppressed in the interest of society. More often than not, however, the courts have found that Islam is principally a religious faith and Muslims a religious community despite any political teachings and, as such, are protected by the free exercise clause of the First Amendment.

African-American Muslim inmates have been responsible in large part for establishing prisoners' constitutional rights to worship.[25] In many instances, African-American Muslims have been recognized as a religious group entitled to First Amendment protection.[26] Cases brought by Muslims have established that prisoners have the right to assemble for religious services,[27] to consult a cleric of their faith,[28] to possess religious publications and subscribe to religious literature,[29] to wear unobstrusive religious symbols such as medallions,[30] to have prepared a special diet required by their religion,[31] and to correspond with their spiritual leaders.

Several judicial decisions have expanded prisoners' rights to religious worship and expression. However, the matter of incarceration and, more specifically, its considerable diminution of the constitutional rights of prisoners, complicate the issue of free exercise guarantees. Although the First Amendment right to free exercise of religion has long been a "preferred" freedom, not all courts have protected religious liberty in prisons. Some decisions indicate that prison authorities may curtail freedom of religion. Prisoners may suffer deprivations that are a necessary result of confinement and the institutional structure of prisons. The state can justify an infringement on prisoners' right to free exercise of religion by showing that it is the least restrictive means to attain a compelling interest. The courts have generally practiced judicial restraint and allowed prison officials to exercise their discretionary powers in determining which interests are genuinely compelling and which means are the least drastic or restrictive. Most often the judicial approach has meant the refusal on the part of the courts to substitute judicial supervision for the expert judgment of prison officials in matters of prison management, even when violations of constitutional rights are at issue.[32]

This reasoning was used in *Wright* v. *Wilkins*, in which the Supreme Court of New York upheld Attica State Prison officials' denial of permission to a prisoner to take an Arabic grammar, needed for the prisoner's religious education, into the recreation yard. The court held that "materials which prisoners were permitted to take with them to prison recreational yard or elsewhere in prison was a matter of prison discipline entrusted to department of correction and warden of prison. . . ,"[33] and pertinent regulations did not violate the prisoner's right to freedom of religion.

The courts have recognized that the state, in some instances, may have an interest that is important enough to outweigh the individual's interest in religious expression. Not all burdens on religion are unconstitutional, and the state has a preeminent obligation to promote security, order, and rehabilitation in its penal system.[34] In addition, prison inmates, by virtue of incarceration, give up some of their constitutionally protected rights.[35]

In *Brown* v. *McGinnis*, where Muslim inmates claimed the right to constitutional protection of their religious activities, the New York Court of Appeals noted that "freedom of exercise of religious worship in prison is not absolute, but rather a preferred right, which cannot interfere with laws enacted for preservation, safety, and welfare of the state."[36] According to this reasoning, the rights to religious worship and expression are subject to reasonable rules and regulations designed in the interest of proper discipline and management of the penal system.

Similarly, in an oft-cited passage from a 1964 federal court opinion which denied African-American Muslim inmates access to controversial religious literature, the court argued: "No romantic or sentimental view of constitutional rights or of religion should induce a court to interfere with the necessary disciplinary regime established by officials."[37] The Supreme Court of California, relying on judicial precedents set by prisoners making nonreligion First Amendment claims, held in *In Re Ferguson* that "inmates of state prisons may not be allowed to assert the usual constitutional rights guaranteed to nonincarcerated citizens."[38] Although the right to believe is absolute, the right to act on those beliefs—for example, assembling and discussing "inflammatory Muslim doctrines in a prison situation"[39]—is not.[40]

When a highly preferred interest such as the free exercise of religion is at issue, however, the courts have generally attempted to place the burden on the state to prove a substantial government interest related to the suppression of religious liberty.[41] In *Brown* v. *McGinnis* the Court of Appeals of New York wrote, "speculation as to the dangers inherent in dissemination among prisoners of beliefs . . . of . . . Islamic faith . . . did not warrant prison officials' alleged denial of right to exercise Islamic faith."[42] The Court of Appeals for the Fourth Circuit noted in *Brown* v. *Peyton* that "a prisoner does not shed his First Amendment rights at the prison portals," and held that the prisoner's desire to practice his religion could be restricted by prison officials only upon "a convincing showing that paramount state interests so require."[43]

In *Fulwood* v. *Clemmer*,[44] the U.S. District Court for the District of Columbia "balanced" the state's interest in prison security and the Muslim inmates' First Amendment claims in a decision that found in favor of the prison officials in part and in favor of the Muslim inmates in part. On the one hand, the court condoned the prison officials' decision to discipline a Muslim inmate for inflammatory remarks at a prayer meeting on a baseball field where many non-Muslims were within earshot. In doing so, the court invoked the "fighting words" doctrine, claiming that inflammatory words are not protected by the First Amendment.[45] In addition, the court held that the prison officials' refusal to allow Muslim inmates to correspond with their spiritual leader or to receive a newspaper containing a column written by that leader was a proper exercise of prison administrative discretion.

On the other hand, the court found other deprivations to be impermissible. The denial of rights to wear religious medals and to conduct prayer services, when the state not only allowed but encouraged and supported religious services and the distribution of medals of other religious faiths, was ascertained to be discriminatory. Also, the disciplinary measures against the inmate who spoke the inflammatory words were judged to be too severe. The punishment was determined excessive because it was imposed not only for the offense but for the improper "purpose of suppressing . . . the Muslim religion in the prison."[46]

Major Issues

Discriminatory Treatment

In many cases, the courts have had to deal with allegations by Muslim inmates of religious persecution and discriminatory treatment. Islamic practices have often been prohibited in prison settings while the practices of other religious denominations are not. Most court decisions have been favorable to Muslim inmates, recognizing Islam (or, as it is sometimes referred to by the courts, "Black Muslimism") as a religion deserving First Amendment protection, and affording Muslims the same rights granted to adherents of other faiths.

Instances of interference with religious freedom, discriminatory treatment, and punishment inflicted as a result of attempts to practice their religious faith[47] have been proven through the effects of Muslim inmates to claim their constitutional rights to free expression and equal protection. When Muslim inmates have been able to demonstrate convincingly that they have not received the same treatment as other religious groups in prison, the courts have generally been inclined to protect their constitutional claims. Most courts have ruled that suppression of religious liberty,[48] if applied unequally at the expense of Muslim inmates, results in an impermissible denial of the constitutional guarantee contained in the First Amendment.[49] In *Fulwood* v. *Clemmer*, Muslim inmates alleged, and the U.S. District Court held, that the District of Columbia promoted and underwrote the religious services and activities of Protestants, Catholics, and Jews in its penal institutions while denying the same rights to Muslim inmates.[50] The court ordered prison officials to make religious facilities available in a nondiscriminatory manner. In *Brown* v. *McGinnis*, where Muslim inmates alleged that prison authorities discriminated against them by prohibiting Muslim religious services, the New York Court of Appeals ordered the Commissioner of Prisons to issue rules and regulations that would secure the rights guaranteed by the Constitution in a nondiscriminatory manner that did not severely compromise considerations of prison security and discipline. Similarly, in *SaMarion* v. *McGinnis*, the Supreme Court of New York held that prison rules and regulations "providing for opportunity for practice of religion of Black Muslimism in state prison system which limited attendance at Muslim services to inmates who were 'presently affiliated' or 'professed' the religion of Muslimism were too restrictive and denied free exercise of religion to prospective members of the Muslim faith."[51]

In *Brown* v. *McGinnis*, an inmate of Green Haven State Prison in New York alleged that he "is of the Islamic faith by religious choice and profession and seeks spiritual advice, ministration, and religious services"[52] from the local temple of Islam and from its minister, Malcolm X. Further, inmate Brown charged that prison officials discriminated against him and his coreligionists by prohibiting religious services, spiritual advice, and ministration from recognized clergy of the Islamic faith. Specifically, the New York Commissioner of Correction did not allow Muslim inmates to communicate with or be ministered to by Malcolm X because of his criminal record. The court ruled that the fact that the temple from which inmate Brown sought ministrations was headed by a person with a criminal record did not warrant the denial of his right to exercise the Islamic faith in a manner similar to that of inmates of other denominations.

The counsel for the state in *Cooper* v. *Pate* sought to show that the "Black Muslim Movement despite its pretext of a religious facade, is an organization that outside of prison walls, has for its object the overthrow of the white race, and inside prison walls, has an impressive history of inciting riots and violence."[53] The state's effort to justify the denial of the Muslim inmates' constitutionally guaranteed right to religious liberty on these grounds, however, was unsuccessful. The U.S. Supreme Court ruled in favor of the Muslim inmates, basing its decision on a finding that prison rules regarding the receipt of religious publications were applied in a discriminatory fashion.

In *Walker* v. *Blackwell*, African–American Muslims sought to extend their religious privileges in the following ways: (1) to be served a specified restricted diet after sunset during the month of December (observed as the Fast of Ramadan by the Nation of Islam as taught by Elijah Muhammad), (2) to listen to the national weekly radio broadcast of their spiritual leader, (3) to receive the Nation of Islam's newspaper, *Muhammad Speaks*, and (4) to correspond directly with Elijah Muhammad. The Court of Appeals for the Fifth Circuit stated that, when claims of religious discrimination and denial of religious liberty were at stake, "the government must show some substantial and controlling interest which requires the subordination or limitation of these important constitutional rights, and which justifies their infringement; and, in the absence of such compelling justification the government restrictions are impermissible infringements of these fundamental and preferred rights."[54] Applying this rationale to the facts in this case, the court then found that considerations of security and administrative expense outweighed the Muslim inmates' claims regarding special meals, and that the omission of Elijah Muhammad's radio broadcast from the prison radio system was not a denial of equal protection, since no programming was available for any religious denomination. However, the appellate court found that the Muslims were entitled to receive *Muhammad Speaks* and to correspond with Elijah Muhammad because inmates of other religious persuasions were permitted to receive religious literature and correspond with their spiritual leaders.

The U.S. District Court, N. D. California, held in *Northern* v. *Nelson* that prison authorities were required to pay a Muslim minister to perform religious services in prison facilities at an hourly rate comparable to that paid to chaplains of Catholic, Jewish, and Protestant faiths. In *Finney* v. *Hutto*, the U.S. District Court for the Eastern District of Arkansas held that Muslim inmates of an Arkansas state prison were entitled to the same privileges of religious worship as were granted to inmates of other faiths. When Arkansas prison authorities appealed, they did not contest the district court decision on religious worship. Instead, they chose to appeal only that part of the decision regarding the treatment of Muslim inmates; allegations were made that solitary confinement, daily meals of less than one thousand calories, overcrowding, and inadequate toilet facilities violated the ban on cruel and unusual punishment contained in the Eighth Amendment.

In one of the few cases rejecting a free exercise claim when combined with an equal protection claim, the Supreme Court of California took the position that Muslim religious practices could be prohibited. In *In Re Ferguson*, Muslim inmates contended that their rights to religious freedom had been violated by prison officials. Unlike the Protestant, Catholic, Jewish, and Christian Scientist groups of Folsom State Prison, the members of the Muslim Religious Society were not allowed a place to worship. They were not allowed to discuss their religious doctrines or to possess "an adequate amount" of their religious literature, their meetings were disbanded, often by force, and prison visits by their religious leaders were prohibited. The Muslim inmates sought relief in one of the following forms: (1) accord Muslims the status of a religious group with religious privileges equal to those allowed to other prison religious groups; (2) deny religious privileges to all prison religious groups across the board; or (3) release Muslims from prison so that they may pursue the Islamic faith unencumbered by discriminatory prison regulations.[55]

The Supreme Court of California, however, held that the director of corrections had not acted unreasonably in refusing to allow Muslim convicts to pursue their religious activities while in prison. As a result of the alleged racist content of the Muslim Religious Society's doctrine of black supremacy and its adherents' rejection of the authority of nonadherents, the court took the position that Muslim activities may be prohibited: "In light of the potentially serious dangers to the established prison society presented by Muslim beliefs and actions, it cannot be said that the present, suppressive approach by the Director of Corrections is an abuse of his discretionary power to manage our prison system."[56] As a result of this decision it is, in effect, within the discretionary power of prison authorities to prohibit dissemination of beliefs and literature expressing an unpopular point of view, even when it is of a religious nature.

More recently, in *Thompson* v. *Kentucky*, the Court of Appeals for the Sixth Circuit held that prison officials did not violate the free exercise of

religion or the equal protection clauses by allocating six and one-half hours of
chapel time per week to Muslim inmates while allocating twenty-three and
one-half hours per week to Christian groups, or in failing to provide funds for
a Muslim prison chaplain while providing for one part-time and two full-time
Christian chaplains. Although the claims involved equality of treatment, the
appellate court found that the prison's policies were justified because they
reflected the different numbers of Christian and Muslim inmates, and thus
were not discriminatory. Furthermore, the court opinion states, "The Free
Exercise Clause guarantees a liberty interest, a substantive right; that clause
does not insure that all sects will be treated alike in all respects."[57]

Although judicial treatment of Muslim prisoners' claims under the free
exercise clause has been far from consistent, a general trend toward recognition
of these claims, when framed in the context of discrimination, has been
gradually emerging in the courts. Decisions such as the one reached in
Thompson v. *Kentucky*, however, may indicate a reversal of this trend and
demonstrate the need to continue to press for the protection of prisoners' rights
to religious liberty. Recent court decisions have been somewhat remiss in
imposing a consistent standard in the evaluation of prisoners' free exercise
challenges. The consequences of many of the decisions are that the religious
practices of Muslims in prison have been significantly curtailed. The impact of
court decisions on various prison religious groups has differed, falling more
harshly on Muslim inmates. A review of the major issues of diet, grooming,
and prayer demonstrates the qualitative differences in treatment.

Diet

Judicial responses to prisoners' deprivations with regard to diet have been
inconsistent. Several cases have dealt with the denial of the right to be served a
pork-free diet[58] and the failure to accommodate the Fast of Ramadan.[59] Islam,
like Orthodox Judaism, prohibits the consumption of pork or pork derivatives.
According to the testimony of one Muslim minister, even "if our lives depended on it . . . we can't eat pork."[60] However, because of the low cost of
pork and pork by-products, they are served frequently in prison dining facilities, sometimes to the extent that abstaining inmates cannot get adequate
nourishment. In addition, prison regulations rarely permit food in the cells,
which prevents those who do not eat pork from independently observing
religious dietary restrictions.

Analogous claims made by Muslim and Jewish inmates have resulted in
dissimilar court rulings.[61] In *Moorish Science Temple, Inc.* v. *Smith*, Muslim
inmate Smallwood-El alleged that although Jewish inmates were provided with
alternative diets consistent with their religious beliefs, prison officials refused
to provide him with a suitable diet. The appellate court remanded the case to
the lower court for additional proceedings on the Muslim inmate's claims. The
Court of Appeals for the Second Circuit, in its 1975 term, upheld Jewish
Defense League leader Meir Kahane's claim that the denial of kosher food in
prison was a violation of the First Amendment. In *Kahane* v. *Carlson*, the

appellate court noted that "the courts have properly recognized that prison authorities must accommodate the rights of prisoners to receive diets consistent with their religious scruples,"[62] and held that the denial of kosher food to a Jewish inmate was not justified by an important government objective. The following year, in *Jihaad* v. *Carlson*, the same court remanded for a hearing on the merits a Muslim inmate's complaint that he was placed in segregation for refusing to shave his beard and then was fed only pork sandwiches and oranges. Since Islam prohibits the consumption of pork, Jihaad was reduced to eating only oranges. The court, in its decision, cited the precedent set in *Knuckles* v. *Prasse*: "The prisoners are not entitled to a special dietary program. Of course they will not be forced to eat pork products."[63] On the basis of the facts before them, however, the court was unwilling to declare unconstitutional the prison officials' denial of a Muslim diet.

In another case, *Barnes* v. *Virgin Islands*,[64] the federal district court ordered prison authorities to provide Rastafarian and Muslim prisoners with food complying with their religious dietary restrictions. The court relied in this decision on *Barnett* v. *Rodgers*, in which the D.C. Circuit Court, in remanding the case to the district court, suggested that "a modest degree of official deference to . . . religious obligations [was] . . . constitutionally required. . . ."[65] A reasonable effort to accommodate religiously sanctioned dietary needs was urged on prison authorities but, unlike in *Kahane* v. *Carlson*, was not required by the courts.

Members of the Nation of Islam observe the Fast of Ramadan during December. The fast consists of restricting the consumption of food to the period before sunrise to after sunset. Special arrangements for the proper celebration of the Fast in prisons are rarely made. Requests for special dining hours and ritual foods have been denied by prison administrators on the grounds of cost, convenience, and security.[66]

The Court of Appeals for the Second Circuit, in *Barnett* v. *Rodgers*, however, was more accommodating to Muslim inmates' claims; the court noted that the inmates' request for one pork-free meal a day "represents the bare minimum that jail authorities . . . are constitutionally required to do, not only for Muslims, but indeed for any group of inmates with religious restrictions on diet."[67] In an unusual decision, a federal district court held that there is no justification for failing to identify foods prepared with pork in prison dining facilities, and ordered the immediate implementation of such a procedure on behalf of Muslim inmates.[68]

Grooming

Nearly all prisons have regulations concerning inmate appearance and grooming. The justifications for such regulations include hygiene and the fact that beards, hair, and clothing can conceal contraband and identity. Muslim inmates, on the other hand, have claimed in various court cases that the enforcement of prison regulations prohibiting facial hair and prayer caps and robes interferes with their free exercise rights. They have testified, for instance, that their religion required them to "let their beards flow."[69]

The Court of Appeals for the Second Circuit, ruling in *Burgin* v. *Henderson*, in which Muslim inmates alleged that prison authorities were interfering with their free exercise of religion by compelling them to shave their facial hair, suggested that the personal appearance of a prisoner is a legitimate concern of the state.[70] The court stated: "It may well be that the state's interest in hygiene and identification of inmates outweighs the prisoner's interest in growing a beard as required by his religion,"[71] but the evidence before the court did not provide an adequate basis on which to rule. In this case, the prison officials also prohibited the wearing of prayer caps in accordance with regulations prohibiting hats and the performance of prayers five times a day because it conflicted with the prison schedule. Rather than decide the case on the basis of the evidence before the court, the judge remanded the case to the district court for a factual hearing on the state's justification for the prison regulations under challenge as well as the sincerity of the religious belief requiring facial hair, wearing of prayer caps, and extensive praying. In remanding the case to the lower court, however, the appeals court judge made a clear distinction between the right to wear a beard for reasons of personal appearance and for religious reasons and indicated that the latter were constitutionally protected.

Burgin v. *Henderson* has helped guarantee the right of a prisoner to wear facial hair if it is done for religious reasons. It has been cited as a precedent in several subsequent cases involving both Muslims and non-Muslims.[72] In *Monroe* v. *Bombard*[73] the district court held that, on the basis of an investigation of competing interests as suggested in Burgin, Sunni Muslims had a constitutional right to grow beards as an aspect of religious freedom and that no government interest sufficient to overcome this had been shown.[74] Institutional requirements with respect to security and prisoner identification could be satisfied by other less restrictive means than a total ban on beards.

In *Shabazz* v. *Barnauskas* the Court of Appeals for the Fifth Circuit held that the district court had erred in dismissing a Muslim prisoner's challenge to a Florida state prison's "no beard" regulation without conducting a hearing into the plaintiff's religious beliefs and the state's justifications for its prison regulations.

Without scrutinizing the reasonableness of prison shaving regulations, the Supreme Court of New York in *People ex rel. Rockey* v. *Krueger*[75] held that evidence of discriminatory application of the rules in question invalidated the requirement that a Muslim inmate shave off his beard. In this case, Muslim inmate Rockey was held in solitary confinement because he refused to shave his beard on religious grounds. The jail supervisory officer admitted in his testimony that he would not require an Orthodox Jew to shave, and that while the Jewish inmate would be isolated from other prisoners, he would not be placed in solitary confinement. Since the regulation was applied admittedly in a discriminatory manner, the court required that the Muslim inmate be released from solitary confinement.

In *Jihaad* v. *Carlson*,[76] Petitioner Jihaad claimed that his religious beliefs require him to wear a beard and the prison's shaving requirement violates his right to freely exercise his religion. The U.S. District Court held in this case that "[i]t is clearly within the power of prison authorities to require appropriate attire and grooming of prison inmates."[77] However, the court refused to hold that the prison's interest in requiring inmates to shave is a compelling one, and ordered an evidentiary hearing to examine the competing institutional and inmate interests.[78]

An examination of the court records reveals that Muslim inmates have contributed substantially to the defense of a prisoner's right to wear facial hair for reasons of religious belief in spite of the state's claims of security, prisoner identification, and hygiene interests. However, the courts have been more reluctant to recognize Muslim prisoners' claims than the claims of adherents of other faiths. While the right of American Indians to wear their hair long has been protected against prison regulations concerning hygiene,[79] and the right of individuals who attach private religious significance to their hair length has been protected,[80] the right of Muslims to refuse to shave off their beards in accordance with religious prescriptions has not been upheld as readily. In cases involving Muslim inmates, the courts have often conceded that prison policies might be defensible, and have called for further examination into both the sincerity of beliefs of Muslim inmates and the legitimacy of the prison regulations in question.

Prayers

Muslims are required by their faith to perform prayers at prescribed hours five times a day. These are accompanied by prescribed ablutions and prostration; "without any one of these forms the prayers would be incomplete."[81] Prison schedules sometimes interfere with Muslim prayers. In *Bethea* v. *Daggett*,[82] in which a Muslim prisoner contended that he was not permitted the right to pray five times daily, the court held that there was no impingement on religious liberty by the prison schedule because it allowed ample opportunity for prayer, although not at the Islamically prescribed hours.

After a July 27, 1973, riot at the McAlester facility of the Oklahoma State Penitentiary, prison officials imposed a total ban on group worship. In *Battle* v. *Anderson*, a prisoner held in McAlester brought suit on behalf of inmates, including Muslims, who claimed that the ban on corporate religious services was a violation of their First Amendment rights and was not justified by any legitimate security concerns. The federal district court averred that the prohibition "appears to have had a greater impact on the Muslims, because [corporate] services provide for their only opportunity for religious guidance. Protestants and Catholics at the penitentiary have at least the services of a civilian chaplain with whom individual consultations may be arranged however brief or unsatisfactory they may be."[83] In effect, the court suggested that the ban on gathering for worship combined with the failure to provide a

Muslim chaplain placed a heavier burden on Muslims and may be inherently discriminatory.

In a recent U.S. Supreme Court case, in which Muslim inmates challenged New Jersey prison policies that prevented them from attending Friday services, the Court, Justice Rehnquist writing for the majority, held in part that "prison officials had acted in a reasonable manner by precluding Islamic inmates from attending weekly Friday religious services and prison regulations to that effect thus did not violate the free exercise of religion clause of the First Amendment."[84] The Court found that the reasonableness of the policies in question was supported by the fact that, although some Muslims are prevented from attending Friday services because of work assignments, Muslim inmates are not deprived of all forms of religious exercise. All Muslims who wish to may, at one time or another, participate in a number of Muslim religious ceremonies.[85]

Despite the fact that Friday prayer services are of paramount importance to the Islamic faith, which the Court acknowledged, it was still determined that "the very stringent requirements as to the time at which [Friday services] may be held may make it extraordinarily difficult for prison officials to assure that every Muslim prisoner is able to attend that service."[86] Since other means of religious worship are available, the Court held that the Constitution does not require prison officials to "sacrifice legitimate penological objectives"[87] to accommodate inconvenient Muslim religious practices. Further, it was held that prison officials need not demonstrate that the policies in question are imperative to further an important interest such as security, discipline, or rehabilitation, and are no more restrictive of prisoners' constitutional rights than is necessary to achieve prison objectives. Even when First Amendment rights are concerned, the Supreme Court will not substitute its judgment for that of prison officials.[88] The Court essentially shirked its responsibility to protect the "preferred" right of religious freedom, guaranteed by the First Amendment, in deference to the discretion of prison authorities in the execution of their duties.

It is worth noting that in his dissent in this case, Justice Brennan cited the brief for Imam Jamil Abdullah Al-Amin et al. as Amici Curiae to illustrate that attendance at Friday Muslim prayer services is obligatory.[89] The Friday services, Brennan argued, "cannot be regarded as one of several essentially fungible religious practices."[90] The opportunity to participate in other religious activities in prison does not compensate for the Muslims' forced absence at the central service of Islam. Brennan compared the situation of Muslims who are not allowed to attend Friday services to that of a Catholic prisoner denied the right to attend Mass on Sunday; "few would regard [the latter] deprivation as anything but absolute, even if the prisoner were afforded other opportunities to pray, to discuss the Catholic faith with others, and even to avoid eating meat on Friday if that were a preference."[91] The fact that other types of religious worship are available in prison does not warrant the deprivation of the opportunity to participate in the central religious ceremony of one's faith, a time when adherents "assert their identity as a community covenanted to God."[92]

Other Religious Issues

In *Abdullah* v. *Kinnison*,[93] inmates Abdullah and Akbar challenged an Ohio prison regulation restricting prisoners' use of white Hanafi Muslim prayer robes to the prison chapel only. The Muslim inmates assert that under Islamic law, Hanafi Muslims should wear white prayer robes at all times, if possible, and must wear them while performing prayers five times a day.[94] Until November 1977, Southern Ohio Correctional Facility inmates of the Hanafi Muslim faith were permitted to keep prayer robes in their cells. A new directive restricted the use of white prayer robes to the chapel. Prison authorities imposed this restriction in response to an incident in which a prison guard took one of the white robes from a prisoner's cell and used it to frighten another inmate by imitating a Ku Klux Klan member. The restriction was thus justified as a "control mechanism" to prevent similar incidents from occurring in the future.[95] In addition, the robes were described by prison officials as a security risk, since they were loose-fitting and could be used to conceal weapons, contraband, and food, or to resemble civilian dress to aid in escape.[96]

The Court of Appeals for the Sixth Circuit held in this case that the burden imposed on Muslim inmates' right to free exercise of religion was minimal, because the new prison policy merely limits, and does not forbid, the use of the Hanafi Muslims' white prayer robes. The fact that the ban on white prayer robes outside the chapel impinges on the right to perform prayers in the prescribed fashion outside the chapel appears to have had no bearing on the court decision. Further, the court accepted without question the prison officials' assertion that their objectives in promulgating the restrictive regulations were legitimate and justified an abridgment of the Muslim inmates' First Amendment rights.

In *Madyun* v. *Franzen*,[97] a male Muslim inmate held in the Pontiac Correctional Center in Illinois refused to comply with a female security guard's order that he submit to a limited frisk search[98] on the grounds that the Islamic religion forbade such physical contact with a woman other than his wife or mother.[99] The Court of Appeals for the Seventh Circuit held that, although a limited frisk search by a female security guard might be incompatible with Islamic tenets, it would not impermissably violate a male Muslim inmate's First Amendment right of free exercise of religion, since it is justified by the important state interests of providing adequate prison security and equal opportunity for women to serve as prison guards.[100] Equal opportunity for women in hiring is cited by the court as a legal obligation of the state.[101] To provide such opportunity in state prisons, female guards must be able to perform all the tasks associated with their positions, including limited frisk searches. The court found the equal opportunity in hiring interest to outweigh the Muslim inmate's free exercise of religion interest.

As we have seen, the circumstances presented by incarceration have often led the courts to sanction the abridgement of the rights of Muslim inmates' to free exercise of their religion. The general judicial approach has been deference to the authority and expertise of prison administrators, often resulting in the uncritical acceptance of stated institutional need at the expense of Muslim prisoners' religious liberty. In an unusual opinion, a lower court argued that the analytical tools needed to define the scope of religious liberty

> do not change merely because the context of enforcement is a prison. Up-holding of a subjugation of preferred First Amendment rights by deferring to the discretion of the prison warden . . . falls short of the duty of a federal court. This does not mean that the circumstances peculiar to prison confine-ment are irrelevant.[102]

The court records here examined demonstrate that Muslim inmates' religious liberty claims, challenging prison regulations that impinge on the free exercise of the Islamic faith, have been accepted only under certain circumstances. First, Muslim inmates have been most successful in pressing their claims when they have clearly been subject to discriminatory treatment. However, even in such cases the courts' reluctance to substitute their judgment for the judgment of prison officials has often overridden the inmates' claims to equal protection. Second, the fundamental interests of the state in upholding competing claims such as women's claims to equal opportunity in hiring or the prison administrators' need to maximize efficiency in maintaining correctional facilities often compromise prisoners' claims to First Amendment protection. Third, prison security is of paramount concern and has been used at times to justify a diminution of Muslim inmates' rights to practice their faith when it is perceived to present a security threat.

Finally, in *O'Lone* v. *Shabazz*, Justice Brennan in his dissent argues in favor of the Muslims' claims for accommodation of Friday services in prison by drawing attention to the similarity between Islamic and Catholic tenets concerning the obligatory nature of Sabbath services. In making this cultural equivalence Brennan intends to elucidate the importance of Friday prayers and, in the process, fits Islam within the Judeo–Christian religious tradition. Although this reasoning was not compelling enough to garner the support of a majority of the Court, it is significant in that it both ascribes to Islam an air of familiarity and attempts to fashion out of the American milieu an imperative for religious accommodation.

The values associated with the free exercise clause of the First Amendment exist in the prison community to the same extent that they exist in society at large; that is, the protection of unpopular beliefs, and those who hold them, from persecution at the hands of the majority is a "preferred" right. Religious liberty is a fundamental principle of the Constitution. Deference to prison officials, who are not always disinterested persons in resolving prison problems, jeopardizes the rights of adherents of nonconventional faiths in particular to practice their beliefs and leads quickly to religious intolerance.

The courts by and large have been sympathetic to the situation of small religious groups and have treated them with greater care than mainstream religious groups. In famous free exercise cases involving the Amish and Jehovah's Witnesses, the courts, in most cases, have found in favor of the individual, rather than the state. In *Wisconsin* v. *Yoder*,[103] for instance, the Supreme Court held that the impact of an accommodation of Amish religious practices on secular goals would be small.[104] Similarly, in *Thomas* v. *Review Board of Indiana Employment Security Division*,[105] the Court determined that the threat presented by Jehovah's Witnesses to the advancement of the state's interest in the secular goal of reduced unemployment was not substantial enough to preclude accommodation.

However, the courts' treatment of Islam has not been uniform and provides little guidance in determining with any certainty how Islam and Muslims will fare in asserting Muslims' civil rights. In the prison context, the courts have deferred, more often than not, to the discretion of prison administrators in deciding when a state interest is compelling enough to preclude accommodation of Islamic practices. This has led to an erratic, ad hoc application of justice with regard to religious liberty inside prison walls.

Possible resolutions to foreseeable conflicts between the state and the individual Muslim remain uncertain. Conflicts may arise in a number of areas: for example, observance of the Sabbath, religious holidays, and attendance at prayer services conflict with the demands of the workplace, schools, the military, hospitals, and prisons.[106] Muslim dietary restrictions and religiously inspired choices in attire, such as veiling and prayer caps, also require a degree of religious tolerance and accommodation. With the extremely narrow conception of what constitutes the Judeo–Christian tradition of our society gaining in popular use, the Muslims of the United States stand in need of constitutional protection now perhaps more than ever before. The ability of the courts to extend such protection to Muslims has been made clear by the precedents set by other religious minorities. The courts' willingness to treat Muslims equally, however, remains unclear.

Notes

1. Arther A. Cohen, *The Myth of the Judeo–Christian Tradition* (New York: Harper & Row, 1970), p. ix. Cohen writes, "We can learn much from the history of Jewish–Christian relations, but one thing we cannot make of it is a discourse of community, fellowship, and understanding" (p. xiii). See also Martin E. Marty, "A Judeo Christian Looks at the Judeo Christian Tradition," *The Christian Century*, October 8, 1986, p. 858.

2. Although President Reagan has often spoken of the Judeo–Christian tradition, his religious references are decidedly Christian. See Chapter 5 (especially pp. 74–77), Paul D. Erikson, *Reagan Speaks, The Making of an American Myth* (New York: New York University Press, 1985).

3. President Reagan, in his 1983 speech to the National Association of Evangelicals in Orlando, Florida, warned of the encroaching spirit of "modern-day secularism" and the designs of liberals and "secular humanists" who "proclaim that they're freeing us from superstitions of the past" in order to destroy the "tried and time-tested values upon which our civilization is based," Erikson, *Reagan Speaks*, p. 77.

4. Yvonne Y. Haddad, "A Century of Islam in America" [*The Muslim World Today*, Occasional Paper No. 4] (Washington D.C.: Islamic Affairs, 1986), p. 9.

5. Martin E. Marty, "A Judeo-Christian," n. 1, p. 859; see also Erikson, *Reagan Speaks*. Erikson writes of the language Reagan uses "that seems almost calculated to make non-Christians uncomfortable. 'Our only hope for tomorrow is in the faces of our children,' he said in 1983, 'And we know Jesus said, "Suffer the little children to come unto me, and forbid them not, for such is the Kingdom of God."'" (Erikson, *Reagan Speaks*, p. 76.)

6. See Lawrence Tribe, *American Constitutional Law* (1978), p. 830; also, the Court stated in *Thomas* v. *Review Board of Indiana Employment Security Division*, 450 U.S. 707 (1981) at 714: "The resolution of that question [what constitutes religion] is not to turn upon a judicial perception of the particular belief or practice in question; religious beliefs need not be acceptable, logical, consistent or comprehensible to others in order to merit first amendment protection."

7. U.S. Constitution, Amendment I: "Congress shall make no law respecting an establishment of religion, or prohibiting the free exercise thereof."

8. *Reynolds* v. *United States*, 98 U.S. 145(1878) (prohibition of polygamy applied to Mormons); *Church of Jesus Christ of Latter Day Saints* v. *United States*, 136 U.S. 1(1890); *Davis* v. *Beason*, 133 U.S. 333 (1890); "The term 'religion' has reference to one's view of his relations to his Creator, and to the obligations they impose of reverence for his being and character, and of obedience to his will," *Reynolds*, p. 342.

9. For example, *United States* v. *Lee*, 102 S.Ct. 1051(1982); *Wisconsin* v. *Yoder*, 406 U.S. 206(1972).

10. For example, *Cantwell* v. *Connecticut*, 310 U.S. 296(1940); *Cox* v. *New Hampshire*, 312 U.S. 569(1941); *Prince* v. *Massachusetts*, 321 U.S. 158 (1944); *Thomas* v. *Review Board of Indiana Employment Security Division*, 450 U.S. 707(1981).

11. *Sherbert* v. *Verner*, 374 U.S. 398 (1963).

12. For example, *People* v. *Woody* 394 P.2d. 813 (Sup. Ct. of Ca. 1964).

13. *Robinson* v. *Foti*, 527 F. Supp. 1111 (E.D. La. 1981).

14. *International Society for Krishna Consciousness, Inc.* v. *Barber*, 650 F.2d 430 (2d Cir. 1981).

15. *Africa* v. *Commonwealth of Pennsylvania*, 662 F.2d 1025 (3d. Cir. 1981), cert. denied 456 U.S. 908 (1982). In this case, the Appeals Court rejected the claim that MOVE was a religious organization because it "is not structurally analogous to those 'traditional' organizations that have been recognized as religions under the first amendment," *Africa*, p. 1036. This conclusion was reached after the court found that MOVE conducts no regular services, observes no religious holidays of its own, and has nothing which passes for scripture.

16. See Freeman, "The Misguided Search for the Constitutional Definition of 'Religion,'" *Georgetown Law Journal*, 71 (1983). The author cites seven cases and twelve articles that deal with the elusive definition of religion. See also p. 1611, Note, "Soul Rebels: The Rastafarians and the Free Exercise Clause," *Georgetown Law Journal*, 72 (1984).

17. See *Davis* v. *Beason*, 133 U.S. 333, 345–48(1890); *United States* v. *Macintosh*, 283 U.S. 605, 633–34(1931).

18. Freeman, "The Misguided Search," p. 1525.

19. *United States* v. *Ballard*, 322 U.S. 78, 86–87(1944).

20. *Ballard*, 69–70.

21. 380 U.S. 163(1965) at 165–66.

22. See Note, "Soul Rebels," p. 1612; see also *Witmer* v. *United States*, 75 S. Ct.

392(1955), in which Supreme Court Justice Clark held that the ultimate question in conscientious objector cases is the sincerity of the objector's beliefs.

23. For example, *International Society for Krishna Consciousness, Inc.* v. *Barber*, 650 F.2d 430(2d Cir. 1981); *Melnak* v. *Yogi*, 592 F.2d 197 (3d Cir. 1979); *Founding Church of Scientology of Wash.* v. *United States*, 409 F.2d 1146 (D.C. Cir. 1969).

24. "Muslim faith is 'religion' within the constitutional provisions as the freedom of religion." *Fulwood* v. *Clemmer*, 206 F. Supp. 370 (1962) at 373.

25. William Bennet Turner, "Establishing the Rule of Law in Prisons: A Manual for Prisoners' Rights Litigation," *Black Law Journal*, 1, 2 (Summer 1971), p. 106.

26. See, for instance, *Walker* v. *Blackwell*, 411 F.2d 23 (5th Cir. 1969) (Black Muslims' religious interests recognized under the First Amendment); *Barnett* v. *Rodgers*, 410 F.2d 985 (D.C. Cir. 1969); *Cooper* v. *Pate* 382 F.2d 518 (7th Cir. 1967) (a determination that beliefs of Black Muslims do not constitute religion would require a comparative evaluation of religions, which is beyond the powers of the courts); *Sostre* v. *McGinnis*, 334 F.2d 905 (2d Cir. 1964), cert. denied 378 US 892 (1964) (accommodation of Black Muslim religious practices in prison settings); *Knuckles* v. *Prasse*, 302 F.Supp. 1036 (E.D. Pa. 1969); *Bryant* v. *Wilkins*, 265 N.Y.S. 2d. 995("Islamic group known as Muslims, followers of sect led by Elijah Muhammed constitutes a 'religion.'"); *Banks* v. *Havener*, 234 F.Supp. 27(1964) (". . . the Black Muslim movement as here taught and followed is a religion.").

27. For example, *Battle* v. *Anderson*, 376 F.Supp. 402(1974); *Knuckles* v. *Prasse*, 302 F. Supp. 1036(1969), cert. denied, 403 U.S. 936(1971); *Walker* v. *Blackwell*, 411 F.2d. 23 (1969).

28. For example, *Northern* v. *Nelson*, 315 F.Supp. 687(1970); *In the Matter of Brown* v. *McGinnis*, 225 N.Y.S. 2d. 497(1962); *Finney* v. *Hutto*, 57 L.Ed.2d. 522(1976).

29. *Northern* v. *Nelson*; *Brown* v. *McGinnis*; and *Finney* v. *Hutto*. Also, *Cooper* v. *Pate*; *Battle* v. *Anderson*; and *Rowland* v. *Sigler*, 327 F. Supp. 821(D. Neb.), aff'd. sub nom. *Rowland* v. *Jones*, 452 F.2d 1005(8th Cir. 1971).

30. For example, *State ex rel. Tute* v. *Cubbage*, 210 A.2d 555 (Del. Super, Ct. 1965); and *Fulwood* v. *Clemmer*.

31. The court decision in *SaMarion* v. *McGinnis*, 284 N.Y.S. 2d. at 508(1967), reads in part: "diet of inmates shall be left to the discretion of the Wardens but where reasonable and practicable and consistent with the ability to do so, religious dietary habits should be accommodated." See also *Battle* v. *Anderson*, 427; *Waddell* v. *Aldredge*, 480 F.2d 1078(1973); *Long* v. *Parker*, 455 F.2d 466(3d Cir. 1972); and *Barnett* v. *Rodgers*.

32. The U.S. Court of Appeals for the Fourth Circuit held in *Sewell* v. *Pegelow* that "[m]aintenance of discipline in prison is an executive function with which the judicial branch ordinarily will not interfere," 291 F. 2d. at 196 (1961).

33. *Wright* v. *Wilkins*, 26 Misc. 2d. 1090, 210 N.Y.S. 2d. 309 (Sup. Ct. 1961).

34. The Court of Appeals for the Seventh Circuit has stated: "the balance between [the prisoner's] right to free exercise and the state's interest in applying to him its prison rules and regulations tips toward the state." *Madyun* v. *Franzen*, 704F.2d 954(1983) at 958.

35. Prisoners "cannot expect the same freedom from incidental infringement on the exercise of his religious practices that is enjoyed by those not incarcerated," *Madyun* v. *Franzen*, 958.

36. *Brown* v. *McGinnis*, 497.

37. *Fulwood* v. *Clemmer*, 370.

38. *In Re Ferguson*, 361 P.2d 417(1961) at 421.

39. *In Re Ferguson*, 422.

40. For a discussion of the two concepts—freedom to believe and freedom to act—embraced by the First Amendment, see *Cantwell* v. *Connecticut*, 296. Although the Cantwell case does not address religious liberty in prisons, it has often been cited as an authoritative source in cases that do; essentially, the right to practice one's religious beliefs is subject only to regulation for the protection of society.

41. The recent Supreme Court decision in *O'Lone* v. *Shabazz*, 107 S. Ct. 2400(1987), is a noteworthy exception. The Court (Rehnquist writing) held that the appellate court erred in placing the burden on the prison officials to prove that no reasonable method existed by which inmates' religious rights could be accommodated without creating bona fide security problems.

In *Sewell* v. *Pegelow*, the U.S. Court of Appeals for the Fourth Circuit held that "[p]risoners lose certain rights and privileges, but are not entirely bereft of all civil rights or every protection of the law," *Sewell* v. *Pegelow*, 196.

42. *Brown* v. *McGinnis*, 497.

43. 437 F.2d 1228(1971) (Black Muslim inmate alleged denial of permission to subscribe to *Muhammed Speaks*, to order religious buttons, and to hold prayer meetings).

44. 206 F.Supp. 370(1962) (Muslim inmates allege denial of constitutional right to communicate with counsel concerning infringement of religious liberties; of right to wear religious medal although other religious medals were supplied at public expense to inmates; of right to hold religious services although some other religious groups were allowed to hold services at public expense).

45. For the "fighting words" doctrine, see *Chaplinsky* v. *New Hampshire*, 315 U.S. 568(1942).

46. *Fulwood* v. *Clemmer*, 379.

47. See Note, "Beyond the Ken of the Courts: A Critique of Judicial Refusal to Review the Complaints of Convicts," *Yale Law Journal*, 72 (January 1963), 540–44.

48. For example, the prohibition of prayer meetings and other forms of discriminatory treatment.

49. In *Pierce* v. *LaVallee*, 203 F. 2d. 233 (1961) and *Sewell* v. *Pegelow*, two federal courts held that discriminatory treatment on the basis of religion is prohibited by the Civil Rights Act, and cannot be justified merely for the sake of efficient prison administration. In *Cooper* v. *Pate*, the Supreme Court held that claims of Black Muslims of religious suppression and discrimination stated a federal cause of action.

50. *Fulwood* v. *Clemmer*, 373.

51. *SaMarion* v. *McGinnis*, 505; also, see note 31.

52. *Brown* v. *McGinnis*, 498.

53. *Cooper* v. *Pate*, 518.

54. *Walker* v. *Blackwell*, 23.

55. *In Re Ferguson*, 420. Inmates argued that religious persecution constituted cruel and unusual punishment, violating their Eighth Amendment rights, and thus warranted their immediate release.

56. *In Re Ferguson*, 422.

57. *Thompson* v. *Kentucky*, 712 F.2d 1078(1983) at 1081.

58. For example, *Moorish Science Temple of America, Inc.* v. *Smith*, 693 F.2d 987(1982); *Battle* v. *Anderson*; *Elam* v. *Henderson*; *Walker* v. *Blackwell* (citing administrative expense as the prevailing concern); *Knuckles* v. *Prasse*; *Barnett* v. *Rodgers*; *Waddell* v. *Aldredge*; *Long* v. *Parker*; *Abernathy* v. *Cunningham*, 393 F.2d 775(1968).

59. For example, *Cochran* v. *Sielaff*, 405 F.Supp. 1126, 1128(S.D. Ill. 1976); *Walker* v. *Blackwell*; *Barnett* v. *Rodgers*.

60. *Barnett* v. *Rodgers*, 998.

61. See *Moorish Science Temple, Inc.* v. *Smith*; *Jihaad* v. *Carlson*, 410 F. Supp. 1132(1976); *United States* v. *Kahane*, 396 F.Supp. 687, aff'd sub. nom. *Kahane* v. *Carlson*, 527 F.2d 492 (2d Cir. 1975).

62. *Kahane* v. *Carlson*, 495, citing *Chapman* v. *Kliendienst*, 507 F.2d 1246, 1251(7th Cir. 1974); *Ross* v. *Blackledge*, 477 F.2d 616(4th Cir. 1973); *Barnett* v. *Rodgers*.

63. *Jihaad* v. *Carlson*, citing *Knuckles* v. *Prasse*, 302 F. Supp. 1036, 1059 (E.D. Pa. 1969), aff'd, 435 F.2d 1255 (3d Cir. 1970)1 cert. denied, 403 U.S. 936, 91 S. Ct. 2262, 29 L. Ed. 717(1971).

64. 415 F.Supp. 1218 (D.V.I. 1976).

65. See notes 26, 31, and 57, and accompanying text.

66. See *Cochran* v. *Sielaff*; *Elam* v. *Henderson*, 472 F. 2d 582(5th Cir.), cert. denied, 414 U.S. 868(1973); *Walker* v. *Blackwell*; and *Barnett* v. *Rodgers*.

67. *Barnett* v. *Rodgers*, 1001.

68. *Battle* v. *Anderson*, 376 F.Supp. 402(1974).

69. *Shabazz* v. *Barnauskas*, 598 F.2d 345(1979).

70. *Burgin* v. *Henderson*, 536 F.2d 501(2d Cir. 1976).

71. *Burgin* v. *Henderson*, 504. Also, Black Muslims believe that "it is against the nature of the creation of Allah, that one should shave the hair off his face and thus resemble women, defacing the nature of man." M. Sayed Adly, About the Beard of Muslims 1 (sermon) (1976), cited Comment, "The Religious Rights of the Incarcerated," *University of Pennsylvania Law Review*, 125, 812 (April 1977), n. 12, p. 814.

72. For example, see *Wright* v. *Raines*, 457 F. Supp. 1082(1977) (Sikhs inmates filed challenge to prison regulations that interfered with their free exercise of religion).

73. *Monroe* v. *Bombard*, 422 F. Supp. 211, S.D.N.Y. (1977).

74. *Monroe* v. *Bombard*, p. 211.

75. 306 N.Y.S. 2d 359(1969).

76. See note 61.

77. *Jihaad* v. *Carlson*, 1134.

78. *Jihaad* v. *Carlson*, 1134.

79. *Teterud* v. *Gillman*, 385 F.Supp. 153 (5th Cir. 1976).

80. For example, *Brooks* v. *Wainwright*, 428 F.2d 652 (5th Cir. 1970) (divine revelation commanded plaintiff inmate not to shave); *Brown* v. *Wainwright*, 419 F.2d 1376 (5th Cir. 1970) (prisoner alleged that he was "an offspring of God and a mortal," and that moustache was a gift from God). See also Comment, "The Religious Rights of the Incarcerated," *University of Pennsylvania Law Review*, 125: 812 (April 1977).

81. *Burgin* v. *Henderson*, 501.

82. 329 F.Supp. 796 (N.D. Ga. 1970).

83. *Battle* v. *Anderson*, 419.

84. *O'Lone* v. *Shabazz*, 107 S.Ct. 2400(1987).

85. *O'Lone* v. *Shabazz*, 2401–402.

86. *O'Lone* v. *Shabazz*, 2406.

87. *O'Lone* v. *Shabazz*, 2406.

88. *O'Lone* v. *Shabazz*, 2400.

89. Id. at 2410.

90. Id.

91. Id.

92. Id., citing Brief for Imam Jamil Abdullah Al-Amin et al., as Amici Curiae, at 32.

93. 769 F. 2d 345(1985).

94. Id. at 347.

95. Id.

96. 769 F.2d at 346, 347, 349.

97. 704 F.2d 954(1983).

98. The standard limited frisk search entails contact along most of the body excluding the genital–anal area. See Id. at 956 n. 1 and 2.

99. Id. at 956.

100. Id. at 954.

101. Id. at 960.

102. *Rowland* v. *Sigler*, 327 F.Supp. 821, 827 (D. Neb.), aff'd. sub nom. *Rowland* v. *Jones*, 452 F.2d 1005(8th Cir. 1971).

103. Supra, note 10.

104. Id. at 225.

105. Supra, note 11.

106. Regarding the Sabbath, see the recent U.S. Supreme Court decision, *Estate of Thornton* v. *Caldor*, 105 S.Ct. 2914(1985), in which the Court held that a Connecticut statute providing employees with an absolute right not to work on their Sabbath violated the establishment clause of the First Amendment. The Court determined that the State's "unyielding weighting in favor of Sabbath observers over all other interests . . . ha[d] a primary effect that impermissably advance[d] a particular religious practice," (at 2918) and placed an unacceptable burden on employers and coworkers.

11

Islamic Education in the United States and Canada: Conception and Practice of the Islamic Belief System

Nimat Hafez Barazangi

This chapter examines the way immigrant Muslim parents and their offspring perceive Islam and view its practice in the context of the societies of the United States and Canada.[1]

Historically and at present the worldview of North American Muslims has generally differed from that of other groups who are either natives of or immigrants to North America. Yet not until recently[2] has any substantial research been done on the presence of Muslims in North America, let alone on their learning patterns or the role of their different worldviews in the education of their children.

Assumptions and Propositions

Four underlying propositions are central to this chapter and to the contrast between the Islamic[3] and Western worldviews:

1. It is possible for North American Muslims, or any believing group, to maintain their view of life within a society that operates, or seems to operate, on a secular[4] basis.
2. As long as a belief system does not remain merely a set of assumptions, but is objectified,[5] as the Islamic belief system should be, the perception of such a belief system should be studied in context and not as a set of abstract codes.
3. Shifting between paradigms, in this case from the Islamic view of life to its Western counterpart, is also possible. Basically, the gap between the two paradigms is viewed here as being resolvable by the way the issues are approached. That is, instead of judging the values or the moral codes, symbols, or rituals that are being transmitted or discussed within the two paradigms, I address the transmission process of a generally

157

accepted ideology by North American Muslims to their offspring within a context that these Muslims generally view as conflicting (in reality or in appearance) with their ideological or cultural heritage.

4. My concern with the process does not mean that I underestimate the variations in the content and principles between the two preceding paradigms. Yet the primary concern of this study is with the objectification of both the content and the principles in a certain context, and not with a set of verbalized values or moral principles. It therefore not only examines Muslims' expression of the principles but also how these expressions are applied in practice, in different contexts, by different Muslim individuals or groups.

I am working with the presupposition that basic differences in the Western and Islamic worldviews impinge strongly on the ways in which their respective philosophies of education are set forth. That Muslims must attempt their own educational programs within the context of Western educational systems raises obvious questions.

Four assumptions about the dominant Western worldview seem to be relevant:

1. Western ideology assumes secularism—the separation[6] of church (representing spiritual life) and state (representing worldly, mundane life)—a concept that is alien to Islam. Under this assumption, which characterizes multicultural soceites, decision makers are not supposed to recognize one belief system over another, even though their personal views and epistemology might be based on a particular belief commitment. Therefore, separation of church and state is emphasized here on the institutional level and not on the individual level.

2. God, Lord, or Creator may be considered a religious entity that can be separated from other aspects of life, and common epistemological assumptions underline this worldview. These common epistemological assumptions contradict the basic Islamic assumption that God is not only the Creator but also the Source of value and knowledge.

3. The human being is considered the master of nature or self; he or she is considered to have full authority on earth, to practice his or her functions in isolation from God.[7] Historical accounts not only provide evidence for separation of the spheres of knowledge but also contradict the basic Islamic assumption that the purpose of education is to understand natural laws so the individual can serve as Allah's khalifa (viceregent) on earth.

4. Rules become the rules of man (whether of the individual or the society), and authority becomes that of man over others, at least as practiced in institutions and in legislation. Rules are drawn by policy makers on the basis of assumptions made by the political founders of secular institutions or by a philosophical view that ignores metaphysics and belief systems.[8]

In contrast to this are the basic assumptions that underlie Islamic thought and its view of human knowledge and morality: first, the human knowledge consists of the product of human reasoning plus revealed knowledge and, second, the human learning, conception, and valuing should be guided by Allah (God) as stated in the Qur'an[9] and according to Allah's natural laws.[10] These two assumptions represent the basic difference between the religious view—in the wide sense of the word—and the secular view of the relation between faith or the belief system and knowledge.

A distinction must be made here between the Western view of public policy (secular and compartmentalized) and of personal behavior. In the latter, a connection between spiritual and mundane life is often advocated, usually respected, and sometimes achieved. Although pluralistic societies tend to subordinate particular ideologies in favor of egalitarianism,[11] it is unrealistic to ignore the fact that Islam benefits, to a certain degree, from the secularism in North America that it finds so alien.

The basic contribution of this study lies in the attempt to bridge the gap between practical concerns of the Muslim community of North America, on the one hand, and the views of "Islamic intellectuals,"[12] curriculum theory and practice, basic and practical research, and conceptual views on learning and understanding, on the other. The significance of this study lies in its investigation of the role of faith and belief systems in the process of education. More specifically, the impact of this study is not limited to believing Muslims, nor to the Muslims of North America. It is basically a study of perception and transmission of a faith and its belief system in a pluralistic, secular context, and it can be applied to any other faith, immigrant group, or pluralistic society.

Finally, because it was instigated in response to a practical need, this study can contribute to understanding the relationship between faith and knowledge. It is an attempt to recognize the differences in human conceptualization of faith by trying to understand the differences and similarities in the perception, as well as the practice, of the particular faith. Its emphasis, therefore, is not on the differences but on the interaction between perception and practice based on these differences. It also attempts to show faith as a determinant in the process of conceptual change, understanding, curriculum planning, and educating.

Summary of Method

Members of forty immigrant Muslim families (140 subjects) of several national and ethnic origins were interviewed in five major cities in the United States and Canada: Buffalo, Montreal, New York, Toronto, and Washington, D.C. The interviewees volunteered through the centers or personal contacts. Attempts to reach nonparticipant/nonmember Muslims (that is, community members who chose not to participate in the study or Muslims who do not frequent these centers) were not successful.

In spite of the difficulties encountered in getting participants, thirty-one sets of matched data (fathers, mothers, and youth, 118 individuals in total) were secured. The cooperation of community leaders, center presidents, and mosque imams (leaders) made this study possible. We will see in the data analysis that the selection process may have skewed the mean scores of the entire population, particularly of the parents, toward the high end of the scale. The scale ranged from 2 to 12, and the mean scores were between 8 and 10. The only criterion for participation was that the families have children between the ages of fourteen and twenty-two who were reared mainly in North America.

The choice of subjects was made to facilitate an intergenerational comparison in the perception of the Islamic ideology and to determine whether Muslim parents were able to transfer the basic belief system in its totality as a way of life. The choice was also intended to provide an insight into the different practices of these Muslim families as influenced by the home country of the parents and the North American societies. The families were interviewed in small groups of fathers, mothers, and youth, and they completed two sets of questionnaires individually to elucidate the points raised here. The data were analyzed qualitatively and quantitatively to determine the variations in parents' and youths' perceptions.

Description of the Population

Confidentiality dictates designating communities of families that were interviewed together with Latin numerals without specifying the place. Arabic numerals were assigned to those cities to conceal the communities' identities as well.

Community I

Contact with this community, as well as with Community II and three other families that were interviewed separately, was through the local office of the well-established (but not center-oriented) Islamic Circle of North America (ICNA). This organization was started by Indo–Pakistanis, but its membership includes Muslims with other national origins. The basic feature of this organization is its effort to disseminate information, distribute literature, and help in establishing study groups and network circles.

Only three families from Community I participated in this study. The fathers are professional, and the mothers are highly educated. These families live in a prestigious suburb of metropolitan City 1 that has an estimated thirty thousand to forty thousand Muslims living in different sections of the city. Regular Sunday meetings are held in the leader's home. The wife of the leader (who coordinated the interviews) also conducts after-school Qur'anic and Islamic studies once or twice a week for the children of these and other Muslim families in the neighborhood. The common features of the families of this community are that they value school and intellectual achievements, they seem to blend with the non-Muslim neighborhood, and they adhere strictly to and reinforce among their children overt Muslim behavior such as dress and greetings.

Community II

Four families participated from this community. The fathers are businessmen and entrepreneurs, and the mothers are moderately well educated. These families live in a middle-class suburb of metropolitan City 1. They hold regular Saturday and Sunday meetings in the leader's home. This community is more heterogeneous with respect to country of origin and ethnicity than the other communities in this study. About ten families who live in the same neighborhood attend these meetings and classes, but only four had children aged fourteen or above and were able to participate in the study.

The common feature of this community is the members' intimate and open relationships with each other. Very little or no concern was expressed about integrating with the non-Muslim neighborhood. Most of the discussions centered on the availability of community reinforcement (particularly with regard to children's activities) and community facilities. Overt behavior, such as dress and greetings, is not heavily emphasized, especially among the youth. There was no mention of affiliation with a center, although the families participate in the major activities of two different centers in the city depending on the event and their distance from the particular center.

Three other families in the City 1 were interviewed separately because of a time conflict. They belong to the same ethnic background and to a center in the low-middle-income section of the city. Their educational and professional levels are not homogeneous.

Community III

Contact with this community and with Community IV was through a teacher in the local all-day Islamic school located in one of the major and most popular mosques in metropolitan City 2. The Muslim population of this city is estimated at 80,000 with Muslims clustered in five of the major areas. Although the two communities generally participate in this mosque's activities, the mosque's great distance from the residents of Community IV prevents its members from participating on a regular basis. Therefore, members of Community IV are holding neighborhood meetings and attempting to establish a neighborhood mosque.

Community III consisted of families whose children attend a weekly youth dialogue group. The levels of education and socioeconomic status varied within this community, as did their countries of origin. The common feature of this community is its vested interest in the youths' Islamic cohesiveness. The sense of fraternity and smooth, open communication among the youth was obvious. The mothers seemed to know each other better than did the fathers, and they spoke candidly among themselves. A common denominator was evident, however, in the mutual respect among the families of this community and the leaders.

Community IV

This community consists of six families, the majority of whom are from the same country of origin and live in the same neighborhood. The families are from diverse educational and socioeconomic levels, mainly middle-class and teachers. A common feature that distinguishes this community from the others is the high motivation and devotion of the youth. It became apparent during the interviews that most of these families had become involved in Islamic education and work because of pressure from their offspring. These children attend the youth dialogue group in the city and through contact with others have developed a strong interest in understanding their Islamicity. Although some friction was evident between parents and youth, parents seem to have developed a commitment to change themselves in accordance with what they were learning from their offspring and other members of the community.

Community V

Four of the five families who participated from this community live in an upper-middle-class suburb of City 3, which contains roughly ten thousand Muslims. The predominant professional field of both fathers and mothers in these families is medicine. The countries of origin vary, yet this seemed to cause no problem in the members' relationship. More apparent are the community's differences with another community in the same city that belongs to another organization and resides in low-middle-income housing. Despite many efforts (by the investigator and the contact person) to secure interviews with members of the latter community, there was no response. The contact person was the imam of Community V, who was a young immigrant trained in Islamic law.

The common feature among the residents of Community V is their professional affiliation. An obvious interest in eliminating the separation between the two spheres of life, the Islamic and the Western, was evidenced in their discussion of certain issues and in their overt behavior. Although some of the youth were more candid and open in their discussion than others, the majority were very reserved and some barely participated.

Community VI

Although the six families from this community who participated are highly committed to Islamic work and actually work for a major Islamic organization, and although they have high levels of Islamic and Western education, their meeting was the least organized of any. The members originated in different countries but share the same ethnic/linguistic background. They all live in one area around the organization headquarters in a suburb of metropolitan City 4 with an estimated forty thousand Muslims. The common features among the members of this community are their sincerity and strong attempts to acculturate their offspring into Islam. Their efforts vary from holding a local study group to sponsoring regional and national conferences for adults and youth. Some of these families, however, seem to have succeeded better than others in integrating the two cultures, as was reflected by their youths' discussion of issues such as social mixing. Other families seemed to reject everything Western. Two additional families were interviewed separately in City 4, neither of which belonged to an Islamic organization. Both families consist of an immigrant father and an American-born mother.

Community VII

The six families interviewed in this community live in one of the neighborhoods of metropolitan City 5 with roughly one hundred thousand Muslims. They are in the same field, international affairs, and have the same ethnic/linguistic background, although they are from two different countries of origin. The youth in these families vary in their interests, place of education, and understanding of Islam. Yet they all seem to have developed a strong attachment to their "Muslim" or ethnic identity. The international milieu that these youth have grown up in has apparently left them with an attitude of open-mindedness and reciprocity.

Conceptual Contrast Model

The curriculum specialist developing programs in communities with significant Muslim populations must keep in mind the governing ideology of that particular community and the level of ambiguity or lack of knowledge among the residents. The governing ideology includes the belief system, the values and codes drawn from it, and the circumstances that govern its practice.

One of the first North American values that strikes immigrant Muslims, like all other immigrants, is freedom. Drawing a contrast between the Islamic and Western conceptions of freedom is a focal point for understanding the differences in the central concepts of the Islamic and Western views, in the governing ideology, and in the various meanings given to Islamic practice.

The philosophical definition of freedom, such as that stated in the *College Edition of the Random House Dictionary* (1968, p. 527) is "the power to make one's own choices or decisions without constraint from within or without; autonomy; self-determination." Freedom from constraint from within may be defined as "the right of frequenting, enjoying, or using it at will," and freedom from constraint from without as "absence or release from ties, obligations."

These understandings of constraint, however, differ from the Islamic view. Constraints from without are understood to be those other than the ones ordered by Allah. The Arabic word *muharrar* in the Qur'an,[13] for example, means that dedicating Mary to the service of Allah obliges her to obey Allah and serve the house of worship. The constraint from within is understood to be one's consciousness and responsibility toward one's role as Allah's khalifa.[14] Therefore, the basic freedom in Islam is to free oneself from passion and desires. Once an individual achieves this freedom, he or she is able to free himself or herself from the fear of mortal human beings. The immigrant Muslim who understands Allah's purpose from the narrow perspective (that is, to perform acts of worship only) may understand the freedom practiced in the West as freedom from the constraint of social and family customs, not as freedom from Allah's purpose of vicegerency.

As North American Muslims attempt to integrate their own beliefs with the secular ideologies of North America, they may, at times, move away from the main goal to transmit their beliefs to their children. This movement occurs because Muslims themselves are not clear as to what exactly they want to transmit to their children. Two reasons were found for this lack of clarity. The first is the apparent incommensurability between the Islamic ideology based on submission to Allah as the supreme guide and authority and the secular system that interprets religion and faith as a form of worship isolated from other aspects of life. The second, and more important, reason is the ambiguity of the relationship between the central concept of Islam (tawhid, God's oneness) and the central concept of Western ideology (secularism) in the minds and behavior of these Muslims.

Earl A. Waugh[15] demonstrates that today's Muslims face difficulties in their attempt to mediate the classical tradition to contemporary conditions through complex institutional forms that are likely to provoke new interpretations in American culture. For the earliest Muslim immigrants to the new land, freedom meant dissociation from both religious and political elites.[16] The early immigrants, according to Waugh, also realized that they could function and manage their lives away from bondage to the village overlords, family heads, and tribal shaykhs who represented the government structure and incorporated the ordinary Muslim into the Islamic society. Therefore, Waugh says, these bonds remain in the mind of the Muslim immigrant as symbols or as part of Islam. Islam judges individuals by their reasoning and behavior, and this freedom gives Muslims the chance to rethink their Islam and the Islamization of their children. As Waugh puts it: "The experience was heady and freedom came to play a cardinal role in the kinds of institutions he [the Muslim individual] organized and fostered."[17]

North American Muslims' freedom from the authority of the imam and the extended family is merely a freedom from certain cultural and social bondages and may be accompanied by new cultural bondages within the host society. For the Muslim who emigrated with the intention of fulfilling the central concept of Islam, tawhid, freedom from the bondage of the extended family or the imam is instrumental to that intention. If that intention was absent (and continues to be absent), however, and the individual Muslim intended merely to fulfill Waugh's definition of freedom, then such an individual cannot fulfill the central concept of tawhid. Regardless of whether or not he or she claims to adhere to Islam, such an individual cannot achieve the chosen identity in practice because the central concept is missing.

The individual Muslim's level of understanding of the meaning of freedom as it applies in the North American culture thus affects and is affected by the practice of freedom as a component of his or her own ideology. This practice, in turn, shapes a pattern of adjustment that will stamp the individual's conceptual ecology and, hence, his or her ability to integrate his or her own ideology in the host society.

This analysis of the individual's ideological contrast can also be applied to the family and the community. Regarding the family, the question is whether freedom from the social and cultural customs of the home country means dissolution of the principle of "mutual rights and expectations" as stated in the Qur'an.[18] For the community the question becomes one of whether freedom from the bondage of the imam or the tribal chief means the dissolution of the principle of "mutual consultation and consensus," as stated in the Qur'an.[19] Here, too, the Muslim whose ideals are rooted in the concept of tawhid cannot accept the ideas of individual freedom, private family affairs, and the rule of the majority at their face value (that is, as understood and practiced in the host society); otherwise, his or her commitment to tawhid becomes uncertain.

Results and Implications

Parents' Perception of "Practicing Islam"

The study hypothesizes that (1) immigrants who apply Islamic teachings as social codes are more likely to compartmentalize Islamic familial life from Western social life, and (2) immigrants who did not apply Islamic teachings before their arrival are more likely to abandon their Muslim characteristics (becoming more committed to Western views) or to develop a better understanding of Islamic principles (becoming more committed to Islamic views or prioritizing Islam).

The patterns of application before arrival were measured by (1) the respondents' evaluation of their families' position on Islamic knowledge and conduct and on worship and (2) the respondents' opinions on Islamic knowledge and conduct, worship, and human relationships. Family position was rated on a scale of three: "too low" ($R = 1$), "about right" ($R = 2$), and "too high" ($R = 3$). The respondents' opinions were rated on a scale of four: "strongly disagree" ($R = 1$), "slightly disagree" ($R = 2$), "moderately agree" ($R = 3$), and "strongly agree" ($R = 4$).

The patterns of application after arrival were measured by (1) the respondents' feelings toward practicing Islam in North America and (2) their expectation of Muslim behavior in North America (see Table 11.1). It seems that the closer the parents' opinion was to the Islamic central concept (tawhid), the stronger their emphasis on guiding their children toward Islamic patterns of application, and the further parents were from the central concept, the stronger their attachment to the Muslims' patterns of application. It is interesting, however, that the majority of the parents disagreed with methods of punishment that isolate the child or withdraw his or her privileges. These methods,

Table 11.1   Parents' Perception of Practice of Islam in North America

Question/Answer	N	Percentage (%)
(Q25) Do you feel that practicing Islam in North America		
Not sure	2	3
Can be practiced at home	6	10
Irrelevant for general life	1	2
Very difficult	1	2
Practiced with modification	9	15
Possible with hardship	27	45
None of the above	14	23
Total	60	100
(Q29) How do you feel Muslims should behave in North America?		
Adopt North American social norms	1	2
Become like North Americans	0	0
Retain tradition even if it contradicts	7	12
OK to hold on to some important things	16	26
Retain Islamic values even if different	31	52
None of the above	5	8
Total	60	100

being neither exclusively Islamic nor exclusively Western, suggest that, despite their closeness to the Muslim view, parents are more influenced by the relaxed approach or lack of reinforcement of certain behavioral rules. This approach is representative of Western-oriented psychology.

Forty-five percent (27/60) of parents who responded to the question concerning their feelings toward practicing Islam in North America stated that "Islam can be practiced with some hardship" in North America, and they scored highest on both conception (10.1) and practice (9.0) (see Table 11.2). Another 23 percent (14/60) responded that they were able to do so ". . . but" (open-ended answer), and they scored second highest (9.9) on conception, but second lowest (8.7) on practice. Two of the open-ended answers deserve some elaboration.

The first comment, "It is hard to pray five times on the job, when you need to wash more often," was by a father from City 1 of Pakistani origin who was interviewed separately and who works in a physically dirty job on an odd-hours shift. This comment reflects a realistic situation, in which a Muslim feels trapped. No employer will allow his workers to shower five times during a work shift just so they can perform their prayers. During the interview with this respondent it became clear that he was very concerned about whether his children would remain Muslims. He expressed a deep faith in and reliance on the community with its gatherings to keep his children close to other Muslims because he knew that he could not do much himself. Moreover, his view of the

Table 11.2 Mean Scores of Parents and Youth Conception and Practice in Relation to Perception of "Islamic Practice" (Range: 2–12)

	Parents			Youth		
	N	Conception	Practice	N	Conception	Practice
(Q25) Practice of Islam in North America is						
Not sure	2	9.8	8.9	0	0	0
Can be practiced at home	6	9.4	7.7	3	9.1	8.2
Irrelevant for general life	1	9.5	8.9	0	0	0
Very difficult	1	9.2	8.9	4	9.2	8.7
Practiced with modification	9	9.9	9.1	10	9.5	8.9
Possible with hardship	27	10.0	9.0	28	9.6	8.4
None of the above	14	9.9	8.7	11	9.5	8.7
Total	60	9.9	8.8	56	9.4	8.6
(Q29) Feel about behaving in North America as Muslim						
Adopt North American Social norms	1	9.9	8.5	1	8.6	8.0
Become like North Americans	0	—	—	0	0	0
Retain tradition, even if it contradicts	7	9.9	8.5	12	9.7	8.4
OK to hold on to important things	16	9.7	8.6	15	9.3	8.6
Retain Islamic values even if different	31	10.0	8.9	28	9.6	8.6
None of the above	5	9.9	8.9	0	0	0
Total	60	9.9	8.8	56	9.3	8.4

West was so apathetic that he had no hope he would get any support from the environment.

The second comment by a father of Syrian origin from Community VII in City 5 was as follows:

> Concerning worship, there is no difficulty, concerning social interaction, there is no difficulty. Concerning calling others to Islam, there is no difficulty. Yet, concerning the practice of Islamic ideology as a way of life (iqamat al-din) I see that the question is irrelevant because the authority and law is in the hands of non-Muslims.

The basic concern of the Syrian father and the conception that underlies this concern do not differ much from the concerns and conception of the Pakistani father. Regardless of their different ethnic backgrounds and of the variation in their level of education, profession, and reasoning, both respondents were concerned that the Islamic ideology cannot be practiced, in full, in the Western context.

This concern shows the difference between practicing a religion and practicing a belief system in a pluralistic secular society. The preceding responses support the argument that an individual in a pluralistic secular society may have the freedom to practice the religious (worship) aspects, but not be able to practice. The second highest number (26 percent, or 16/60) of parents anacts are only a part.

These two parents' conceptions of the central meaning of al-din (Islamic ideology and way of life) are very close, even though their levels of confidence and ability to express or transmit the meanings to their offspring vary significantly. This was evidenced in the responses of the children of these two parents and in the parents' different levels of hope and confidence in the future of their children's practice of Islam.

One should not underestimate the variations in the living conditions and their effect on religious concepts of the belief systems. Not only does the Pakistani father not have control over his environment—contrary to the Syrian father—but he cannot feel comfortable in performing the most sublime act of worship before God in his dirty overalls, nor can he feel that his prayers will be accepted. Any person in such circumstances will have to compromise either his or her job or religious concepts (worship). Such a complex state of cognitive dissonance may oblige one to conclude that even religious acts may not be possible in a secular society. The conflict remains alive, and it may force some modification in the faith, the conviction, or the level and nature of the belief.

Fifty-two percent (31/60) of parents agreed that "Muslims should retain Islamic values even if they are different from Western values and culture." These parents achieved the highest (10.0) (9.0) scores on conception and practice. The second highest number (27 percent, or 16/60) of parents answered, "It is all right for Muslims to become Americans/Canadians, but they should hold on to the important things from their Islamic life." These parents scored the lowest (9.7) on conception and in the middle (8.6) on practice. Eight percent (5/60) chose "none, but" and their comments ranged from "should be

Muslims" to making no comment even when they circled the open-ended choice.

The level of parents' perception of Islam has more influence on the parents' adjustment process than on their patterns of application. As stated earlier, the closer the parents' perception of Islam is to the central concept level, the more likely they are to abandon Muslim or Western views, and the more emphasis they place on guiding their children to Islam from that level of perception only. The fact that they themselves are not trained in appropriating the central concept (tawhid) in relation to other concepts (particularly human interrelation concepts) may affect their ability to adjust and transmit Islam in the Western context.

Youths' Perception of "Practicing Islam"

The study hypothesized that Muslim youth, like youth of other immigrant parents, identify primarily with American values and secondarily with the Islamic value system their parents communicate. The indicators for identifying with the Islamic value system are those related to conception and practice of Islamic principles. The patterns of practicing these principles were measured by (1) the respondents' feelings about practicing Islam in North America and (2) their expectation of Muslim behavior in North America (see Table 11.3). It seems that the youths perceive the Western value system to be more prevalent than the Islamic belief system. This perception is reflected in their patterns of practice, which, in turn, influence their perception of Islam.

Table 11.3 Youths' Perception of Practice of Islam in North America

Question	N	Percentage (%)
(Q25) Do you feel that practicing Islam in North America		
Not sure	0	0
Can be practiced at home	3	5
Irrelevant for general life	0	0
Very difficult	4	7
Practiced with modification	10	18
Possible with hardship	28	50
None of the above	11	20
Total	56	100
(Q29) How do you feel Muslims should behave in North America?		
Adopt North American social norms	1	2
Become like North Americans	0	0
Retain tradition even if it contradicts	12	21
OK to hold on to some important things	15	27
Retain Islamic values even if different	28	50
None of the above	0	0
Total	56	100

Fifty percent (28/56) of youth who responded to the question concerning their feelings toward practicing Islam in North America stated that "Islam can be possible with some hardship" and scored highest on conception (9.6) and second to lowest (8.4) on practice (see Table 11.2). Another 20 percent (11/56) who responded they were able to do so, "but" (open-ended answer), scored second on both conception (9.5) and practice (8.7).

The open-ended answers ranged from "It is simple" by a sixteen-year-old male of Pakistani descent to "can be possible with determination" by a twenty-one-year-old male of South African descent. These responses support the argument that youth identify primarily with North American values, since, in contrast with some parents, they did not see the difference between practicing a religion and practicing a belief system in a pluralistic secular society. The preceding two responses were from youths from Community III, which takes pride in its youth dialogue group's commitment to and striving for Islamic life.

Fifty percent (28/56) also agreed that "Muslims should retain Islamic values even if they are different from Western values and culture." These youth maintained high (9.6 and 8.6) scores on conception and practice (see Table 11.2). The second highest number (27 percent, 15/56) of the youth answered, "It is all right for Muslims to become Americans/Canadians, but they should hold on to the important things from their Islamic life." These youth scored second to lowest (9.3) on conception and high (8.6) on practice.

The results allow us to conclude that the level of youths' perception of "Islamic practice" has more influence on their perceived action than does with their conception of Islam in the North American context.

Curricular Objectives

The discussion of the critical role played by Muslims' perception of Islam and their knowledge of the Western context raises certain questions about their educational objectives in North America: (1) Is it realistic to expect Islamic instruction to integrate North American Muslims rather than merely help them relate between the Islamic and Western views? (2) How can we expect the different groups of Muslims to change—or at least examine—their fundamental assumptions so that they can consider and deal with new ideas? The problem is not limited to the fact that neither the parent nor the youth is aware of his own fundamental assumptions. Many complications are added by the linguistic, ethnic, geographic, age, and other variables that need to be dealt with before group instruction can be feasible.

If an affirmative answer is given to the first question, the contents of the previous sections of this study suggest that we aim at developing among North American Muslims the following preliminary objectives:

1. An awareness of their basic assumptions and of those implicit in Islamic and Western views.

2. An awareness of the epistemological and historical foundations of Islamic and Western views.
3. Some sense of satisfaction that the new conception may resolve the remaining conflict.
4. A requisite for consistency between their beliefs about the world and their practices in everyday matters and within the new context.

The objectives of the curriculum for which the ground was described earlier are to help North American Muslims do the following:

1. Ground their beliefs in knowledge by enabling them to achieve the following:
   - to clarify the Islamic belief system;
   - to understand the principles of such beliefs as the bases of practice;
   - to separate elements of the belief system evidenced in Qur'anic teachings from other elements that come from ethnic or sentimental sources.
2. Understand the organization of the two belief systems (Islamic and Western) and arrive at a synthesis for their own beliefs. This synthesis may, in turn, help parents communicate the Islamic belief system to their offspring in the Western context, avoiding potential conflict between the different elements of the two systems.
3. Abate separation or compartmentalization of Islamic and Western knowledge, but without losing the basic principles of the Islamic system or eradicating group security, such as ethnic or linguistic identification.

Options for the Muslim Community

Fulfilling these objectives requires attention to the Muslim beliefs and concepts about each of the two belief systems. It was mentioned earlier that the Western secular system is not as explicit as the Islamic one to North American Muslims. Therefore, *educational intervention* starts at one of the following three points (Figure 11.1):

1. Make the Western secular system explicit and identify its central concept(s) first. Then describe the different levels of Western and Islamic systems separately or concurrently. Teach the details of the Islamic central concept and its principles (subject matter). Finally, attempt to reconcile the two systems by developing practical examples.
2. Identify the structure of a belief system in general, then describe its implications for both Islamic and Western systems. Teach the subject matter (Islamic central concept and principles). Finally, reconcile the two systems.
3. Teach the subject matter first (Islamic concepts), then place the concepts in their proper levels. Compare them with similar concepts from the Western system and attempt to relate them at the same level or at

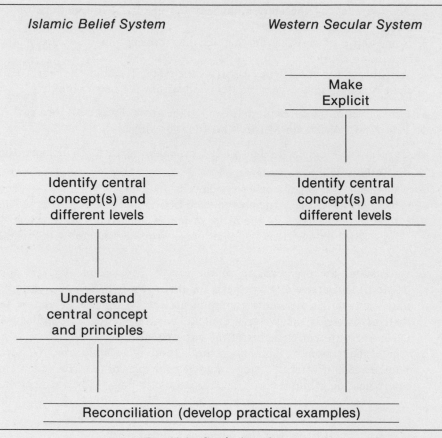

Fig. 11.1   Curricular schema.

different levels to develop practical examples and to examine their consequences for reconciliation or for conflict, respectively.

Communicating Islam among North American families can be viewed as a case study for understanding and exploring the role of metaphysical beliefs and concepts in the learning process. The problem of North American Muslim youths' connection to Islam will not be resolved by merely teaching the principles (schooling), or by teaching certain practices and applications (informal training). Future educators of Muslims need to realize these facts and move away from them. A new pedagogical approach for education in North American Muslim communities must relate the epistemological, metaphysical, and conceptual elements of both the Islamic and Western systems.

The intention of such an approach is to preserve the Islamic identity in an integrative[20] manner within the pluralistic Western society. Whether this intention can be facilitated by schools similar to parochial schools or the old Islamic madrasa system is a subject for future discussion and study. This intention itself suggests theoretical and pedagogical implications that must be addressed if North American societies are to achieve educational systems that allow each group to preserve its identity while maintaining its equilibrium within itself and in relation to other groups in the society.

Notes

1. Many people have contributed directly or indirectly to this author's Ph.D. research on Muslims' perception, practice, and transmission of the Islamic belief system in the context of the Western secular societies of North America, of which this chapter is only a part. In particular, I wish to acknowledge the late Isma'il R. al Faruqi of Temple University, an ad hoc member of my Graduate Committee, and Robert L. Bruce of Cornell University, my academic adviser, both of whom have contributed significantly to shaping ideas, stating concepts, and reporting results. Special thanks are also due to Sid Doan, who helped me prepare the manuscript.

2. See, for example, A. A. Elkholy, *The Arab Moslems in the United States: Religion and Assimilation* (New Haven: College and University Press Publishers, 1966); E. A. Waugh, B. Abu-Laban, and R. B. Qureshi, eds., *The Muslim Community in North America* (Edmonton: University of Alberta Press, 1983); and Y. Y. Haddad and A. T. Lummis, *Islamic Values in the United States: A Comparative Study* (New York: Oxford University Press, 1987).

3. Islam is viewed here as a belief system that constitutes a philosophical foundation of thought and action, incorporating religion (in the narrow sense, and as understood by the secular view) as a system of faith and worship only. (See *Webster's Seventh New Collegiate Dictionary*, 1972).

4. The definitions of "secular" and "secularism" are derived from the *Random House Dictionary* (1968).

5. F. Rahman, *Islam and Modernity: Transformation of an Intellectual Tradition* (Chicago: University of Chicago Press, Center for Middle Eastern Studies, No. 15, 1982), p. 132.

6. Though the Canadian Constitution does not explicitly state the separation of church and state, the general practice of government and institutions indicates that authority rests with the legislatures.

7. See M. Arkoun, "The Islamic Consciousness: A Cultural Profile," *Cultures* 4 (1977) 66–93, in which he adds that in the early twentieth century the human heart transformed the "God of Worth" into the "growth of mind" as the goal and the "social worth" as the criterion.

8. Empiricists from Hume to twentieth-century logical positivists have cast considerable doubt on the possibility of doing metaphysics. On the other hand, empiricism has had much of the flavor of a worldview, generating not just views of knowledge and science, but of psychology, ethics, and politics as well. See Kenneth A. Strike and George J. Posner, "Types of Synthesis and Their Criteria," in Spencer A. Ward and Linda J. Reed, eds., *Knowledge Structure and Use: Implications for Synthesis and Interpretation* (Philadelphia: Temple University Press, 1983), pp. 344–62.

9. Represented in the opening Sura (chapter) 1:1–7.

10. "Fitrat Allah allati fatar al-nas alayha": According to the pattern that Allah has made mankind (S.30:30).

11. J. R. Pole, *American Individualism and the Promise of Progress* (Oxford: Clarendon Press, 1980).

12. "Islamic education" means to F. Rahman (1982) "Islamic intellectualism, for it is the essence of higher Islamic thought that must provide real criterion for judging the success or failure of its educational system."

13. "Behold! A Woman of Imran said: 'O my Lord! I do dedicate unto thee what is in my womb [meaning Mary the mother of Jesus] (free) for thy special service'" (S.3:35).

14. "I have only created jinns and humans, that they may worship me [proclaim my unity]" (S.51:56), and "Behold, thy Lord said to the angels: 'I will create a vicegerent on earth'. . . . And He taught Adam the nature of all things. . . . We said: 'O Adam! dwell thou and thy spouse in the Garden . . . ; but approach not this tree, or ye run into harm and transgression'" (S.2:30–31 and 35).

15. E. A. Waugh, "Muslim Leadership and the Shaping of the Umma: Classical Tradition and Religious Tension in the North American Setting," in Earl Waugh et al., *The Muslim Community in North America* (Edmonton: University of Alberta Press, 1983), pp. 11–33.

16. Though the representatives of these two institutions became separate in the eleventh century, Muslim polity continued to consider them as one entity.

17. Thus it would be an error, Waugh adds, to consider immigrant Islam as merely the transferral of a creed to a North American environment. We must also consider how the Islamic immigrant perceives his past and how he understands it to inform his new situation, then, how he must deal with the new situation with yet more understanding drawn from his past experience. It would be too much to expect that these complex movements could occur without friction or conflict ("Muslim Leadership and the Shaping of the Umma," pp. 11–33).

18. "O mankind! Reverence your Guardian—Lord, who created you from a single person, created of like nature, its mate, and from them twain scattered countless men and women; reverence God, through whom ye demand your mutual (rights) and reverence the wombs (that bore you); for God ever watches over you" (S.4:11).

19. "Those who hearken to their Lord, and establish regular prayer; who (conduct) their affairs by mutual consultation, who spend out of what we bestow on them for sustenance" (S.42:38).

20. The term *integrative* is used here to indicate the ability to maintain the Islamic belief system at its central concept level, tawhid, and to objectify this belief system in the Western secular environment without (1) compromising the Islamic principles, (2) sacrificing national/ethnic group attachment, (3) living dual, but separate lives (Islamic and Western), or (4) withdrawing from the outside society.

V

MUSLIM WOMEN
IN INTERCULTURAL
PERSPECTIVE

12

African-American Muslim Women

Beverly Thomas McCloud

Most scholars writing about Islam in the African-American Muslim community have focused their efforts on the examination of the teachings of the Nation of Islam.[1] In particular, their interest seems to have centered on a critique of the Nation's philosophy concerning the origin of the Caucasian race, a preoccupation of non-Muslim as well as Muslim writers.[2] This obsession with the teachings about race has led to two major lacunae in our understanding of the dynamics of Islam in society. First, we have relatively little informed data about the growth and development of an equally large Islamic population outside the Nation of Islam, that of the Sunni African-Americans who have been active in the major urban areas of the United States since the first quarter of this century. Second, there is no analytical writing about the role of women in the African-American Muslim community, including the Nation of Islam.

The conversion of African-Americans to Islam is a twentieth-century phenomenon. In a major way it is a response to American racism as a consequence of which black Americans found themselves experiencing what it means to be "a problem," with the constant knowledge of the hatred that white Americans have for people of dark skin.[3] It is also a reaction to white America's solution for "problem races," evident in its treatment of American Indians, a solution that aimed at eradicating the problem by genocide or containment. Consequently, black Americans saw two options for their survival. These were articulated by various leaders as accommodation and separation.

The accommodationists operated within the general framework of "proving the worth of the black American to white society." They stressed that the black citizen is worthy of equal status in the land, especially those black people with "acceptable" skills in areas such as home economics and trades. Booker T. Washington, the chief proponent of this school, was supported by Christian ministers from various denominations who emphasized an underlying ideology centered on the maintenance of good conduct, good work habits, efficiency, and good moral living.

The separatist movement, on the other hand, operated within the general framework of "double consciousness," which Dubois articulated as the mental state of black Americans, "the sense of always looking at one's self through the eyes of others—the twoness—an American, a Black."[4] This movement was divided into two groups. The first was the widely supported "Back to Africa" movement advocated by Marcus Garvey, who called on blacks to prepare themselves for a reconciliation with Africa.[5] It provided hope for black Americans who were being tortured, beaten, and killed daily.[6] The second was the "nation within a nation" movement that insisted black Americans had a claim to America since it was founded on their blood, sweat, and tears. They believed America had a debt to pay; it must be forced to provide compensation for its sins.

Conversion to Islam fits within the orientation of the "nation within a nation" movement. Although very few references explain how ideas about Islam became available in the black community,[7] it is clear that this religion promised a new identity, a feeling of "somebodiness" denied by the dominant culture, a liberation from Christian domination and from relegation to insignificance. The new adherents shed Christianity, which they perceived as the root of their oppression in its glorification of suffering and promise of redemption in the hereafter.

That African-American women have opted to reject adherence to Christianity and chosen to convert to Islam has given rise to a number of important questions. These questions betray their source in fear, prejudice, and general confusion both in the dominant society and among African-Americans. They range from "What is this Islam that they believe in?" and "What went wrong with the Christian Church?" on the one had to "Why would a woman who has fought for freedom willingly convert to oppression?" or simply, "Is she crazy?"

The conventional use of the term *conversion* often implies an emotional or a irrational retooling of faith. It projects a resolution of some internal conflict whose core is faith. Conversion also involves an apparent total negation of the old self and the implantation of a new one. Changes in belief, in turn, influence and transform behavior. This understanding of conversion is rooted in the Pauline paradigm.[8] The recent proliferation of cults in America, however, has fostered a new look at conversion, one that takes seriously the fact that the religious seeker is engaged in self-definition, in "taking action to change."[9] The conversion of black American women to Islam is discussed in the context of individuals, stable or destabilized, who are striving to achieve fundamental changes in their life experiences through religious conversion.

My study of African-American women who have converted to Islam is in progress. The sample on which I am drawing is the community in Philadelphia. Since the material gathered is primarily from oral histories, I will use descriptive language that is as close as possible to the language of the group I am studying. What is presented in the following pages are some preliminary findings based on taped interviews with women ranging in age between nineteen and sixty-seven.

Like the majority of African-Americans, the women in this study are poor. The only apparent available avenue out of their perpetual poverty is education, an option promoted by what can be called "the American Dream." Unfortunately, American education is not designed to override the racism and oppression experienced by African-Americans. In fact, education as a tool for the realization of the American Dream is generally ineffective. For the vast majority of African-Americans, education does not eradicate poverty.

On some level, every African-American woman dreams the American Dream knowing full well that without financial resources, education, and emotional support her dream will always be a fantasy. The women in my sample mainly represent an invisible force in both the society at large and within the context of the African-American group. Their invisibility is a product of their position in both societies. Universally, they are perceived as females who work for others and who have questionable morality.[10] While the African-American woman's efforts at visibility are often subsumed under the labels of "superwoman" or "lazy woman," they sometimes manifest themselves in "conversions." One such conversion is to Islam.

Who, then, are these women who convert to Islam? A preliminary analysis of the material I have gathered suggests four general categories. These categories are based on the ways in which the women describe themselves before and after conversion. It is important to remember that the categories do not represent all converts; what follows is an attempt to provide the major characteristics shared by certain clusters of women and to identify those experiences that distinguish the various constituents. The history of the women before conversion is very significant to the general patterns of their religious life and self-understanding. The names and descriptions I have given to the several categories of women who convert to Islam are ones that are prevalent within the African-American community, as both folklore and real characterizations.[11]

The first type is "Peaches,"[12] who characteristically comes from an environment in which each day is lived as if there were no tomorrow. There are no thoughts of the future in terms of plans, goals, or careers. Peaches usually leaves the educational system early in life, because she has either not been encouraged to pursue education or she is ill-equipped to handle the demands of school in America.[13] She is (as an adult) often depicted as an un- or undereducated premature mother who will spend her life in welfare lines. Each day is spent in despair because of lack of security. Peaches usually assuages her humiliation and pain with drugs or excessive play. Even in the temporary escape from the trials of black America, Peaches knows from the television that there are alternative life-styles where black women are "somebodies." "Somebodiness" has many levels, one of which is the positive visibility through which one can attain respectability. The problem is access. In the absence of career and educational goals, "somebodiness" seems virtually unattainable.

Contrary to popular belief (in both the Christian and Islamic worlds), the women in this group are not devoutly Christian. Peaches knows neither the Christian world nor the activity of Christianity except to sense that it is at the root of her problems. In one of her last efforts to find "something better," Peaches decides to investigate Islam. She usually already knows an African-American Muslim male who explains how she would be "better off" as a

Muslim woman. This male claims that Muslim women are given the highest respect of any on earth; all the men who are "about something" are Muslim, and a good Muslim husband will straighten out her life. Peaches is drawn to Islam in search of that instant husband and "somebodiness."

It is now both privately and publicly affirmed that Peaches will "cover her body," pray, abstain from contact with any men other than her husband, avoid alcohol, and in general eschew Western values forever—if she does not want to go to hell. Peaches says: "Befo' I could ketch my breath, they was tellin' me about all the layers of clothes I had to wear so nobody could lust after me. When did anybody ever lust after me? What is lust? They said that the men cain't control themselves when they see the woman's form so I have to be modest and look plain, wear black."

She begins a self-hypnosis[14] that transforms her thought patterns. In the name of Islam she can now disclaim, reject, and curse the Western system that has humiliated her. She has a valid reason to refuse to participate in her own community, not to vote, not to help the needy or the poor on the grounds that the larger society consists of nonbelievers. She no longer has to feel inadequate as a provider, because those other material things that she struggled for were wrong in the first place. The welfare check ceases to be a degradation and becomes an inner source of power. The focus is on the capacity for self-determined action. Peaches has children. She can say she does not know anything about their father because the person to whom she is talking is non-Muslim and therefore does not deserve the truth. She has given her unemployment concrete validation—"they won't hire me, 'cause of what I wear, and I have to wear it 'cause I'm Muslim." Peaches knows that welfare cannot deny her "even though they hate me." This is power. Peaches is a walking condemnation of their "nakedness." "I felt like I was somebody, lookin' down on sin and evil, a reminder of chastity and modesty to a naked, immoral woman. I felt good. America ain't nothin' and all of them will burn. They owe me."

Then the realities begin to surface. Gradually she becomes aware of the special kind of disdain and prejudice that is reserved for African-American Muslim women. Seeking for the "epitome of respectability," that is, marriage, she is faced with the necessity of having to decide on a husband without the consultation of persons who have known and loved her. She must use only criteria provided by a book she is ill-equipped to understand, or mimic some Muslim culture of which she knows nothing. What she knows of relationships is buried back in black America.

At the same time the interior and exterior transformations are occurring, Peaches is obligated to learn the prayers in the Arabic language. Because of her lack of education, she resorts automatically to oral tradition and memorizes the mispronunciations of other converts. Peaches gets information on the "do's and don'ts" of Islam, correct or incorrect, from an equally unknowledgeable convert.

The most urgent demands are that she "dress right" and get married. She performs some self-hypnosis and becomes the woman who will marry someone whom she does not know and whose past is erased with conversion. She pushes aside reason and puts on faith. Faith? "Faith that God will lead her to make the right decision." Peaches performs this self-hypnotic act at least four times before she gives up on marriage. For Peaches, Islamic marital life is very similar to her pre-Islamic live-in arrangements—abusive arguments, physical fights, profanity, and a general air of discontent. In her Islamic marital life, however, there is the ironic addition of polygamy. Peaches is in constant anxiety over the possibility of becoming a "cowife" (reminiscent of her pre-Islamic fights over other women). Two of the more unfortunate consequences of this anxiety are an outward hostility toward other single women and an acceptance of a certain amount of abuse (to stay married as long as possible).

Peaches continues to see herself as being as strong as she always was. She is strong because she is able to get over on the system, to take the necessary abuse to feed and clothe herself and her children. The problem is that now she is not herself in any other respect. The reality of no bridges for return and the possibility of no future without Islamic identity are usually enough to silence Peaches behind her veil.

The second and third categories of African-American women who convert to Islam represent a very complex group whose roots go back to the underpinning of the "double consciousness" dilemma of Americans of African descent. As representatives of this "double consciousness," I will discuss "Kiswana"[15] and "Safonyah"[16] together. The two samples present great variety in terms of family backgrounds, but the factor that bridges the gap in their diversity is education. At some point in their recent past, both women have focused on blackness and made a conscious decision regarding the way they are to play the role of African-American women. These women are cultivated; through travel, reading, or personal contacts, they have widened their horizons and acquired an expanded worldview. Their exploration of the race problem in America and their exposure to other cultures has led them to at least two discernable and divergent paths. One path includes activity and participation in black political/ cultural groups or movements, while the other path aims at survival—survival as achievement in the white establishment.

Kiswana, who assumed her name, has subscribed to black political/cultural movements, becoming aware of and supporting Third World perspectives. Her name gives her a voice; it is the embodiment of "somebodiness." She seeks security and permanent identity through attempts to promote and help bring about justice, or protesting its overwhelming absence. But the revolution in which she has wrapped herself proves to be as temporary as were her personal relationships. She has come to realize that the larger society (white) does not acknowledge the black voice of "somebodiness." Kiswana finds herself with child(ren), broken dreams, and alone.

Safonyah, on the road to assimilation, looks to the mostly male-dominated professions to attain her goal, such as medicine, engineering, and finance. Though she has plenty of drive, true success eludes her. The identity she seeks in the American Dream is elusive and illusionary. Her path converges with Kiswana's in the domain of "superwomen."[17] Safonyah is also with child(ren), broken dreams, and alone.

The changes these women implement in their lives are conversions because they seek to break away from the norm in an effort to take on a new identity. Both find that whether through experimentation with the "Black Revolution" or by assimilation through achievement, "somebodiness" is defined as "really belonging." Kiswana, during her revolutionary days, had converted to an African-oriented religious group that was non-Christian. After that phase, communities such as the Nation of Islam and the Moorish Science Temple held an overwhelming attraction. Safonyah had originally converted to yoga meditation and dallied with Buddhism. Alternatives such as these continue to whet her rational appetite.

Pursuit of the rational, spiritual, and revolutionary leads these women to Islam. They generally read all the available literature on Islam and first become "Islamic sympathizers," political allies of Islam seeking the justice that Christian America denies them. The final conversion to Islam is not as difficult as their first attempts at alternative identities. It is seen as the end of a journey.

Kiswana and Safonya are both tired of being forced to live up to the "superwoman" image. Islam, they are taught, will put an end to their distress. In Islam, Kiswana knows that she can pursue her social/political goals because a major tenet is the establishment of social justice. Kiswana sees the women in the masjid, and their appearance provokes familiar thoughts of "the unity" of the old days of the revolution. For Safonyah, the appearance of Muslim women is new, fascinating, and intriguing. In Islam, both Kiswana and Safonyah can be "real women"—expected to be dependent and coveted for that dependency.

Interestingly, both women describe their internal conversion as a series of stages beginning with the phrase, "in my temporary insanity." These women find themselves constantly in internal turmoil, trying to maintain their self-esteem. They are taught that their secular knowledge is a hindrance to true belief in Islam. They cannot use most of what they knew. The community does not encourage either education or ambition. Music is *haram* (forbidden); reading literature other than Islamic literature is haram; singing, dancing, professions that entail contact with men are haram; professions involving banking are haram; and so on. They generally find themselves being forced into nothingness.

Both Kiswana and Safronyah are outnumbered by women whose experiences are totally different from theirs. The only things they have in common with the others are color and gender. There are many dichotomies present in the internal selves of both of these women. Safronyah did not succeed at assimilation, even though she obtained education. Kiswana saw herself crowned queen of a no-land; she fought a revolution to become servile. Both read about themselves as beautiful, while their black male peers "went off with white women." Now both are in a position where they have to design a strategy for battle that is subtle enough to distinguish them from their sisters in Islam.

Kiswana and Safonyah are also plagued by harassment from without. Their jobs are immediately in jeopardy after their conversion. The clothing change usually initiates the harassment. Both men and women stare at them in disgust because they have covered their hair. Most of their coworkers even begin a temporary campaign of intimidation to get the convert to "uncover." They are told that the image presented is not in line with the company image. Usually the campaign succeeds, and the Muslim woman is forced out of work. Kiswana and Safonyah do not usually put up much of a fight, because they are beleaguered on all sides. Finding another job becomes almost impossible because of their dress. They are then reduced to another great humiliation in the life of victims—welfare.

Another option for African–American women in this group is to try to alter their life-styles again with a characteristic return to a blend of their Third World predisposition and Islam. They take off their Islamic dress, go back to work, repurchase furniture, and generally participate with the general African-American community only on holidays and at special events. At those times they put on "proper" clothing, though they remain aloof from the women and disappear at the close of the event. They also tend to move away to neighborhoods where there are not likely to be African-American Muslims living.

These African-American Muslim women finally settle into Islam as a way of life that allows them actually to practice Islam and push aside neither their cultural heritage nor their aspirations. They are not considered "good Muslim women," however, and are usually not treated with either respect or courtesy by other Muslims.

The fourth type, "Sarah,"[18] is distinguished neither by poverty nor by level of education. She is differentiated by a deliberate religious quest. Remarkably, her quest for understanding usually begins in childhood.[19] She typically grows up in a home in which church is attended regularly by all family members. She waits out the ferment of the "Black Revolution" and does not have a particular driving professional ambition. She is, however, in love with knowledge, especially of other cultures. At the university she attends, most of her time is spent wherever there are international students. She reads psychology, history, and literature and lives vicariously in a million places. Her mind is tantalized by religious theories whether obscure or evident. Sarah is truly a truth-seeker and not prone to undertake superficial inquiries. These interests have led her to join several religious groups.

The strife of African-American life has not eluded her and racism is something that her whole family has experienced. Sarah's pursuit of "somebodiness" is muted by her more intense pursuit of truth. Because of her moral stand, she does not have the need for "somebodiness" as a balm for the strain of poverty and discrimination. Her value system stresses collectivity, sharing, affiliation, obedience (albeit not unquestioning) to authority, spirituality, and respect for the past. Sarah understands the "victim system" that America has forced on her, and while she has no desire to fight like Kiswana or to assimilate like Safonyah, her presence is an act of protest against injustice. Her investigation of Islam comes after many such investigations into the literature of world religions. She reads the Qur'an from cover to cover and then enrolls in university classes to acquaint herself with the history and philosophy of Islam.

Sarah's conversion to Islam, unlike that of her sisters in the previous groups, includes her family. She takes them to the masjid and asks the imam to provide answers to their questions. She also provides family members with literature on Islam to complement what the imam has said. Although she does not expect her family to convert, she does consider her pursuit of truth to be a family affair. Interestingly, Sarah feels no need to change her name and proudly asserts that it is the name a loving mother and father bestowed on her.

Sarah prefers to help from the periphery of the African-American community in Islam. She had tried to "jump in the middle of things" only to later spend days in depression and confusion. After a few of these episodes, she returned quickly to the margin. Sarah's family's absorption of Islamic principles and articles of faith, however, is systematic and thorough. The family assimilates Islamic values rather than the cultural values of other ethnic groups of Muslims. Because of this, her family is not functioning under pressure to live the life of another. Although they are different from their next door neighbors, the dissimilarity does not produce discord. Sarah settles down in "good neighborly relations." When Sarah invites Muslim women to her home, there is generally an air of festivity and warmth. The women are all named Sarah, and their lives in Islam are both pleasant and satisfying.

The obvious need fulfilled by the Islamic alternative in the lives of black Americans in the Progressive Era of this century cannot be discussed adequately in this chapter. Islam satisfied the inner hunger of black people to be acknowledged as human. As many blacks threw away their crosses in response to the burning of crosses by the Christian Ku Klux Klan, Islam stepped in to fill the religious void and to give hope in a new and different way. This hope allowed blacks to separate spiritually and yet remain in the midst of white America. It allowed blacks the ultimate protest—the discarding of Christianity. It provided an avenue of belonging to a world perceived as greater than America, one that would one day subdue America and make it responsible for its sins.

But still today many black women are locked into a system under which they are slaves to the American system. The welfare program of this country humiliates and degrades women before it provides the level of subsistence it is designed to give. In this system women are asked about their personal lives and often treated with extreme impertinence while they apply for public assistance. Social workers cannot deny this assistance to female applicants who have children under five years of age, even those wearing Islamic dress, but the price paid in loss of self-esteem can be high.

The African-American Muslim woman who is forced to pursue this form of survival usually has a "double dose" in store for her. She is questioned about the reality of the religion that "forces its women to beg" and is confronted with such questions as "Why don't you ask your people who have all that money?" When she shows up without a husband (it is extremely difficult to have a husband and receive welfare) the question may well be: "What good did it do you to put on all those clothes and still the man that makes the babies doesn't take care of them?"

That there is a "women's world" in Islam is known. What is not known is that there is little place in it for African-American Muslim women. The carefully built structures of security and power among Muslim women in Islamic countries[20] have no gates of entry for outsiders. These groups of women are extremely ethnocentric. Contact with the Islamic world for African-American Muslim women is through the men of that world. Muslim men from the Islamic world have been the primary propagators of Islam in America. They generally have given African-American Muslim women instructions on how to be Muslim women. They hold classes and give seminars to expound on womanhood in Islam. Their wives, however, are not usually present.

Initial inquiry into African–American Muslim women's communities thus far reveals a series of small subgroups within the larger communities. Generally speaking, these subgroups are related to the position of husbands within the community. There is minimal interaction between groups, as position is based on education, income, and status. Although the class boundaries are acknowledged in the communities, the women have been helpful, genuinely considerate, and caring across boundaries. This may be because the Islamic "circle" is already a closed system within the larger African-American community and the need for cohesion is great.

The roles of women in the various African-American Islamic communities constitute a story that is larger than the confines of this chapter. What can be said is that the roles differ from community to community, and there are different ratios of typologies by group. Most of the women see themselves as recovering the role of mother, wife, and homemaker in a positive sense. They are keenly aware of the out-of-the-house role that black women have been forced to assume and welcome the traditional roles for women. Competitive efforts are made to "be good at homemaker and mother." Emphasis is placed on nurturing children and shielding them from the "evils of America." The stability of the home environment is sought at all cost.

My extrapolation from interviews thus far reveals that African-American Muslim women do believe Islam *can* provide a better life. Discovering how that better life can be achieved provides a multitude of tensions. It is extremely difficult to be the pioneers and to struggle through a maze without even the support of the larger community of women. The reality of being African-American is a direct challenge to traditional Islamic norms for the roles of women, that is, veiled, maintained, and shielded. The American system of racism and oppression looms ever present in the lives of African-American women. Clearly tensions are heightened when the African-American woman converts to Islam—she is a visible protest to everyone else. There are also new oppressions: these women now are held in contempt not only for their blackness, but also for conversion to a perceived enemy system.

"Somebodiness" is partially achieved. There is the assurance of having found the way to God, but also the despair of trying to carve an absolutely different way of life in the midst of an old familiar one. The habits of survival and the instincts for survival are ever present and a new pattern is not yet developed. These women have to establish their "women's world" because they have been made acutely aware of the closed-door policy of other Muslim women. They are also aware of the ambivalent nature of their existence in the

Islamic world as a whole. In the words of Kiswana: "The Islamic world is proud to count us for statistics, but they have no interest in assisting us toward freedom in this land where they are also pursuing the American Dream."

Notes

1. C. Eric Lincoln, *The Black Muslims in America* (Boston: Beacon Press, 1961); E. U. Essien-Udum, *Black Nationalism* (New York: Dell, 1962); Dorothy Blake Fardan, *Understanding Self and Society: An Islamic Perspective* (New York: Philosophical Library, 1981); Clifton E. Marsh, *From Black Muslims to Muslims: The Transition from Separatism to Islam, 1930–1980* (Metuchen, N.J.: The Scarecrow Press, Inc., 1984).

2. See, for example, Raymond Hall, *Black Separatism in the United States* (Hanover, N.H.: Dartmouth College University Press of New England, 1978).

3. W. E. B. DuBois, *The Souls of Black Folk* (Greenwich, Conn.: Fawcett Publications, 1961), p. 16.

4. Ibid.

5. Edmund David Cronon, *Black Moses: The Story of Marcus Garvey* (Milwaukee: University of Wisconsin, 1955), p. 31.

6. Ibid., pp. 31–36.

7. It can be presumed that there was early contact through converts and immigrants. Prominent among the former was Muhammad Russell Webb, editor of *The Moslem World*. (His biography is being written by Akbar Muhammad, director of the African American Studies Department, State University of New York at Binghamton.) Among the immigrants, special note should be made of the Ahmadiyya Movement that counts tens of thousands of blacks in its membership (see Maulana Muhammad Ali, *The True Conception of Ahmadiyyah Movement* [Lahore: Ahmadiyyah Anjuman Isha'at Islam, 1951], p. 258) and of the work of Sheikh Daoud and his wife, Sayeda Khadijah, editor of *Sahabiyat*, a bimonthly educational magazine for Muslim women.

8. Walter Conn, *Christian Conversion* (Mahwah, N.J.: Paulist Press, 1986), p. 5.

9. James T. Richardson, "The Active vs. Passive Convert: Paradigm Conflict Conversion/Recruitment Research," *Journal for the Scientific Study of Religion* 24 (1985), 119–236.

10. Carrie Allen McCray, "The Black Woman and Family Roles," in *Black Woman*, ed. La Frances Rodfers-Rose (Beverly Hills: Sage Publications, 1980).

11. The names for the characterizations are taken from the recording, *Wild Is the Wind* by Nina Simone and Gloria Naylor's *The Women of Brewster Place* (New York: Penguin, 1983).

12. "My skin is brown, My manner is tough. I'll kill the first mutha I see, my life has been rough. I'm awfully bitter these days, cause my parents were slaves. What do they call me? My name is Peaches." [Nina Simone]

13. Public education in America technically is free. The costs occur in trips for children, school supplies, and dress codes.

14. The methodology used in self-hypnosis is the same as when Peaches conditions herself to absorb the mental and emotional blows distributed by America's social agencies.

15. "Kiswana has still insisted on cutting her own hair, but it was so thin and fine-textured, it refused to thicken even after she washed it. She never forgave Wilson for telling her she didn't look African." (Naylor, *The Women of Brewster Place*, pp. 81–82]

16. "My skin is yellow, my hair is long, between two worlds I do belong. My father was rich and white, he forced my mother late one night. what do they call me? My name is Safonyah." [Nina Simone]

17. This phrase is carefully elucidated in Michele Wallace's *Black Macho and the Myth of the Superwoman* (New York: Dial Press, 1978). The definition is the woman who does everything, that is, works outside the home and takes sole care of her children, usually expressing uncompromising strength.

18. "My skin is black, my arms are long, my hair is wooly, my back is strong. Strong enough to take the pain inflicted again and again. What do they call me? My name is Aunt Sarah." [Nina Simone]

19. In taped interviews with women in this group, they all expressed that they had problems with religious doctrines at early ages sometime between eight years and ten years. Taped interviews numbers 5 and 14.

20. See Jane Smith, "The Experience of Muslim Women: Considerations of Power and Authority," in *The Islamic Impact*, ed. Yvonne Haddad et al. (Syracuse: Syracuse University Press, 1984).

13

Two-Way Acculturation: Muslim Women in America Between Individual Choice (Liminality) and Community Affiliation (Communitas)

Marcia K. Hermansen

The main premise of this chapter is that shared worlds of experience and communication for Muslim women exist in America, whether these women have emigrated from abroad or come from Caucasian or black American backgrounds, and exchanges within this world facilitate the process of adaptation in which all groups participate.

While acculturation is a term that has various connotations in the social science literature, initially referring to the process by which colonized or dominated native populations adapted to the ways and values of their oppressors, in less power-laden terms it has also come to indicate the adaptation process followed by immigrant populations in a new setting.[1] Using the term for both American and immigrant Muslim women may be slightly dissonant, given the difference in their overall experience. On the other hand, it does focus the discussion on the role of "culture" and its relation to the process of developing religious ideology and expression in a new context. Therefore let me define *acculturation* here as the process of confronting a new cultural context and worldview and having to choose where to adapt to aspects of that context or worldview in one's own life.

In the case of Muslims in North America, issues of acculturation in this sense are always present, ranging from the implicit to more and more explicit and conscious domains. The situation of the emergent Muslim communities in North America is unusual since, as one of my informants pointed out, we have Muslims by choice living in a "Christian-based" culture.[2] For Muslim immigrants this involves the need to rationalize one's choice and motives for being in such a situation where, by definition, many norms and laws of Islam cannot be applied, in addition to adjusting to the obvious impact of dislocation from familiar customs and the kin network. As indicated in the literature on immigrant communities in general, and Muslims specifically, the self-perception of the community has, over the past decades, passed through a number of stages. These transitions have been influenced by increases in the number of immigrants present which enable them to constitute more and more closely defined subcommunities, the changing social and economic background of the immigrants, and events—political and ideological—affecting the North American perception of Islamic identity.[3]

Americans who become participants in the community have interacted both with these changes, and, I argue, with generational shifts in their own culture. The experiences of women from both American and immigrant groups therefore reflect a mosaic of circumstances, choices, and individual factors that can only provisionally be organized into a broader framework of interpretation.

I therefore begin by discussing some of the patterns and symbols used by Muslim women in America to demonstrate how they are making choices of how to express components of their identity as Muslims in America. I then discuss two areas in which the women's world cuts across ethnic or national boundaries, women's religious meetings, and marriage arrangements.

The research on which I am drawing is, I should indicate, of the participant–observation type based on relatively short periods of residence in various North American cities including Berkeley and San Diego, California, as well as Montreal, Canada. The study is therefore largely descriptive and features observations of those "active" Muslims who do participate in organized gatherings and institutions. To focus and verify certain of my perceptions I scheduled personal interviews with women members representing each of the groups I discuss and with several women who have been long-term participants in the organized community.

Let me briefly summarize the institutional contexts of my observations. Muslim women in the areas covered by this study reside primarily in large urban centers. The women in Montreal are part of a community that has reached a level of organization sufficient to maintain an Islamic Center (the Muslim Community of Quebec) and a new Islamic elementary school. The formal establishment of a women's group was at the time of my interviews, however, still in the initial phase. Women at this center attend lectures and other functions, generally eating in a separate room and having the option of attending lectures or listening to them broadcast or video-transmitted into a separate area. Women from a wide range of ethnic and social backgrounds attend the center's activities and are active participants in administering and advising on community affairs. Attendance at women's educational meetings might range from twenty-five to forty ladies, with more attending social functions involving their families as well, such as the evening meals breaking the fast in Ramadan. In Montreal, a number of other mosques and centers also function,[4] and the overall size of the Muslim population is estimated at around thirty thousand, with about five thousand attending the Id (festival) prayers, and perhaps three hundred really active members involved with ongoing activities at the MCQ center.

The San Diego community took shape in the 1970s and is now rapidly organizing around four centers, Masjid Abi Bakr al-Siddiq of the Islamic Society of San Diego, Masjid al-Taqwa, Masjid Nur, and the Ribat. The Islamic Society is the largest center where some three hundred persons attend Friday prayers at a local recreation center hall. A new mosque building, Masjid Abi Bakr al-Siddiq, the first to serve the area's Muslims, is in the final stages of construction. A number of informal women's groups have constituted themselves among members of the various centers, and smaller ethnic (Saudi and Kuwaiti) prayer and women's groups also meet. Female attendance at Friday prayers is quite limited or totally absent at most of the centers, but appropriate facilities would permit greater participation.

The overall Muslim community in the San Francisco Bay area comprises over one hundred thousand persons with a total of perhaps fifteen functioning Islamic Centers or mosques including Masjid al-Islam (Oakland), Hussaini Center (San Jose), Masjid Muhammad (Oakland), Masjid an-Noor (Santa Clara), Masjid Jamea (San Francisco), Masjid Nur (Richmond), Islamic Center of San Jose, Hayward Masjid, Islamic Center of San Francisco, Islamic Center of Fremont, American Muslim Mission (San Francisco), Fiji Muslim Mosque (South San Francisco), Masjid Abi Bakr al-Siddiq (Berkeley), and two student groups at the University of California Berkeley. The community also features a number of smaller, less formal congregations. The small women's student group described later functions in Berkeley and operates on its own, unaffiliated with any local center, a pattern true of many smaller ethnic or interest groups or those in outlying or remote geographic areas. Members of these smaller groups will travel to larger centers to participate in special activities, such as lectures, Iftār (Ramadan evening fast-breaking and prayers) and Id prayers.

The American Muslim Woman: Patterns and Symbols of a New Identity

In this section I consider four types of American Muslim women: first-generation immigrants, and three types of American-born—Anglo–American, African–American, and the "new generation" children of Muslim immigrants to America, many of whom are now young adults.

Muslim women who have immigrated to America must choose the degree to which their ethnic and Muslim identity is symbolized and apparent within the new cultural environment. Major factors affecting an individual's choice are the time at which she immigrates and the region in which she resides. Large urban centers where Muslim and ethnic groups can constitute subcultures mean less pressure to acculturate. Previous generations' immigrants were more subject to the pressure of the melting pot, while overall the multicultural environment of Canada may be more supportive of maintaining Islamic dress and language than the United States.

Most immigrant women come as members of family groups and thus keep pace with their family's views of religious practice and the degree to which dress and life-style overtly reflect religious commitment. Single females generally are either students or divorcees and face greater pressure to assimilate to American culture unless they can find circles of friends from the original ethnic background, for example, Malaysian student groups, where female students largely associate with each other and often maintain Islamic-style dress.

The experience of Caucasian American Muslims may be characterized as permanent or prolonged liminality. As participants in a series of subcultural communities such individuals experience constant confrontation of choice and commitment, which on the one hand sets them apart and at the same time can propel them toward a powerful though transitory sense of community. In using the term *liminal* I draw on the well-known theories of Van Gennep[5] and Victor Turner,[6] who characterize the ritual process associated with major life transitions as moving the person through the three stages of separation (from the original personal status and social structure), liminality (a transitional, anxiety-ridden state between detachment from "the old" and attachment to "the new"), and reintegration into the community (communitas), which in turn reenergizes the structure and reinvests an individual's commitment to it.

In the case of the American Muslim experience, communitas is apt to be small but powerful. Although I do not wish to blur the individuality and uniqueness of each person's experience, it is nonetheless true that Caucasian–American women's involvement in Islam may be seen as following the generational patterns that are strong in American culture—witness our capacity to stereotype an artifact or attitude as 1950s, 1960s, or 1980s.[7]

My observation, corroborated by conversations with a number of interviewees, is that the attitudes and experiences of Caucasian–American Muslim women correlate extensively with their time of "coming of age" in America.

Most American women exposed to Islam in the 1950s and 1960s were those who met Muslim students from abroad in the course of their studies. At this time awareness of Islam in America was minimal, and marriages often occurred on the basis of shared intellectual and social worlds with little attention to religious commitments. As time passed these women often returned with their husbands to South Asia or the Middle East and faced real issues of culture shock. In some cases marriages lasted and were transformed as the wife found a commitment to Islam that revitalized and cemented it. In other such cases, marriages failed under the pressures of cultural difference. Women of this group, whether in the United States or abroad, became organizers, activists, and in many cases pillars of the Islamic center movement in America as they realized early the need for institutions to supplement and support the family setting in transmitting religion to their children. The patterns and symbols associated with the Muslim component of identity in these women's lives continues to develop as they participate in the growing Muslim presence in North America. I learned of the case of some American-born women with very secularized Muslim immigrant spouses who, through the participation of their teenage children in Muslim camps and youth groups, had begun to more strongly represent their Muslim identity through behavior modification. Women who have been married and Muslim for upwards of twenty years generally feel established and comfortable with either a very American image or by observing strict dress norms over a long period.

A contrast to this is the experience of the Caucasian–American Muslim woman who, for example, accepted Islam in the 1970s (although she came of age in the 1960s). Often propelled by the search for meaning of her cohort generation, she may have sought out information about the Islamic religion on her own since more information had by this time been disseminated in the culture. Much of the information available featured Sufism as one element of the Islamic tradition which offered a path to personal spiritual transformation. Such women often marry American Muslim males of similar orientation, realizing that such a personalist interpretation of religion as a path to transformation is ideally shared. These couples are usually more peripheral in the Islamic center movement and have less involvement, although in some cases there may be a bridge through their concern with Islamic schooling for their children. Some are working in developing alternative or home education systems for Muslim children.[8] The social networks of these couples usually consist of other couples like themselves. It is only in these smaller groups of couples of similar background that the liminality of being both Anglo–American and Muslim may be forgotten. A number of such persons, while having extreme misgivings about their native culture, at the same time find it familiar and at many levels sustaining. Another response of couples of this generation has been to constitute alternative communities of like-minded persons. For such individuals, I propose, the background of American culture is very strongly present in the awareness that one cannot totally reject or escape it since the freedom to explore personal growth through Islam emerged for them in that environment. On the other hand, the choice to "countermodernize"[9] must be made concrete for such persons through symbols of identification and cogent intellectual argument.

The homes or inner private worlds of such individuals are usually symbolically marked "Islamically" to a greater degree than the outer worlds, and persons who do not marry Muslims from the East may feel a need to more strongly integrate their Muslim identity by learning Arabic, traveling to Muslim countries, and furnishing their homes in traditional Islamic style. In the case of females the liminality issue is likely to be more strongly sensed. It would be hasty to attempt to characterize the outer life patterns—such as dress and socializing of this group—since a number of variables depend on the status of the person as single, married, or part of a larger subcommunity. The more isolated the individual woman, the less likely she is to symbolize her identity outwardly as Muslim, but the issues exist every day, perhaps every hour. For some, outer symbols—largely dress related—are dealt with contextually, that is, at Muslim functions or in Muslim countries one would adapt to local pattern while in the American world modes of dress chosen would be modest but not unusual. Some women pass through an initiation period of covering the hair and then gradually rationalize that it is not required in the American context, on the basis of modernist[10] or personalist/Sufi concepts. The choice, once rationalized at the personal level, is still raised overtly or subconsciously when associating with other Muslims.

Black American Muslim women also experience this tension, and it has been suggested that the generational shifts are less influential than a series of role models existing simultaneously for that community.[11]

For Muslim women the issue of multiple worlds is more pronounced than it is for men because of the issue of dress and visibility. Dress, whether one identifies with it as an issue or not, has a subconsciously powerful impact. One interviewee spoke to me of the sense of schizophrenia in transiting from her work role—dressing like any other American—to home life and contact with other Muslims. In women's meetings in which a variety of opinions are represented it is probably this issue that receives the most discussion and has the strongest effect on personal lives. One informant complained that the content of women's meetings in her community almost always focused on either issues of "covering" or issues of "obeying one's husband."

Issues of culture are entangled with the means of fulfilling dress requirements or expectations. This, while an obvious point, raises interesting issues, since an American Muslim woman, to a greater extent than her male counterpart, faces the possibility of acculturating to Islamic cultural norms at a visible level and encounters greater pressure to modify aspects of her life-style even in the most ordinary processes of daily social interaction.

In summary, the options open to the American Muslim woman in choosing to express the elements of her identity are to (a) not overtly express the fact of being Muslim; (b) express her Muslim identity context-dependent; (c) visibly express being part of the Muslim minority in America, but continue regular career and social activities; (d) totally modify her life-style.

The Caucasian–American Muslim of the 1980s is yet another type. One informant described as typical a woman in her twenties who found in Islam the structure she missed in a liberal, laissez-faire home where no standards were set and she was told to "be yourself." Such a woman is drawn to accept a totally observant Islam consonant with the dress and behavior norms advocated by the current "Islamic movement" and usually perpetuated in America in a milieu informed by Arab immigrants. After her initial commitment to Islam the supportive Muslim community arranges her marriage with a young student from the Middle East and she returns home with him.

Interestingly, interviews with such women indicate that they feel less liminality in America because their total commitment to an alternative view expressed visibly gives them a strong, clearly defined sense of identity—buttressed by the reactions around them even if these are disturbed or hostile. In fact, one such woman expressed a sense of greater liminality once she settled in Saudi Arabia with her spouse. There the statement she had made in adopting Islamic dress was considered a normal part of the culture, but being American, she was by definition alien. Women of this generation speak of the Muslim community they have joined as supportive in a way that American culture is not, particularly in terms of the strong female-bonding in personal relationships. These are experienced by them as being more genuine and noncompetitive than ones among American non-Muslim women. The importance given to family life and responsibilities within the family to children and parents is also a strong factor of the new identity that appeals to these women.

The patterns and symbols of acculturation for American Muslim women of this generation therefore tend to be overt, total, and identified with norms established by the current Islamic movement as being properly Islamic.

Women from the black American community whom I interviewed, on the other hand, seem to have a different attitude to their identity as Muslims, that is, those women who have been through the transition from the Nation of Islam to the American Muslim Mission. They do not seem to experience the same sort of liminality and culture choice issues. For example, members of one such group expressed comfort with making dress choices—frequently saying it is natural and feels right, and citing positive, admiring reactions to their Muslim personas from the surrounding culture.

For those who operate mainly within this community, issues of culture and foreignness are modified, since the Muslim identity is seen as the original or more authentic one. One respondent noted that "our grandmothers dressed this way (modestly) and this was our culture." Participants stated that "we feel that now we are where we were supposed to be" and "once we found al-Islam, we felt the pieces coming together like a puzzle."

For black American women who participate in more ethnically diverse groups or marry Muslims from Africa, issues of culture and liminality may be more prominent. A recent divorcee, for example, commented on her impressions that a certain clique of Arab male leadership in the community chose to interpret Islam for their own benefit. Another woman mentioned her impression that a study group attended mainly by younger Caucasian–American Muslims projected a lot of rigidity, emphasizing generic dress and attitudes.

Once out of the formal mode of the interview in their self-presentations, the conversations of women from the black community disclosed the presence of issues of culture, not in terms of abstract symbols or ideologies associated with being American versus being Muslim, but in terms of family relationships and expectations. One woman mentioned her Christian mother's concern about Muslim burial customs since her image of her daughter's funeral (hopefully far in the future) no longer meshed with her fantasy of being laid out in one's Sunday best for the family wake; and with immediate burial, how could the geographically far-flung relatives be expected to assemble in time?

Overall one can observe a pattern of "prolonged liminality' in the case of Anglo–American Muslims, and oscillating liminality for black Americans depending on which Muslim group they are associated with. In the light of my observations of American Muslim women I find that it is the group that initially had the highest sense of power and participation to American culture that seems to experience the greatest sense of being liminal on accepting Islam.[12]

The New Generation

The first generation of American-born Muslims is now coming of age. Many of this group grew up in settings where only a small support network was to be found. In other words, they attended American schools and had limited contact with other Muslim young people. This group deserves a study of its own; my own observations are limited to the regions with which I am familiar.

Among the trends of which I have been informed is a higher attrition rate (from the community) for males than females, making marriage for females with spouses committed to Islam more difficult. Intercultural marriages, for example, between Arab and Pakistani–American children are occurring more frequently. One reason for this is that young people who are highly committed to Islam feel that this should be the criterion for choosing a spouse rather than ethnic heritage. Although this does conform to the teachings of the religion, for those of their parents' generation it is a startling trend. The young women in the group are often able to integrate Islamic and American identities more comfortably, for example, to the point of wearing Islamic dress and being committed to Islamic activist ideology while choosing visible and demanding careers in business, law, or academia. Up to this point these are women who went through the American school system. In the future I wonder if the products of Islamic or home school systems will feel issues of liminality more strongly?

Women's Religious Meetings

The women's meeting provides an important arena for Muslim women of diverse ethnic and class backgrounds to interact and share; a tolerant, support-ive, inclusive attitude pervades these gatherings since simply being a "Muslim sister" is enough of a bond to ensure a sense of community that overrides issues of age, dress, race, or ideology. This is an attractive feature remarked on by those who participate in the groups—the discovery of a commonality and closeness that transcends other factors of diversity.

It is clear that meetings of Muslim women in America vary with the purpose, setting, and level of structure of the groups. The gatherings held to celebrate social and life-cycle events more readily reflect aspects of specific ethnic cultures. The Islamic centers offer Friday and Sunday prayer services, lectures, and classes that women may attend or that may be organized specifi-cally for them. Outside the centers more informal groups offer exchanges of religious information and shared devotional practices. In these meetings women from diverse backgrounds may meet, affirm their community and Islamic identity, and increase their knowledge of the religion. Male authorities such as the imam of the center are occasionally invited to the women's groups as resource persons for question-and-answer sessions. In the less formal, smaller groups, members are often assigned rotating presentations on topics such as prayer and fasting, which may lead to informal discussion and sharing of personal views and experiences. As a participant of a small Qur'an study meeting occurring in the Black Muslim community said, "We have to learn the religion for ourselves." Interestingly, her group's sourcebook is an English translation of *Tablight Nisab* by Muhammad Zakariyya of the Tablīghī Jamaat.[13]

Women's meetings take place in a wide variety of settings and contexts— privately organized in a participant's home, on university campuses, in rented church halls and community centers, and in Islamic centers. The women drawn together in such meetings often come from diverse social and cultural backgrounds, one aspect of the Muslim experience in America being that such encounters expose women from different backgrounds to a range of friendships and social contacts which are truly unique. Such contacts would be unavailable in any one Muslim country and even in a typical North American setting are rare.

The scope of such meetings varies with both the region of the country where they are held and the setting and orientation of participants in the meeting. A pattern observed by a number of women is a tendency for the broader, more eclectic social and ideological content of the meetings that existed before the 1980s to have become more and more particularized along ethnic and, especially, politicized lines. As previously noted, both increasing numbers of women available to constitute groups and the politicization of the community are factors influencing this trend.

A need has emerged to explicitly define the group as open and accepting of any and all interested women in the face of more purist tendencies, which are more subtly coded in a commitment to shared behaviors of dress code, favored books on tafsir (Qur'an interpretation), and the like. Participants quickly sense which group fulfills their needs.

One example of such a shift is the change that occurred in a women's Qur'anic study group which met regularly once a week over a number of years. This was an eclectic group gathered around the focus of a major university. The group drew on the student and student wife population from overseas as well as the black and Caucasian–American communities. Initially the group concentrated specifically on the study of Qur'an, which consisted of recitation of the text in Arabic by women able to do this, followed by an English translation and tafsir (interpretation) according to a standard classical resource such as Ibn Kathir. Selections from the hadith collections were also studied. Interested non-Muslims were accepted as participants and the women, in addition to participating in the structured meetings, arranged occasional special events in Ramadan, and on one occasion a weekend retreat in the mountains, which for some of the women from the Middle East was the first time they had experienced a meeting of this type away from home and husbands. These special meetings included further religious practices such as extra devotional prayers after midnight (tahajjud) and recitation of pious litanies (dhikr). The trust and community engendered through shared participation in such

Islamic groups led women from foreign cultures to experience some aspects of American life as a retreat away from home. This group fragmented in the 1980s into smaller subgroups along ethnic and ideological lines. By contrast, a Qur'an study group in the same area attended primarily by Arabic-speaking spouses of Muslim students focuses on reading from Qur'an, group memorization of five verses, followed by a reading of interpretation (tafsir) by Sayyid Qutb (a contemporary activist-oriented interpretation),[14] and a weekly topic such as purity (Ṭahara). The meetings are held entirely in Arabic.

Leadership in women's meetings emerges under the influence of a number of factors. An important feature of such meetings is the transmission from Arabic which clearly distinguishes the Arabic-speaking members of the group as transmitters of the tradition, especially those with religious education enabling them to recite or read accurately. The importance of being literate in Arabic as a criterion of leadership may either integrate a group or provide a divisive factor for a group. In one ethnically mixed meeting sponsored by an Islamic center, an Arab woman was recognized as the main teacher—she can read and simultaneously translate and explain the Qur'an. In another group, an Arab woman with credentials in Islamic fields was not able to integrate with and become the leader of an ethnically mixed group; in this case, her preliminary command of the English language and unfamiliarity with American culture were the deciding factors. It seems that a person must integrate both traditional knowledge and an understanding of the new environment to successfully lead an ethnically mixed group. Within groups functioning as parts of Islamic centers there is sometimes a need to choose liaison representatives to meet with male boards and mosque committees. In this case leadership qualities were a prime factor, while married women were preferred, consonant with Islamic norms of propriety.

Marriage

The typical Muslim concept of what marriage is and the way it is contracted differs greatly from the typical American view.

For the immigrant Muslim woman in America, the issue of marriage arises less often since she is normally married before arriving here. Most Muslim women immigrating to the United States have come as members of families, usually as spouses, which is consistent given their cultural and religious backgrounds. In a few isolated cases Muslim women have come alone, either as students planning to return home, or as women—perhaps divorced at home—coming to strike out on their own to establish themselves or help their families.

In terms of marriage, such women as the latter initiated two new patterns. In some cases women student activists found in the context of the Islamic movement in America spouses of like ideology from their own cultural background. In others, a number of single Muslim women who came in the 1960s or early 1970s married non-Muslim Americans. With the shift of increased awareness of their Islamic identity and a larger community with which to identify, these women experience increasing stress on their marriages and identity.

In the case of unmarried daughters, immigrant families face the problem of keeping their daughters within traditional norms and out of American practices such as dating; they also have the problem of a limited pool of suitable spouses from similar backgrounds and smaller networks of persons to involve in the matchmaking process. This in turn may induce families to return to the home country to locate suitable matches there.

For the new generation of Muslims, the first growing up in America, patterns of marriage include more intercultural marriage across Muslim ethnic lines (i.e., Pakistani–Arab) as degree of religious commitment and socio-economic level have become more important criteria than ethnic background. Young people are encouraged to socialize with other Muslims through youth groups, camps, and larger regional gatherings.

For "new" Muslims of American background, marriage is one area in which a lot of adjustment may be required. Among the most recent group of American women who have become Muslim, many accepted arranged marriages, meeting only briefly with spouses from Middle Eastern countries. This cannot be considered "traditional," since none of the family and cultural context surrounding Muslim marriages abroad exists. It may, however, be considered in conformity to "Islamic" rather than any specific culture's norms. This pattern of marriage was observed in a large city where no consolidated Islamic center exists. I would expect that under the aegis of such centers, a more moderated form of marriage, one that makes some concessions to American expectations of premarriage counseling or the intended spouses getting to know each other, would exist.

The issue of the single Muslim woman takes on new significance in the American context. Note that in traditional Muslim cultures such a term would not have much applicability, since daughters stay at home until they marry, normally at a relatively young age. Unmarried career women are rarely observed, and they almost never live alone but rather become part of an extended family or reside in institutional settings, such as girls' school teachers or matrons.

One interviewee—a divorced black American Muslim, commented that she felt under great pressure because of the sentiment that "if you don't stay married, you're not a good Muslim." It is generally more difficult to find acceptance in the Muslim community as a single woman; one informant mentioned "a reaction of fear and suspicion," whether one is an immigrant or American.

This problem is typical of the 1970s generation of female American Muslims. It is more difficult for them to marry either as divorcees with children or as single women who, now in their thirties, are considered "older women."

Very strict observance of Islamic norms and dress often facilitates marriage, since in many circles it is considered a pious action to marry such a woman "in the path of God," and a number of such marriages do take place. One female informant from Pakistan suggested this increased possibility of entering married and family life (increasingly difficult for many single women in America) as a motivation for their becoming Muslim. This is probably not outside the realm of possibility.

With respect to the religious dimensions of acculturation, first let me note that of the Muslim women who have immigrated to North America, a significant number probably have little previous assocation with religious symbols except for name and some few life-cycle events. Among those who retain a concern with the religion, a broad distinction can be made between those who acknowledge their new situation in America and do make choices about how to acculturate and those who consider themselves "in transit" as wives or students and remain relatively isolated within a small kin or ethnic-based subculture.

Several patterns may be observed among those immigrant women who face the challenge of being Muslim in America. The first is the rediscovery of Islamic identity. This has been discussed in a number of previous studies.[15] It is due to both a growth in the size of the community, the worldwide Islamic resurgence, and the experience of raising children in America.

A second pattern concerns the exposure to new forms of religious participation. A simple example is attending mosque services, such as Friday prayer, lectures, or functions. The practice in most Muslim countries is that women do not attend the prayers, and such attendance is in fact discouraged or prohibited according to the four Sunni schools of law. In North America, it is important as a source of social and religious reinforcement, although the majority of women still do not practice it. There are discussions of how women should be separated, given the constraints of spaces not designed for the purpose of segregated prayers, how to deal with child care during the services, and the newness of the experience in general. Another novel experience for women is participating in the previously discussed study groups composed of Muslims from various ethnic backgrounds, including American Muslims who, in some sense, symbolically bridge the cultures.

For the immigrant, religion is not normally the central issue relating to her placement in a new situation within which she has to adapt One exception is the female educator–activist who comes principally to do Islamic work in America, in which her self-definition precludes acculturation. In one case, such an activist shortly after her arrival in the community found the rather informal authority structure and decorum of the local woman's meeting unacceptable and constituted a new group along traditional lines with herself as the leader. Another female immigrant who states that she and her husband came to America to work for the cause of Islam among non-Muslims seems to experience her situation as one of hardship and deprivation. She refuses to attend the local Islamic center although her husband does, since she feels women should not participate in such mixed environments. However she works publicly in a service industry wearing ethnic dress and covering her hair.

In the case of American Muslims, acculturation raises a different set of issues. This is true for several reasons—one is the experience of a conversion as opposed to transition or alternation. Conversion is defined by one social scientist as moving outside of the prescribed mode of discourse,[16] and by another as constituting identity based on a "new operative Archimedean point."[17] In contrast to most immigrant Muslim women, for the American convert or "new" Muslim, religious identity is a central issue.

Among such women an "elective affinity"[18] exists, which matches styles or generational patterns within American culture with possible perceptions of Muslim identity. Such perceptions transcend any specific ethnic culture, but rather involve interpretations of the essence of how to be Muslim—activist, Sufi, or whatever. For the majority of American Muslims the adaptation and rationalization of new patterns of social interaction, marriage, and home life are inspired by Islamic norms.

In many cases the challenge of being Muslim in America calls for an ijtihad (interpretation of Islamic law and values), which in its radical nature reasserts the initial impetus of the Islamic revelation to break down tribal/ethnic identifications. The question of whether this will have a significant impact on the intellectual and religious life of the larger world community, or whether assimilation is the ultimate destiny of this group will be answered by the coming generation.

Notes

1. Edward H. Spicer, "Acculturation," in *Encyclopedia of the Social Sciences*, 1 (New York: Macmillan, 1968), pp. 21–26.

2. That is, Muslims in America (or Europe) have chosen to leave "dar al-islam" (abode of submission), the Islamic order where at least in theory Islamic law is implemented and Muslim norms are upheld, and to permanently reside in a non-Muslim environment. For a majority this choice is made primarily on the basis of economic motives.

3. Yvonne Haddad, "Muslims in Canada: A Preliminary Study," in *Religion and Ethnicity*, eds. Harold Coward and Leslie Kawamura (Waterloo: Wilfrid Laurier University Press, 1978), pp. 71–100.

4. For example, the large Islamic Center of Quebec in St. Laurent, Masjid al-Umma, and Fatima Mosque in the downtown area, the South Shore, Pierrefonds, and West Island Islamic Centers, and Twelver Shi'a and Isma'ili Muslim Congregations.

5. Arnold Van Gennep, *The Rites of Passage* (Chicago: University of Chicago Press, 1960), pp. 189–194.

6. Victor Turner, *The Ritual Process* (Ithaca, N.Y.: Cornell University Press, 1977), pp. 94–130.

7. Ronald Robertson, in a sociological analysis of "Conversion and Cultural Change" (*Meaning and Change: Explorations in the Cultural Sociology of Modern Societies* [New York: New York University Press, 1978]) indicates a cultural shift in that "the extreme conceptions of the fluidity of identities, lifestyles and states of consciousness are already waning and will continue to wane vis-à-vis their 1960s and early 1970s highpoint." He further proposes that the mid-1970s concern with life-cycle issues, theories of adult development, and moral and cognitive development "suggest above all a concern with greater fixity in the sphere of individual patterns of living."

8. For example see Noura Durkee, "Primary Education of Muslim Children in North America," *Muslim Education Quarterly*, 5, 2, (1988), 54–81.

9. "Countermodernization" as a reaction to the "homelessness" of the modern mind is an analytical category formulated by Peter Berger as "an intense nostalgia for the integrative symbols of the past, resulting in a traditionalism that defensively reaffirms ancient symbols of community" (cited in Peter Homan's *Jung in Context. Modernity in the Making of a Psychology* (Chicago: University of Chicago Press, 1979), pp. 201–2. Becoming Muslim, in the case of an American, is rather more complex, since one at the same time is traditional and affirms community while identifying in many cases—modernity and American culture as alienating forces.

10. "Modernist" in the sense of the Islamic modernist trend of interpretation which views historical–critical approaches to tradition as legitimate and desirable.

11. As presented in the unpublished "Muslims in America" conference paper of Susan McCarthy Brown.

12. This concurs with Catherine Walker Bynum's reassessment of Victor Turner's theory, in that in her research on medieval Europe she found that the process of a dissolution of structure and return to communitas was more relevant to the experience of the male elite. "Women's Stories, Women's Symbols: A Critique of Victor Turner's Theory of Liminality," in *Anthropology and the Study of Religion*, eds. Robert L. Moore and Frank E. Reynolds (Chicago: Center for the Scientific Study of Religion, 1984), pp. 105–25.

13. Muhammad Zakariyya Kandhlawi, *The Teachings of Islam. Tablīghī Nisab*, Vol. 1 (New Delhi: Iḍara Isharat-e-Diniyat, 1981). This work, disseminated by the Tablighi Jamaat, contains sections of the lives of the Prophet's companions, prayer, the Qur'an, Ramaḍan, dhikr (reciting pious litanies), and invoking blessings on the Prophet.

14. For a discussion of the life and thought of Sayyid Qutb see Yvonne Y. Haddad, "Sayyid Qutb: Ideologue of Islamic Revival," in *Voices of Resurgent Islam*, ed. John L. Esposito (New York: Oxford University Press, 1983), pp. 67–98.

15. For example, in Yvonne Haddad, "The Impact of the Islamic Revolution in Iran on the Syrian Muslims of Montreal," in *The Muslim Community in North America*, ed. Earle H. Waugh et al. (Edmonton: The University of Alberta Press, 1983), pp. 165–81.

16. Richard V. Travisano, "Alternation and Conversion as Qualitatively Different Transformation," in *Social Psychology Through Symbolic Interaction* ed. Gregory P. Stone (Waltham, Mass.: Xerox College Publishing, 1970), p. 601.

17. Robertson, *Meaning and Change*, p. 211.

18. Robertson, *Meaning and Change*, discussing Max Weber's concept of the relationship between individual modes of existence and cultural change, pp. 193–94.

VI

AMERICAN MUSLIMS AND
THE QUESTION OF IDENTITY

14

Islamic Issues for Muslims in the United States

John O. Voll

Muslims in the United States face a variety of challenges. Many of these are similar to those faced by other minority communities in America. However, Muslims also face challenges and opportunities that are tied to the character of Islam. The Islamic faith and its practice involve special obligations and responsibilities that shape the way Muslims as individuals and groups respond to the conditions of American society. Often people become involved in examining the "American" issues faced by distinctive and minority communities in the United States forgetting that the special characteristics of the community are also important. Significant Islamic issues are involved in the life of Muslims in the United States as well as important American issues.

These Islamic issues should not be viewed simply as special problems or difficulties. Some issues do involve problems, but others involve challenges that are significant opportunities as well. The ways that Muslims respond to changing conditions in the United States may provide important guidelines for Muslims elsewhere and for non-Muslims in the United States, since at the heart of Islamic issues there are universal concerns.

There are two different types of Islamic issues for Muslims in the United States. First, are what might be thought of as the "classic" issues for Muslim minorities everywhere. In these, the "key concern is how to live an Islamic life in a non-Muslim country."[1] Here the basic issues are maintaining Islam as a way of life in a context where that is difficult, and deciding the meaning and implications of community-faith concepts such as *hijra* (emigration), *jihad* (exertion), and *da'wa* (mission or calling) in the American context. In some ways these issues are similar to those faced by Muslim minority communities throughout the history of Islam.

A second type of Islamic issue also is directly related to the special conditions of the contemporary world. These are the issues involved in the great transformations of human society which have been taking place in the past decades. These changes have been described by some as the emergence of postindustrial society[2] while others speak of the development of postmodern perspectives and institutions.[3] Whatever descriptive title is given to the processes, the transformations of recent decades create the conditions within which special issues arise for Muslims and others living in the emerging "postmodern" society in the United States.

The "Classic" Islamic Issues

The Islamic issues facing Muslims in the United States are shaped by the basic nature of Islam. The worldview and guidance for behavior provided by Islam contain specific elements as well as general approaches that are specially affected by the nature of American society.

Islam as a "Way of Life"

It is often noted that Islam is not "just a religion," but a total way of life. This observation is made by both non-Muslims and Muslims when they are discussing the nature of the Islamic faith, obligations, and experience.[4] It refers to the comprehensive and inclusive nature of the Islamic ideal. Muslims have a guide and model that covers "the most mundane aspects of everyday life and behavior as well as the general principles directing the community."[5]

All major religious traditions in some way attempt to guide humans in their lives. Christian and Jewish aspirations define "ways of life" and, in some contexts, have presented comprehensive ideals for believers. The worldview of medieval Western Christendom provides an example of a comprehensive Christian social ideal, as does the worldview of orthodox Judaism. However, in the modern era in Western societies the secularization of worldview has been a prominent development. This has meant that a growing proportion of society accepts a differentiation among the various sectors of life—religious, economic, political.

In many ways, the process of secularization became most widely accepted and most clearly implemented in the United States of the twentieth century. The separation of church and state became almost a political dogma. Similarly, "religion" in the United States has come to be seen by many as a "private" and individual matter rather than a public one. To a remarkable extent, social attitudes and political expectations in the United States are built on an asseumption that the basic faith of an American will, in a significant way, be "just a religion." The expectation is that religion can be separated from politics and a sense that the United States is a secular society.

The context and basic social framework within which Muslims live in the United States is in some important ways secular. One of the major issues for Muslims is how Islam, which defines a comprehensive way of life, can function within such a secular context. Muslims are not alone in facing this issue. Christians and Jews have also had to define the relationship between the implications of their faiths and the expectations of a secular society. Muslims, however, do face a special challenge of operating within a legal and social framework in which church–state relations have been defined primarily in relation to Judaism and Christianity.

In recent years, the concept of American society as a secular society has been refined and challenged. Some say there is a "civil religion," which in some way provides a religious foundation for politics and the social order.[6] There is also a recognition of American acceptance of a general monotheistic morality based on Judaism and Christianity. In this context, the distinctive characteristics of Islam raise special Islamic issues for Muslims in the United States.

The three major monotheistic religions in America have many similarities, but there are also some distinctive differences. The special American adaptations to Jewish and Christian practices do not necessarily solve similar problems for Muslims. These often have implications for basic issues of the relationships between religion and society, and religion and politics, in the United States.

The issue of prayer in public schools can be used as an example of how American church–state issues relate to Islamic experiences. At the present time, the subject of whether or not prayer should be allowed in American public schools is hotly debated. The vigor of the debate shows that many Americans, possibly a growing proportion, do not accept the full implications of secularism for American society.

The purists supporting separation of church and state have successfully maintained in the courts that separation should allow no general prayer opportunity, not even a moment of silence at some appointed time. Others have suggested a variety of measures, ranging from the moment of silence to more formal prayers.[7] The debate on this issue, however, tends to be stated in terms that assume a relatively Christian definition of prayer.

None of the most visible or prominent groups involved in the debate has discussed the situation in a context within which a Muslim would be able to fulfill the obligation of *salat*, the prescribed five daily prayers. Much of the school prayer debate uses the basically Christian approach, which assumes prayer to be a private communication between the believer and God. As has often been pointed out, salat "are somewhat different from 'prayer' as used in the Christian sense, although personal supplication and glorification of God (known as *du'a*) are also a very important part of the Muslim worship."[8]

The specific conditions requisite for the regular prescribed prayers are not readily available in American schools (or in offices and factories). In addition to the need for released time at the proper hours, the believer also needs facilities for the preliminary ablutions and an appropriate space. As relatively large Muslim communities develop in American cities some facilities are being made available. (A room in a high school in Dearborn, Michigan, for example, has been set aside for Islamic prayer.) However, in general terms, none of the proposals for prayer in public schools make salat significantly easier for the Muslim students.

On this important issue in American religious life, Muslims do not have an obvious or clear choice between the existing alternatives. The "prayer in school" option has an appeal because it recognizes the importance of actions of faithful believers within the context of daily life. Yet it tends to impose a definition of prayer on the school child that can be confusing and possibly even misleading. This alternative strengthens the pressures already existing in society to "Christianize" the religious practices of all Americans. In this sense, there could be the same type of pressure that non-Christian families feel with regard to Christmas trees and other socially secularized Christian customs.

For Muslims to support the opponents of prayer in school would be for them to accept the assumptions of a secularized society. In particular, this position encourages the attitude that religion is a personal rather than a public matter and, therefore, its activities should not be practiced in public places. The issue thus challenges the sense of Islam as a total way of life. There are believers in Islam as well as in Judaism and Christianity who accept secularist assumptions, but they are challenged by more fundamentalist believers, as in the other religious traditions.

For the American Muslim, then, an important task is to redefine issues of religious life in America in such a way that an Islamic alternative is possible within the debate. Such an alternative would recognize in some way the special character of Islam as a total way of life, in both the public and private arenas. The prayer in school issue reflects the type of concern involved in such an effort.

It is possible to see a number of similar issues raised by the specific expectations and requirements of Islam. In these cases, again, the issues involved often affect believers other than Muslims, but the debate has taken place in terms that are not specifically Islamic or open to an Islamic option.

In recent years, this has been apparent in issues of prisoners' rights. A long series of cases had decided the First Amendment rights of prisoners with regard to the free exercise of their religions. It was recognized that a prisoner's rights were subject to a variety of restrictions related to his or her status as a prisoner but, at the same time, it was recognized that any limitations on First Amendment rights had to be justified in terms of security or rehabilitation efforts.[9]

Many of the early cases were specifically applied to Christians, and not until the late 1970s and 1980s did the specific requirements of Muslims begin to receive attention. Among the issues to which particular attention was given were those of prayer and worship in group settings, especially the Friday prayers, the wearing of particular religious garb, and equal recognition for use of chapel facilities. For the most part, though not without exception, court resolutions have gone against requests by Muslims for considerations that would facilitate the practice of their Islamic faith and, in many cases, would offer them no more than has been made available to Christians and Jews in prison contexts.

The cases of prisoners represent extreme situations, but they reflect the broader context of American society. Specific practices of Muslims involve schedules and activities most institutions in the United States have not traditionally recognized. Muslims and other nonmajority groups face the issues of changing their practices or violating regulations in their work, school, or recreation. Even when the broad issue has already been decided (for example, that prisoners have some rights to assemble for worship), the procedures are usually adapted to Christian practices rather than generalized. Even though Judaism has been more integrated into the general American religious scene than has Islam, Jews have similar problems.

The challenge for Muslims is to create responses that will provide recognition of the special character of Islam in both private and public life without creating unnecessary conflict. Muslim responses to issues such as prayer in school and worship in prisons may help all Americans create more general and universal practices that are not shaped exclusively by traditional Christian practices.

"Classic" Response Concepts

The situation of Muslims in the United States has many elements that are not unique in the history of Islam. In many different eras and areas, Muslims have found themselves in societies where they are not the controlling group or the majority. As a result, over the centuries certain concepts have developed which define modes of response to the situation of living within a non-Muslim majority. Some of the most important of these are hijra, jihad, and da'wa. Each of these concepts is important in defining a specific way of responding to the minority situation.

Hijra can be translated in a number of ways. The core of the meaning is the act of leaving one place and moving to another, often with the implication of seeking refuge but sometimes simply as a process of emigration. A "hijra experience" is at the heart of the historic development of the Islamic community during the lifetime of the Prophet Muhammad.

The hijra of the Prophet marks the beginning of the Islamic calendar era. It was a significant transition in the nature of the community of followers of Islam. Muhammad began his prophetic mission in Mecca, where he presented the revelations he received as a preacher in an already established community. The leaders and controlling elite in Mecca did not accept the message Muhammad preached and placed limitations on him and the small number of people who had accepted Islam. Then, in A.D. 622, Muhammad and the rest of the Muslim community moved to another town, which later became known as Medina. It is this movement from Mecca to Medina which is called the Hijra in Islamic tradition.

The Hijra of the Prophet represented a major transformation of the Islamic community. In Medina, Muhammad organized his followers into an effective community, and the Islamic message defined the full way of life of that community. In this historical context, hijra is an escape from persecution and unbelief, but it is also an emigration to a new context within which the Islamic community can flourish as a full way of life.

The idea of withdrawing from a society to live a life in accord with one's faith appeals to many communities. This may involve staying within the geographical boundaries of society but withdrawing socially, and sometimes even spacially. Such a response can be seen among some Christian communities in the United States, such as the Amish. This might be thought of as the sectarian–hijra response, using *sect* as defined by Bryan Wilson in his studies.[10]

This sectarian–hijra response is not restricted to the American context. Fundamentalists in Egypt during the 1970s, for example, debated whether or not it was necessary to withdraw from Egyptian society, which some of them felt had become a society of unbelief.[11] In the United States it reflects some of the spirit of the early experience of the Nation of Islam and other groups with special needs of protecting and supporting their members. There was no special emphasis on the specific concept of hijra, but the idea of withdrawal from a persecuting and unbelieving society was a strong part of the sense of community within the Nation of Islam and similar groups.

This sectarian–hijra involves separation but not isolation. It is, in many ways, an act of witness and challenge to the existing society. In this way, sectarian withdrawal can become an expression of the desire to create a transformed broader society, with the sectarian–hijra community constituting the core of this new society. In this way, the hijra can lead to one form of proclamation of the mission or da'wa. Within the Islamic message this proclamation is a major imperative, which does not allow simple withdrawal into self-contained and isolated communities. Because of this, Muslim sectarian–hijra communities are never as withdrawn as such Christian groups as the Shakers or Amish.

A second hijra type of response to the minority situation is the actual act of physical emigration, moving to an Islamic society. In some traditional Muslim discussions of the obligations of Muslims, believers are said to have the alternatives of emigration or jihad if they live in a society that is not Islamic.[12]

Most Muslims living in the United States have good reasons for not wanting to emigrate. Many are members of groups and families that have been here for generations and have little desire or incentive to move. Movements calling on black Americans to emigrate to Africa had little success in the 1920s and 1930s, despite the racial discrimination they suffered, and Muslims from the black American communities today show a similar attitude toward moving to Islamic countries.[13]

In addition, many Muslims in the United States at present are themselves immigrants, often coming from societies where Muslims are a majority. "The number of Muslims in America has risen dramatically in the last half century through immigration, procreation, and conversion. About two-thirds of the total are immigrants from Muslim countries, mostly in the Middle East, and their descendants."[14] For these people, emigration from the United States is not a likely option.

It is worth noting that this does not make Muslims in the United States particularly different from other minority Muslim communities. Despite the suggestions from traditional teachings, hijra has not often been the option taken by Muslims in non-Muslim areas. Such Muslims have either adapted themselves to non-Muslim conditions or have worked to transform the societies within which they live.

The dynamic expansion of Islam in world history has, in fact, depended on Muslims who did not emigrate when they found themselves in non-Muslim societies. Muslim merchants and traveling teachers, for example, were important vehicles for the expansion of Islam in sub-Saharan Africa and Southeast Asia. In other contexts, Muslim minority communities have survived and adapted to non-Muslim societies in China, the Balkans, and now in the Soviet Union. In such situations, any hope for the conversion of the society as a whole to Islam is a long-term vision, but the communities have been able to maintain an authentic sense of Islamic identity.[15]

The experiences of Muslims in China and in Sub-Saharan Africa define two rather different responses. Neither response involves a physical departure from the non-Islamic society. However, the Chinese Muslim communities have tended to establish rather clear boundaries for their identity, either in ethnic terms (as among peoples like the Uighars) or socially (as with the Hui, or Chinese-speaking Muslims). The Chinese Muslims have enacted a kind of hijra into a special social identity that can be integrated into the broader dynamics of society.

The experience of Muslims in Sub-Saharan Africa identifies the other alternatives: rather than hijra, Muslims should work to transform the societies in which they find themselves. This option includes two important concepts arising out of the Islamic tradition. They are related to each other and to a sense of hijra as well. These are da'wa, which can be translated in this context as mission or call or message, and jihad.

Despite the fact that many writers, both Muslim and non-Muslim, have tried to explain the broader meanings of jihad, it remains a very misunderstood term in the West. If average, non-Muslim Americans heard the statement that Muslims, even those in the United States, accepted the responsibility of jihad in the path of God, they would assume that this meant that those Muslims were obligated to engage in acts of violence in the name of their religion. *Jihad* is most frequently translated simply as "holy war." While jihad does, in certain contexts, mean holy war, it has a much broader meaning within Islamic consciousness. Jihad in the path of God is an active striving for righteousness. At times this may mean fighting for one's faith, but it also involves the more general sense of actively serving God in every way possible. It is jihad in this broader sense that becomes the responsibility of all Muslims, whether they are living in a Muslim or a non-Muslim society. There is, however, a special sense of the need for each Muslim actively to affirm Islam in non-Muslim contexts.

Muslims, wherever they are, are expected to strive for recognition of God's oneness through social justice and a properly ordered society. In one sense, at least, the message of many of the writers in the current movements of affirmation of Islam throughout the world is that no society at the present time is truly Islamic, and therefore Muslims everywhere are to work for the presentation of God's message to humanity.[16] Although this striving at times involves fighting, it is primarily a struggle to win the hearts of humanity. This is the methodology of the Islamic revolution, for example, as described by a major Islamic revivalist thinker, Mawlana Mawdudi.[17]

For Muslims in non-Muslim societies, this striving may take many different forms, both independently and in cooperation with other forces in society. In the struggle against drug sales and drug-related crimes in Brooklyn, for example, a mosque took an active role in cooperation with the police. Reports of this noted that Muslims "risked personal safety to defend the area against drug dealers" and resulted in local non-Muslims saying, "Thank God for the Muslims."[18] A similar activist Muslim program has helped reduce drug dealing in some housing projects in Washington.[19] Activities like these reflect a type of jihad that is working for the transformation of non-Muslim society. Elsewhere, programs for control of alcohol abuse and gambling and recreation programs for youth have a similar impact.

Related to this jihad effort is the active effort to present the message positively to the people in the non-Muslim society. This mission or call is da'wa. In the perspective of Islam as a total way of life, as one Muslim leader expressed it, "living in surrender to Allah cannot be actualized fully unless other people join us in our endeavor, unless the whole society lives in surrender. Hence, at least inviting others to join our venture, that is Da'wah, is an essential part of being a Muslim."[20]

Bearing witness within society represents a traditional Islamic alternative to the two types of hijra, either social withdrawal or emigration. Ismail Faruqi related this sense of mission to a special kind of hijra, seeing Muslims in the West as having made a hijra *to* the West, rather than preaching that they should undertake a hijra *from* Western society. In this sense he was calling for active da'wa. Faruqi urged Muslims in the West to see themselves as "ambassadors of Islam" with a mission to bring Islam to Western society. He said, in an address to Muslims living in the West, "we want to live as if we were . . . Companions of Mohammad from Makkah [Mecca] to Madinah [Medina]. . . . This is our Madinah, we have arrived, we are here. Now that you are in Madinah, what is your task? . . . Your task is . . . the saving, the salvation of life, the realization of the values of dignity, of purity, of chastity, all the nobility of which humans are capable."[21]

This vision of the West as the Medina of contemporary American Muslims is a powerful one. It recalls the efforts of the first Muslims to create an Islamic community where none had existed in the days of the Prophet Muhammad. The charge is that if the early Muslims could transform the non-Islamic society of Arabia, contemporary Muslims should also be able to transform the society to which they have come. For the person who might say that the task is too great, there is the reminder that an "individual imbued with a message and mission may look like an insignificant, ineffective entity. But was not there only one Da'iya [person engaged in da'wa] in Makka? You may say: Ah, but he was a prophet. Yes, but he is *the* example."[22]

This type of thought represents the foundation for a statement of the Islamic mission (da'wa) and identity within the secular, non-Muslim society of the West. It goes beyond the suggestions of traditional Muslim teachers who urge emigration from non-Muslim societies to avoid the contradictions of trying to live Islam as a way of life in a society where that is difficult. It sets a long-term goal for Muslims of the transformation of their society but does not necessarily insist that that goal be achieved immediately. It makes it possible for Muslims to have a sense of Islamic mission while participating in a non-Islamic social order.

The classical Islamic issues for Muslims in the United States are those related to Islam as a way of life. Although many of the general aspects of these issues are similar to issues raised by being a Christian or a Jew in American society, specific Islamic characteristics give these issues a distinctive tone for Muslims. In response to these challenges, basic Islamic concepts such as hijra, jihad, and da'wa take on new implications while maintaining much of their traditional significance. Sectarian hijra and actual emigration are not effective alternatives for most American Muslims. Instead, active, nonmilitant jihad and da'wa appear to be the most effective classical Islamic responses for contemporary American Muslims.

Issues of Islam and American Modernity

In addition to the classical Islamic issues raised for Muslims who are minorities, Muslims in the United States face complex issues raised by the great social transformations of contemporary world history. The emergence of postindustrial or postmodern society creates special problems. All faiths, not just Islam, have had to confront and cope with the conditions created by the modernization of societies. Some people believe there is an inherent contradiction between all "traditional religions" and modernity, and others feel that only if such faiths are significantly altered can they be compatible with the needs of modern society.

The dynamic condition of Muslim communities in the United States represents a significant refutation of these kinds of assertions when they are applied to Islam. It is possible for Muslim communities to survive and thrive in a variety of contexts within American society. There certainly are problems in fulfilling Islamic obligations in the midst of a secular society, but these problems can be resolved in many ways.

It is, however, important to go beyond these observations to the long-term evolution of faith and religion in the United States (and, in fact, in the world in general). The major evolution is in the direction of what some people have called postmodern faith.[23] There is a move away from the secularist perspective and a growing sense, in the major religious communities, of the public dimensions and obligations of their faiths.

Globally, major religious traditions have had an increasingly visible role in the political arena. The forces of the Islamic resurgence have been very important here, although the emergence of Liberation Theology in Latin America and the roles of the Roman Catholic Church in Poland and elsewhere show that this broadening of the sphere of religion is not simply an Islamic phenomenon. One important aspect of this has been in areas beyond the strictly political. The moral and ethical implications of science have become important topics of debate in societies where science has traditionally been considered a "value-free" activity.

Shortly after World War II, Arnold Toynbee identified special contributions that might be made by Islam to the social life of the emerging global "great society." Toynbee, writing in the late 1940s, felt that the race consciousness of modern Western society was a source of danger for humanity and that the message and achievements of Islam in this area were a source of possible strength that could "decide this issue in favour of tolerance and peace."[24] Although it has been argued that the Muslim record was idealized by people like Toynbee,[25] in the context of American society Islam has provided a way to move against at least some aspects of racism. The message of Islam provided a way for a Malcolm X to break away not only from the racism of American whites but also of the early Black Muslim movement, led by Elijah Muhammad. Islam has provided a new perspective for the emerging morality of identity and pluralism in the American context.

The Islamic ideal of informing the total way of life by divine revelation is in tune with the broader movements of moral awareness in the United States. Muslims in the United States have a special opportunity which has been articulated by Muslim activists in terms of da'wa (mission). Ismail Faruqi, for example, has said, "if you look upon this as an event in world history, you will see that Allah, *subhanahu wa ta'ala*, has prepared the course of history to welcome you in the West. . . . By bringing you here . . . Allah, *subhanahu wa ta'ala*, has carved out a vocation for you, a new mission, and this mission is to save the West."[26] Suzanne Haneef, at the conclusion of her introduction to Islam, states, "As the number of indigenous and immigrant Muslims continues to increase in the Western world, it is hoped that they will make very significant contributions to the societies in which they live, side by side with other likeminded people, by making Islam's point of view known, and drawing upon the vast legacy of its teachings to work toward solutions of the many grave problems and dilemmas confronting mankind."[27]

These statements point to two somewhat different types of Islamic issues facing Muslims in the United States. First, there are the classic issues of community survival in a minority context. Islam as a way of life requires certain things that are sometimes difficult to do in the context of a secular society. In that context, concepts such as emigration (hijra), religious exertion (jihad), and mission (da'wa) have special meaning and represent obligations for Muslims.

Second, there are the grand issues of the mission of Muslims in contemporary world history. As modern societies enter the postmodern era, new issues are raised and new approaches must be developed. In this, there is a move away from the old modernist–secularist approaches. Worldviews that see faith and practice as a total way of life may have a particular contribution to make. American Muslims are in a special position and have a special challenge of finding ways to have postmodern society in the United States reflect the Judaeo–Christian–Muslim tradition most Americans share.

Notes

1. Yvonne Yazbeck Haddad and Adair T. Lummis, *Islamic Values in the United States* (New York: Oxford University Press, 1987), p. 155.

2. See, for example, the discussions in John P. Rasmussen, ed., *The New American Revolution: The Dawning of the Technetronic Era* (New York: John Wiley, 1972), Part 1.

3. See, for example, Harvey Cox, *Religion in the Secular City: Toward a Postmodern Theology* (New York: Simon & Schuster, 1984); and Stephen Toulmin, *The Return to Cosmology: Postmodern Science and the Theology of Nature* (Berkeley: University of California Press, 1982).

4. See, for example, Suzanne Haneef, *What Everyone Should Know about Islam and Muslims* (Chicago: Kazi, 1982), p. vii; and Michael Gilsenan, *Recognizing Islam: Religion and Society in the Modern Arab World* (New York: Pantheon, 1982), chap. 1.

5. Gilsenan, *Recognizing Islam*, p. 17.

6. See, for example, the discussions in Robert N. Bellah, *The Broken Covenant, American Civil Religion in Time of Trial* (New York: Seabury, 1975); and Duncan Howlett, *The Fourth American Faith* (Boston: Beacon, 1968).

7. A helpful summary of the views of many organizations involved in the issue of prayers in the schools can be found in Patricia Theiler, "Should States Be Permitted to Allow a Formal Moment of Silence in the Classroom?" *Common Sense* 1:1 (Jan.–Feb. 1985), 35–39.

8. Haneef, *What Everyone Should Know*, p. 43.

9. A short summary of these principles can be found in *1983 Annual Survey of American Law*, published by New York University School of Law. Important cases in establishing this situation are *Price* v. *Johnston*, 334 U.S.266 (1948); *Cooper* v. *Pate* 378 U.S.546 (1964); *Cruz* v. *Beto*, 405 U.S.319 (1972); *Pell* v. *Procunier*, 417 U.S.817 (1974).

10. See, for example, Bryan Wilson, *Religious Sects* (New York: McGraw-Hill, 1970).

11. See, for example, Saad Eddin Ibrahim, "Anatomy of Egypt's Militant Islamic Groups: Methodological Note and Preliminary Findings"; and Nazih N. M. Ayubi, "The Political Revival of Islam: The Case of Egypt." Both of these are in *International Journal of Middle East Studies* 12:4 (1980).

12. Some of the issues and sources for this subject are discussed in John O. Voll, "The Mahdi's Concept and Use of 'Hijrah'," *Islamic Studies*, 26:1 (1987).

13. An interesting discussion of the relationships between the African return movements and the early Islamic organizations can be found in Clifton Ernest Marsh, "The World Community of Islam in the West: From Black Muslims to Muslims (1931–1977)" (Ph.D. dissertation, Syracuse University, 1977), chap. 3.

14. Yvonne Y. Haddad, *A Century of Islam in America* (Washington, D.C.: American Institute for Islamic Affairs, 1986), p. 1.

15. See, for example, the discussion in John Obert Voll, "Soviet Central Asia and China: Integration or Isolation of Muslim Societies," in *Islam in Asia: Religion, Politics, & Society*, ed. John L. Esposito (New York: Oxford University Press, 1987).

16. For one widely read presentation of this type of analysis, see Syed Qutb, *Milestones*, trans. S. Badrul Hasan (Karachi: International Islamic Publishers, 1981).

17. S. Abul A'la Maududi, *The Process of Islamic Revolution* (Lahore: Islamic Publications, 1977), pp. 17–21 and passim.

18. *New York Times*, February 25, 1988.

19. *New York Times*, September 26, 1988.

20. Khurram Murad, *Da'wah Among Non-Muslims in the West* (Leicester: The Islamic Foundation, 1986/1406), p. 12.

21. Ismail R. Faruqi, "The Path of Dawah in the West," *The Muslim World League Journal* 14: 7–8 (Rajab–Shaban 1407/March–April 1987), 56.

22. Murad, *Da'wah Among Non-Muslims*, p. 14.

23. See, for example, Cox, *Religion in the Secular City*.

24. Arnold Toynbee, *Civilization on Trial* (London: Oxford University Press, 1948; reprinted with *The World and the West.* (New York: Meridian Books, 1958), p. 182.

25. Bernard Lewis, *Race and Color in Islam* (New York: Harper & Row, 1970), pp. 1–6 and passim.

26. Faruqi, "The Path of Dawah in the West," p. 55.

27. Haneef, *What Everyone Should Know*, p. 184.

15

American Foreign Policy in the Middle East and Its Impact on the Identity of Arab Muslims in the United States

Yvonne Yazbeck Haddad

Muslim identity in the United States has been influenced by the American environment in general and by individual and corporate experiences of immigrants in various American localities during the last hundred years; it is also conditioned by the distinctive self-perceptions that immigrants bring with them to the United States.[1] This identity is clarified and molded daily by the treatment Muslims receive in their places of residence and employment,[2] in the schools,[3] and by the courts.[4] It is altered and negotiated repeatedly as a result of the discrimination they experience as they deal with the images projected about them by the host society in literature,[5] the movies,[6] and the media.[7] And, in a very dramatic way, it has been shaped during the last four decades by the vagaries of American foreign policy in the Middle East and America's relations with Muslim countries throughout the world.[8]

The Muslim community in the United States comprises a variety of peoples from more than sixty nations who represent different linguistic, national, and racial backgrounds. They have emigrated in several waves, reflecting changes in American immigration policies as well as sociopolitical and economic upheavals overseas. Like other immigrants, Muslims represent myriad interests and goals. Their immigration was initiated in an effort to enjoy the various benefits the United States provides: economic and social enhancement, political refuge, and religious freedom. Over the years they have shaped and reshaped their social and religious organizations to reflect the changing interests and growing concerns of the members of their community. A variety of factors impinge on the formation of their identity,[9] of which this study considers one particularly important aspect—the influence of American foreign policy in the Middle East. Although it is clear that this factor is increasingly significant in forging an American Muslim consciousness among the various ethnic and national groups that constitute the Muslim community in the United States, this study focuses on those persons who seem to be most immediately affected, the immigrants from Arab countries.

Immigration from the Arab world to the United States began around 1880 and has continued to the present. Each wave of immigrants has brought with it the distinctive identity fashioned by its generation. At the turn of the century, Muslims from Arab countries were identified as "Ottoman subjects." The colonial experience formed their identity in relation to specific nation-states; they were seen as Syrian, Lebanese, Palestinian, Jordanian, and so on. More recently, these immigrants have defined themselves first in relation to Arab nationalism, dominant in the postcolonial period, and then to the more recent phenomenon of Islamism.[10]

The immigrants also brought with them their home country's perception of the United States at the time of their emigration. Until the 1950s, America was for many both the land of opportunity, where "gold grows on trees," and a model of virtue. Its popularity was based, among other things, on President Wilson's espousal in 1919 of the right of subject peoples to self-determination. America was perceived as champion of a righteous world political order that endowed national communities with the right to independence and to free choice of their own form of government.[11]

American Foreign Policy in the Middle East

The United States assumed an active role in Middle Eastern affairs some forty years ago. Vigilant against communist infiltration and anxious to fill what was considered a "vacuum" in the area, America through the Truman Doctrine (1947) proclaimed its foreign policy to be one of containment. In assuming the leadership of the free world in the 1950s, the United States became entrenched in a cold war mentality that divided humanity into two camps, free nations and communist nations. Third World countries were increasingly seen as objects of manipulation and reduced to the level of potential puppets to be courted, bribed, pressured, cajoled, or manipulated as clients of the major powers. This mentality generally granted these nations no independent judgment, local interests, separate identity, or national pride unless it was somehow linked in subservient status to the United States or the Soviet Union. It insisted that nations must choose allegiance to one or the other of the two superpowers, doing their bidding and fulfilling their interests—a choice necessitated by the polarization of military strength.

Each succeeding U.S. administration has produced a new doctrine, which has generally been defended as consistent with previous policies and actions of the American government and as a continuing clarification of stated American values of democracy and freedom. However, such presidential doctrines have been perceived in the Middle East as increasingly inconsistent with these values, giving the impression of an erosion in America's support of them. The Muslim community has come to suspect that expedient justification of specific actions plays a major role in the development of succeeding policies.

The Truman Doctrine of 1947 promised U.S. support for free people who were resisting "attempted subjugation by armed minorities or by outside pressures." For many immigrants from the Arab world, this promise should have qualified the Palestinians for American support in resisting the foreign Jewish armed terrorist gangs such as the Haganah, Stern, and Irgun, which were trying to displace them. Consequently, on May 15, 1948, when President Truman recognized the State of Israel eleven minutes after Ben Gurion declared its formation, Arab-Americans perceived this recognition to be without regard for the hopes or even the rights of the Arab people.[12] It shattered the image of American political values held not only by Arabs overseas but by the immigrant communities in this country.

Truman's recognition of Israel initiated forty years of American foreign policy in the Middle East and resulted in what Muslims believe to be an injustice inflicted on the Palestinian people, primarily to win an election. Truman is reported to have explained his action with the words, "I am sorry, gentlemen, but I have to answer to hundreds of thousands who are anxious for the success of Zionism; I do not have hundreds of thousands of Arabs among my constituents."[13] The immigrants were also dismayed at the intense pressure the American delegation to the United Nations applied to other countries to win support for the State of Israel.

America's recognition of Israel and its continuing support for that nation has been wrapped in ethical and ideological justifications. The language used to defend administration policy and actions in the Middle East is experienced by Arabs with intense disappointment as masking subterfuge, duplicity, and hypocrisy. It is clear that since 1947 the stated American foreign policy objectives in the Middle East have continued to be governed by domestic considerations regardless of apparent conflicts with cherished American values.[14] There have been some exceptions from which Arab Muslims have drawn temporary hope. Eisenhower's willingness to apply American pressure to secure the withdrawal of Britain, France, and Israel from Sinai after the 1956 war became the hallmark by which Arabs judged the United States. "If we agree that armed attack can properly achieve the purposes of the assailant," he said on national television on February 20, 1957, "then I fear that we have turned back the clock of international order."[15] His stance was perceived as proof not only that America can influence policies in Israel, but also that, given a strong president, it can live up to its moral and ethical commitments and ideals of an international moral order regardless of partisan politics.

The war of 1967 can be seen as a watershed in Arab-American relations. It followed a period in which the Democratic administrations of John Kennedy (the first American president to sell arms to Israel) promulgated the Kennedy Doctrine, which affirmed, "We will act promptly and decisively against any nation in the Middle East which attacks its neighbors." Lyndon Johnson, by sending American offensive weapons to Israel, had shifted the policy of even-handedness Eisenhower fostered. In the minds of many American Muslims, America's apparent willingness to abandon Eisenhower's principle that nations should not be allowed to hold on to territory acquired by war is the direct cause of present conditions in the Middle East. American acquiescence to Jewish pressures to allow Israel to retain those territories is seen increasingly as being directly linked to two persistent factors: government accountability to the Jewish lobby and Israeli intransigence.[16]

Successive American administrations since the 1967 war have placated Arabs over the rights of the Palestinians in the Occupied Territories while concurrently providing Israel with economic and military support to maintain the occupation. On December 9, 1969, Richard Nixon's Secretary of State William Rogers stated that U.S. policy is to refuse to support changes in recognized political boundaries that are executed through conquest, other than minor ones agreed on for reasons of mutual security. "We do not support expansionism," he said. "We believe troops must be withdrawn as the resolution provides. We support Israel's security and the security of the Arab states as well. We are for a lasting peace that requires security for both."[17] In actuality, however, implementation of American foreign policy in the Middle East has deviated sharply from the Rogers Plan. The last two decades have been marked by frustration on the part of the Arabs and Muslims in America and the Middle East as they have tried to understand what is increasingly described as American "hypocrisy" in the Middle East. Nixon himself seems to have been aware of that hypocrisy when he wrote in his memoirs: "I knew that the Rogers Plan could never be implemented, but I believed it was important to let the Arab world know that the United States did not automatically dismiss its case regarding the occupied territories. . . . "[18]

The 1970s were marked by increased distress in Arab circles that precipitated attacks by the Palestinian Liberation Organization, (PLO) against Israeli targets, resulting in increased anti-Arab sentiment in the United States. A scheme known as Operation Boulder placed Arab-Americans under FBI surveillance and produced some rash statements from American leaders, including the public accusation by then Congressman Gerald Ford that Arab-Americans were agents of Communist China.

Under the administration of Jimmy Carter the perceived double standard continued, culminating in the Camp David agreement. This accord, so highly acclaimed in the West, is perceived by Arabs as a wedge to divide the Arab world, isolate Egypt, and give Israel a free hand to rearrange the map of the Middle East.[19] Early in his tenure, President Carter in a public statement in Clinton, Massachussetts, appeared to affirm the right of the Palestinians to self-determination, saying that "There has to be a homeland provided for the Palestinian refugees who have suffered for many, many years."[20] After the Camp David agreement, however, Israel appears to have assumed the right to continue to establish Jewish settlements in the West Bank by appropriating Arab land. Carter, under strong and vocal pressure from the Israeli lobby, and to the intense disappointment of the American Muslim community, acquiesced.[21]

While other administrations were able to maintain some semblance of evenhandedness, however shallow, the Reagan administration rarely bothered to distance itself from Israel's interests.[22] Ronald Reagan came to the presidency during a period of heightened fear of "things Islamic." The fall of the Shah and the establishment of the Islamic Republic in Iran, coupled with the holding of American hostages for 444 days by Iranian students, were dramatically reported by an American press, which tended to blame Islam and Muslims for everything contrary to the interests of America. Reagan played on this fear during his administration to garner the support of the American people for his policies.[23] His tenure as president was a period of intense stress for the Muslim community in the United States.[24] Statements by members of his administration were seen as racist and derogatory to Arabs and Muslims, and the perception of an administration cast in a religious aura of Judeo-Christian righteousness set on stamping out Islam and Islamic fervor took root.

This perception was aggravated by media reports of the uncompromising militancy of the Iranian regime toward the United States. Having come to power by capitalizing on Carter's moral anguish and apparent indecision in dealing with Iran—which became a symbol of American impotence—Reagan began his presidency with what was perceived as a blatant diatribe against Islam and Muslims. In an interview with *Time* magazine in November 1980, he was quoted as saying that Muslims believe the way to heaven is to lose their lives fighting Christians and Jews. Objections of the Muslim American community to this statement went unheeded.[25] Successive statements and policies articulated during his administration did not dispel Muslim concern, but rather intensified them as the administration became increasingly embroiled in Israeli adventures in Lebanon, Iraq, Tunisia, and Iran. Toward the end of his administration this involvement shifted Reagan's perception of the "Evil Empire" he felt heroically called upon to defeat from Communism to Islam.

It seems clear that when he assumed office, Reagan and his first Secretary of State, Alexander Haig, adopted the Israeli view of the Middle East. They announced that the cornerstone of U.S. foreign policy would shift from human rights concerns to combatting terrorism. In the process, the United States cast an aura of approval over Israeli intervention and heavy-handed exploits in Lebanon. (The Israeli government had adopted the practice of referring to the Palestinians as terrorists with the result that all Israeli policies of destruction of homes, indiscriminate bombings, deportations, and abductions were legitimated as a means of response to terrorism.)

George Schultz, who succeeded Haig as secretary of state, was the strongest supporter of antiterrorism and his most vigorous attacks on terrorist activities were usually staged before Zionist audiences. The Reagan administration appropriated the Likud policy of referring to Palestinians as terrorists rather than as people. Secretary Schultz announced that he favored the Israeli model of dealing with terrorists, leading to the establishment of the Jonathan Institute to combat terrorism with assistance from Zionist sources. The Israeli UN ambassador's book on terrorism was necessary reading for members of the administration. Even the deliberations of members of the Reagan administration were determined by what the Israelis told them were legitimate questions to ask, answers to contemplate, and options to follow. Israel was cast as America's partner in being a target of terrorism. As a consequence, and with unfortunate ramifications for American Muslims, American pluralistic society was increasingly defined by the administration as Judeo-Christian.

The image of America as a nation that fears and hates Islam has been enhanced by a chain of events and cycle of American reactions, generally precipitated by intimate American involvement in the Israeli war in Lebanon. The following evidence can be cited:

• In 1982 massacres were committed at the refugee camps of Sabra and Shatila in which more than nine hundred Palestinian civilians were killed. The Muslim community worldwide was appalled by what one American Muslim termed "the conspiracy of silence" around these atrocities. Although it is argued that the role of the Israelis was probably limited to running interference while the Phalangists perpetrated the atrocities, the United States is held accountable not only because it was American arms, money, and political support that empowered the Israelis to facilitate such actions, but more pointedly, that the United States had guaranteed the security of the civilian population of the camps against such atrocities. Furthermore, while the Kahan Commission (the 1983 Israeli High Commission) determined that several Israeli generals allowed the atrocities to take place, the American government accepted the credentials of one of these generals, General Amos Yaron, who was assigned as military attache to the Israeli embassy despite the protests of the Arab American Anti-Discrimination Committee.[26] The Canadian government, however, denied his credentials.

• In 1985 the Israeli air force bombed the Palestine Liberation Organization headquarters in Tunis, killing sixty-two people, mostly civilians. In commenting on the attack, President Reagan said that it was "justifiable." He later retracted his statement when American diplomats and the press reported the international Muslim outrage and especially Tunisia's hostile reaction to America.

• When the hijacking of the cruiseship *Achille Lauro* resulted in the death of Leon Klinghoffer, an American Jew, President Reagan condemned the act repeatedly on television, in speeches, and in interviews. In his quest to punish the perpetrators, he went so far as to send the air force to intercept the plane carrying the hijackers to bring them to justice. However, when Alex Odeh, an Arab-American Christian, was killed a few days later by a bomb the FBI believes was planted by the Jewish Defense League, President Reagan was silent.[27] The alleged perpetrators escaped justice by taking refuge in a settlement in Israel. To date, the American government has not tried to extradite them, nor has any attempt been made to bring them to justice. Attacks on various mosques and Islamic institutions throughout the United States, including the bombing of the Houston mosque, were met with silence by the administration. This has raised serious questions in the minds of American Muslims as to whether Americans in general and the American administration in particular base the value of human lives on the victim's religious or ethnic affiliation.

• Terrorist attacks on the Rome and Vienna airports on December 27, 1985, were condemned severely and repeatedly by President Reagan, especially because a six-year-old child was killed. When the American air force attacked Azzizaya in Libya on April 15, 1986, Muammar Ghaddafi's adopted two-year-old daughter was killed. Secretary Schultz, asked on television what he thought America achieved by that act, responded, "We feel good about ourselves."

• The duplicity involved in what came to be known as the Irangate Affair is now well known. Claiming to support Iraq and the security of the Arab Gulf nations, America's shipment of offensive weapons to the Khomeini regime in fact undermined that security.

• Hostility toward Palestinians is so evident in the U.S. Congress that some Arabs and Arab-Americans have begun to refer to the American legislative branch of government as "The Hostages on the Hill," a reference to their accountability to Zionist pressure the American Israel Political Action Committee has repeatedly boasted about. It was a bill initiated by Congress that closed the PLO office in Washington.[28]

• In 1987, the Immigration and Naturalization Service initiated deportation proceedings against seven Palestinians and a Kenyan (popularly referred to as the L A 8) who were accused of minor visa violations but "treated as if they were criminal threats."[29] This attempt and the declassified FBI report that revealed the Reagan administration was renovating army camps in the South as a contingency plan for possible internment of Arabs and Iranians have increased the fear and alienation of the U.S. Muslim population.

The Dilemma of the Muslims of America

As these examples suggest, a major element in the experience of the Muslim community in the United States during the last forty years has been a rising sense of the hypocrisy of succeeding presidential administrations. Muslims feel they are living in a country that is hostile not only to their ethnic origins, but increasingly to Islam and Muslims in general. Their situation has been likened to being on a roller coaster on which they are forced to experience new heights of distortion and villification.

Arab Muslims have become increasingly aware of the power of the Israeli lobby, which to them appears to have "hijacked" the American government and subverted it to Israeli interests. Other Americans who have experienced the power of the lobby share their view. To some Washington experts it is quite evident that America is unable to execute an independent American foreign policy in the interest of the United States. Former Assistant Secretary of State Richard Murphy grumbled that American policy is controlled by Israel and its allies, whose approval is necessary before any action can be taken. Identifying Jordan as a friend in need of American assistance against outside aggression and terrorism, he acknowledged that this assistance can be provided only when we are able to persuade Israel that the security of Jordan is in Israel's interest.[30] Donald McHenry, former U.S. Ambassador to the United Nations, expressed a similar opinion when he acknowledged that the Israeli lobby prevents the United States from freely pursuing its own national interests in the Middle East.[31]

American strategic goals in the Middle East are generally listed as maintaining access to Middle East oil, preserving the state of Israel, perpetuating good relations with pro-Western Arab nations, maintaining peace and stability, and preventing Communist penetration of the area.[32] It is clear, however, that American foreign policy has had contradictory results. Growing dissatisfaction with these policies and statements as well as the apparent American distaste for independent Arab nationalist tendencies in the Middle East have been perceived as being inconsistent with American ideals and values and undermining the independence of the Arab nations. They can be seen as the direct cause of Marxist and socialist gains in the Arab world in the 1950s and 1960s. America's uncritical support of Israel since the 1967 war and the growing disenchantment with the U.S. administrations that have supported Israel's demands and policies with seeming disregard for the human, political, and civil rights of the Palestinians have led to growing popular support for radical Islamic ideologies hostile to the United States. Islamic militancy is consistently described by its advocates as a response to Christian, Jewish, and atheistic (Marxist) militancy.

American policies appear to be governed by a variety of considerations and principles, which are increasingly perceived by Muslims worldwide as prejudiced against Arabs, Islam, and Muslims. The proclaimed religious affinity between Israel and the United States based on a heritage shared by Judaism and Christianity fails to acknowledge Islam as a moral force in bringing about peace in the international order. Statements by American government officials, especially members of Congress, have revealed prejudice against the "backward" Palestinians who are to receive the benefits of Israel's sharing of Western enlightenment and civilization. Israel continues to be depicted as the "underdog," a fledgling nation fighting against formidable odds. The massive infusion of American arms into the Israeli arsenal is defended as an attempt to maintain the balance of power in the region. And more recently, some in the Department of Defense have been describing Israel as "the unsinkable aircraft carrier," providing American troops with support facilities for possible future military engagements in the area.

Israel's supporters[33] have increasingly presented Israel and the United States as inextricably bound together in a common destiny in the area. Israel is depicted as the incarnation of American utopian ideals as well as the defender and maintainer of American values in the Middle East. Arabs, however, wonder why Americans, who theoretically advocate separation of religion and state and tolerate varieties of religious expression under the umbrella of pluralism, support Israel in its insistence on Jewish identity as a prerequisite for citizenship, denying the political and human rights of Muslims and Christians under its occupation. Israel not only bans the return of Palestinian gentiles to their homeland, but also restricts its Christian and Muslim citizens to specified living areas[34] and limits their access to resources which are monopolized and confiscated by the state (such as education, water, and land).[35]

The dilemma of Muslims living in the United States is exacerbated by an awareness that the truth about the Arab world, Islam, and Muslims is being distorted for political expediency by those in office. Arabs are repeatedly cast by members of the Congress and administration as intransigent and bent on the destruction of Israel. Yet, in many cases, once out of office these same officials freely admit to the truth. For example, in a joint article in the February 1983 *Readers Digest*, former Presidents Ford and Carter wrote that "the Arab leaders have indicated a readiness . . . to live in peace with Israel." Deputy Secretary of State Kenneth W. Dam said on April 11, 1983: "Today Arab leaders are talking about *how*—not *whether*—to make peace with Israel."[36] Even Syria, considered by Israel as the rejectionist state, has been acknowledged as willing to make peace.[37] Officials who have been candid about the role of Israel in influencing U.S. policies include former Secretary of State Cyrus Vance, former U.S. Ambassador to Syria Talcott Seelye, and William Quandt, of the National Security Council in the Carter administration.[38] Arab-Americans continue to be dismayed that those in public office who have access to accurate information and could set the record straight fail to do so.

American Foreign Policy and the Forging of the Muslim Identity

Arab immigrants at the turn of the century experienced prejudice at the local level, and in some cases were subject to discriminatory immigration policies on the part of the U.S. government. However, since the United States at that time was not heavily involved in the Middle East, American foreign policy had little impact on their identity. With the growth of Zionism in the American Jewish community and its attendant influence on American policy, however, things changed drastically.

The reputed Zionist solicitation of funds in the 1940s with such slogans as "Pay a dollar, kill an Arab" evoked the natural anger of Arab immigrants as they sought to redress this negative propaganda. Their frustration was heightened by the awareness that Arab communities were small and scattered throughout the United States and that they lacked organizational structures to influence public policy. Their feelings of marginality were intensified as they recognized they had no input to shape American priorities, opinion, or foreign policy and insignificant access to the press to help correct the false reports being published about their heritage. In response, a few individuals became involved in gathering information, debating and lecturing to anyone who would listen, trying to present a fair and undistorted image of the Arab people.

By the middle of the century some efforts were being made to provide organization and structure to the Arab Islamic community in the United States. In 1952, under the leadership of the World War II veteran Abdullah Igram, they formed the Federation of Islamic Associations in the United States and Canada (FIA) to bring together more than twenty immigrant Muslim congregations to coordinate efforts to provide for the social, cultural, and religious needs of the community. Modeled on similar associations within American society, the FIA served both to provide a sanctioned context for young Muslim people to gather and to present Islam in its legitimate context as one of the several religions constituting the fabric of America. While some newspapers report Igram's appearance before several civic groups in Iowa to describe the Palestinian situation, the FIA in his time does not seem to have engaged in any significant efforts to raise Arab political consciousness.[39] What it did, however, was provide the bureaucratic structure to seek recognition of Islam as a religion by the U.S. armed services. The gesture by the Eisenhower administration to allow Muslims to declare their religion on their identification tag was seen by the Muslim community as an important step in the legitimation of Islam in the American context.

The 1956 war in the Middle East had an electrifying effect on immigrants from the Arab world. The Eisenhower administration's insistence on the withdrawal from Sinai of the occupation forces of Britain, France, and Israel and its condemnation of Israeli aggression in 1956 restored some of the community's confidence that America would live up to its stated ideals. America once again appeared eager to uphold international law and order. The withdrawal of the tripartite forces was perceived as the final defeat of colonialist subjugation of the people of the area and confirmed Arab beliefs in America's devotion to fair play and justice. Gamal Abdul Nasser, whose position throughout the Arab world was enhanced as a result, became a hero for many Arab immigrants in the United States. They began to identify their Arab heritage with pride rather than to stress the regional or national identities with which they had previously associated themselves. Nasser's resistance to the West fostered the hope that Arabs really could withstand outside forces perceived as bent on destroying the people of the area. His "victory" inspired the new generation, who began to believe in the potential of the future, vindication of the Arab cause, and their emergence as full participants in the modern world. In short, it provided an identity of which to be proud.[40]

By the middle of the 1960s, Arab identity had become a badge of pride for Arabs overseas as well as for the recent immigrants. It superseded regional identification and became a sign of hope that unity under an ethnic and linguistic umbrella could be the key to belonging. The 1967 war and the biased reports it received in the American press heightened the immigrants' awareness of their marginality and inability to get fair coverage of the issues. It gave birth to several Arab-American organizations. These included the National Association of Arab-Americans, the Arab-American Anti-Discrimination Committee, and the Association of Arab-American University Graduates, Inc.[41] (This identity also coincided with American acceptance of the "hyphenated" ethnic identities as a consequence of the Black Power Movement in the United States.)[42]

In 1963, the Muslim Student Association (MSA) was formed on several American campuses, organized by a small group of foreign Muslim students disenchanted with Arab nationalism. The majority were from the Muslim Brotherhood, with a substantial number of Pakistanis who found Arab identity restrictive. The MSA had a very modest beginning, but its membership grew dramatically in the period after the 1967 war, and became especially strong after the war of 1973 in which the United States seemed not even to pretend to be evenhanded in its Middle East policy. It is during the early 1970s, for example, that Ismail al-Faruqi, a Palestinian immigrant noted for his writings on Arab nationalism, was converted to an Islamic identity and became one of the most important leaders of the movement and its most eloquent defender in the United States.

The fall of the Shah's regime has been a very important factor in heightening Islamic identity in the United States. The Shah was perceived as the enemy of the Arab people because of his role in providing Israel with oil. Furthermore, American foreign policy under Kissinger had empowered the Shah at Arab expense. Iran, Israel, and Turkey had been designated as the nations who were to act as surrogates to contain the Arabs, and the United States had allowed the Shah to acquire strategically located Arab islands in the Gulf. His removal from power fueled the belief that an organized Islam could provide the energy to mobilize the masses to remove corrupt rulers as well as Arab regimes perceived as lackeys of the United States and impotent before Israel.[43] This renewed hope in the power of Islam has been extremely significant in the thinking of many Muslims as they seek to define their role in the context of American society.

Several realities have been particularly important in recent years in determining Arab Muslim's sense of self-identification in America. One of these is the growth in the power of the Israeli lobby in the United States, which has had a profound impact on the American Muslim community.[44] American acquiescense in Israel's invasion of Lebanon and the inability of Arab regimes to do anything to protect Arab people from the long arm of the Israeli military has led to further erosion in the perception of America's evenhandedness. Arabs are aware that Israel is empowered by the infusion of $3 billion of U.S. taxpayers's money per year and the use of U.S. veto power in the United Nations. They see this as instrumental in Israel's ability to flount international laws and carry out its colonialist policies in the occupied territories with impunity. They believe that the 1982 invasion of Lebanon and its aftermath of deteriorating relations were possible because of the power of the Israeli lobby through its ability to influence American public opinion and the members of Congress.[45] This concern about the power of the lobby and about the apparent resulting disenfranchisement of Arab-Americans has produced a variety of options for Muslim life in the United States. Some Muslims have abandoned any hope of setting the American government on an evenhanded course and have opted for a marginalized existence in terms of political involvement. Others have made the opposite choice, seeking as much input as possible in the American political process.

It is clear, that American foreign policy has had a profound influence on Muslim identity and on the ways in which Muslims choose to participate in the American process. U.S. dealings in the Middle East over the last forty years appear to have alienated the majority of its Muslim citizens. The last decade has been a particularly difficult period for Muslims as they have tried to function in an atmosphere charged with hostility. As a result they have sought to frame their identity in a number of ways, their choices resulting in special sets of characteristics, perceptions, and attitudes.[46] In very general terms they fall into two major groupings.

1. Some continue to see themselves first as Arab-Americans. Though Muslim, they are generally secularists who see religion as a personal matter between the individual and God. They emphasize an ethnic identity based on heritage and linguistic affinity, which includes Christians and Jews from Arab countries. Comprising the majority of Arab Muslims in America, they are of two general types. Some can be called American Muslims—that is, persons who are consciously both American citizens and members of the community of Islam and want to hold America accountable to its ideals and values. Others are what might be called the "unmosqued," nominally Muslim but finding their identity in ethnic or political organizations.

Arab-Americans have often decided to reach out to other sectors of society and work together for a better America, a place where people outside the Judeo-Christian faith can feel at home, an America that will be transformed to live up to its potential and to its ideals. They include a large number of second-, third-, and fourth-generation American-born Muslims. Among them is Abdeen Jibara, president of the Arab-American Anti-Discrimination Committee, whose leadership he shares with its founder, former U.S. Senator James Aburezk of Lebanese Christian background. This organization, which includes American Christians and Muslims of Arab background, has striven since the late 1970s to sensitize Americans to the presence of Arabs in their midst, to the prevalent racism against Arabs, and to the inconsistent policies of the American government in the Middle East.

Arab-American Muslims take exception to the portrayal of Islam as having a different value system from the Judeo-Christian tradition of the dominant culture, as well as to the frequent accusation that it espouses violence. They are concerned that America itself is not living up to its ideals. This perception is well expressed in the following excerpts from a speech Queen Noor of Jordan delivered in the United States:

> We grow increasingly concerned about the widening gap between America's principled declarations and what we perceive as predominantly unhelpful American actions in the Middle East. . . . I see an America that promotes negotiations between Arabs and Israelites, but itself refuses to open a dialogue with the chosen representatives of the Palestinian people. . . . I see an America that tacitly recognizes the illegality of Israeli settlements in occupied Arab lands, but continues to increase its annual aid to Israel, thereby actively helping to perpetuate those very settlements. . . . I see an America that asks Jordan and the Palestinians and other Arabs to show moderation and boldness, while America's military aid to Israel is characterized by immoderation in quantity as well as a distressing lack of resolve in applying the letter or spirit of the legal sanctions that govern the use of the weaponry it supplies. . . . I see an America that speaks of justice and peace in the Middle East, but helps perpetuate Israel's illegal practices by generous foreign aid. . . . I see an America that claims to value Arab moderation, but pursues policies of virtually unquestioning support for Israel. . . . I see an America that expects the Arabs to enter negotiations for peace without any preconditions, while America's own Middle East policy continues to reflect many of Israel's longstanding pre-conditions. . . . I believe it is time for the United States to

ask itself the hard questions that others are asking throughout the Middle East and throughout much of the rest of the world: Why does this country that gave the world the concept of self-determination refuse to apply it to the Palestinians?[47]

2. A second category includes those who might be called Muslims in America, persons who identify themselves specifically as Muslims and are often alienated from American culture. They, too, fall into two general subtypes.

On the one hand are persons whose feelings of alienation and distrust have led to a withdrawal from social and political life in America. Muslim Americans who have opted out of the political system emphasize the relationship of God to man as primary and do not try to influence the world around them. Caught in the tension between an idealized image of the home country, where brotherhood and community support abound, and the reality of the experience of an uncaring, and at times hostile environment, these immigrants look to a reconstituted community with a coherent and harmonious purpose under the umbrella of Islam as a way of fitting into the context of American society. Theirs is an Islam that focuses all efforts in this life on the hope of recompense in the hereafter. Among these are groups such as the Tableeghi Jamaat, whose emphasis is primarily on spiritual matters.

The other kind of Muslims in America are those who see America's hostility toward Islam as a continuation of the Crusades. They are dedicated to transforming this reality. Their goal is to bring about peace and justice through the conversion of America to Islam. This identity has been appropriated by a growing number of Muslims during the last decade. In this view Islam is a unique order of life established by God for humanity, in which religion and politics must be intertwined to ensure justice and freedom. It provides special cohesiveness and support to a community going through a troubled period of perceived rejection, the object of hate and fear. Muslims who opt for this vision identify with a universal view of brotherhood that does not discriminate among human beings according to race, color, language, or national origin. The scope of this vision is universal; it seeks the conversion of the world. Separateness in the U.S. context is thus contained and experienced not as the result of rejection by the host culture, but rather as a divine commission made necessary because America has deviated from a moral life devoted to God.

Muslims in America react to American distaste for Islam, to rampant prejudice, and to the perception of being ruled out of the system when national leaders call America a Judeo-Christian country. They affirm that Islam must prevail because America and Israel are scheming to destroy the Islamic faith and the Muslim people. Those who adhere to this identity generally despair of changing the status quo or reforming it. America, they believe, has been coopted by special interest groups, which has caused its deviation from the values and vision that previously merited God's blessing. Thus, America needs not only salvation but also radical transformation that can restore it to its mission, to an America that lives in obedience to God and surrenders to His will, an America that dwells in Islam.

This perspective was well articulated in a sermon, delivered at the Islamic Center of Hartford, Connecticut, in the fall of 1984, by Ibrahim Zaid al-Kilani, vice chairman of the Sharia College at the University of Jordan in Amman, then on a visit sponsored by the U.S. Information Agency.

Fellow Muslims, there is an open season on Muslims in the world. Muslims are targeted for slaughter in Lebanon, Palestine, the Philippines and India. And no one cares! You know, Americans are very sensitive people. They are compassionate; they do not like violence; they care for the oppressed. Today, we were in Boston where there was a huge demonstration against experimentation on mammals. They have Greenpeace; they put their lives on the line in order to protect the seals from being clubbed to death. They protest; they lobby; they march and they raise their voices. When it comes to the death of Muslims, they are silent. Their tax money, their airplanes, their tanks, and their bombs are employed to kill Muslims.

Ponder your fate. You as Muslims are treated as less than animals. Have you heard any outcry to stop the carnage? They dubbed west Beirut as "Muslim" Beirut and that gave the Israelis license to level it. They used fragmentation bombs, phosphorus bombs and even "vacuum" bombs to destroy Muslims. What has brought us to this fate? Why have the Christians and the Jews conspired to destroy us? Brothers and sisters, God has revealed to us in the Qur'an that our defeats are due to our faithlessness. As long as we forsake Islam, God will forsake us. As long as we pander after the friendship and approval of the West and ignore God's commandment to obedience and commitment, we shall be the target of elimination by the combined forces of the Judeo–Christian conspiracy.

What has become of the Muslims that we have now become the guinea pigs on which America tests its weapons? What has become of us as a nation that Muslim flesh is chosen for experimentation? Christian bombs are dropped by Jewish boys on Muslims in Beirut in order to determine the potency of phosphorus in burning flesh. Fragmentation bombs are exploded to dismember you. Who is there to defend you? Who will stand up for you? We have no leadership to thunder with your voice, no army to defend you. Why are we helpless? Why has God forsaken us?

The negative media portrayal of things Arab and Islamic has had its toll on the Muslim community in the United States. Muslims continue to wonder what the next chapter in their life in America will be as they struggle to define their future in an atmosphere of apparent continuing hostility towards Islam. Will the Muslims of North America survive as a vibrant religious community, able to participate fully and freely in its religious mosaic and to help define its future as a pluralistic society? The realization that the religion of Islam clearly is not appreciated by many in the United States may mean that some will feel that the only option for Muslims is a marginalized existence in this society, albeit one that is freely and consciously chosen. Whatever the alternative, American Muslims cherish the hope that their children will not so identify with Western culture that they abandon the faith, and that they will continue to espouse and live by the sacred values of their Islamic heritage.

Notes

1. Yvonne Haddad, *A Century of Islam in America* [Occasional Paper No. 4, Islamic Affairs Program] (Washington, D.C.: The Middle East Institute, 1986).

2. Salim Khan, "A Brief History of Pakistanis in the Western United States," Master's thesis, California State University, Sacramento, 1981.

3. Ayad al-Qazzaz, "Images of the Arab in American Social Science Textbooks," and Sharon McIrvin Abu-Laban, "Stereotypes of Middle East Peoples: An Analysis of Church School Curricula," both in *Arabs in America: Myths and Realities*, ed. Baha Abu Laban and Faith Zeadey, (Wilmette, Il: Medina University Press International, 1975); Samir Ahmad Jarrar, "Images of the Arabs in the United States Secondary Schools Social Studies Textbooks: A Content Analysis and Unit Development," Ph.D. Dissertation, Florida State University, 1976; W. Griswold et al., *The Image of Middle East in Secondary School Textbooks* (New York: Middle East Studies Association of North America, 1975); G. Perry, "Treatment of the Middle East in American High School Textbooks," *Journal of Palestine Studies* 4:3 (1975), 46–58; National Association of Arab-Americans, *Treatment of the Arab World and Islam in Washington Metropolitan Area Junior and Senior Textbooks* (Washington, D.C.: NAAA, 1980); Barbara Aswad, "Biases and Inaccuracies in Textbooks: Depictions of the Arab World," in *The Arab World and Arab-Americans: Understanding a Neglected Minority*, ed. Sameer Y. Abraham and Nabeel Abraham (Detroit: Wayne State University Center for Urban Studies, 1981).

4. Phillip K. Hitti, *The Syrians in America* (New York: Doran Press, 1924), p. 88.

5. Edward Said, *Orientalism* (New York: Pantheon, 1978); Janice Terry, "Arab Stereotypes in Popular Fiction," *Arab Perspectives*, April 1982; Janice Terry, "The Arab Israeli Conflict in Popular Literature," *American-Arab Affairs*, fall 1982; Janice Terry, "Images of the Middle East in Contemporary Fiction," in Edmund Ghareeb, ed., *Split Vision: Portrayal of Arabs in the American Media* (Washington, D.C.: American-Arab Affairs Council, 1983), pp. 315–26.

6. "From 1984 to the present, a period of nearly two and one-half years, this writer has documented nineteen films that focus on Arab portrayals. The image of the Arab in most films parallels the image of the Jew in pre-Nazi Germany. The cinema of Nazi Germany offered viewers the Jews, as scapegoat." Jack J. Shaheen, "The Hollywood Arab: 1984–86," *Mideast Monitor*, reprinted and distributed by the Arab-American Anti-Discrimination Committee.

7. Mary C. McDavid, "Media Myths of the Middle East: The U.S. Press on the War in Lebanon," G. Neal Lendenmann, "Arab Stereotyping in Contemporary American Political Cartoons," Patricia A. Karl, "In the Middle of the Middle East: The Media and the U.S. Foreign Policy," and Jack G. Shaheen, "The Image of the Arab on American Television," all in Ghareeb, *Split Vision*.

8. Hatem I. Hussaini, "The Impact of the Arab–Israeli Conflict on Arab Communities in the United States," in *Settler Regimes in Africa and the Arab World*, ed. Ibrahim Abu-Lughod and Baha Abu Laban (Wilmette, Ill.: The Medina University Press International, 1974), pp. 201–22; Michael W. Suleiman, "The Effect of American Perceptions of Arabs on Middle East Issues," in Ghareeb, *Split Vision*.

9. Yvonne Haddad, *The Muslim Experience in the United States*, (New York: Oxford University Press, forthcoming).

10. Yvonne Haddad, "Nationalist and Islamist Tendencies in Contemporary Arab-American Communities," in Hani Faris, ed., *Arab Nationalism and the Future of the*

Arab World (Belmont Mass.: Association of Arab-American University Graduates, Inc., 1986), pp. 141–59.

11. Thus, when the General Syrian Congress in Damascus adopted a resolution expressing a desire to establish a constitutional monarchy based on democratic principles in 1919, it went on to say, "If, however, the peace conference should insist on establishing a mandate, we ask the United States of America to be the mandatory power, of a period not exceeding 20 years. . . . " Quoted in Mohammad T. Mehdi, *A Nation of Lions, Chained* (San Francisco: New World Press, 1962), p. 59.

12. Mehdi, *A Nation*, p. 35.

13. Public Papers of the Presidents of the United States, *Dwight D. Eisenhower*, 1957 (Washington, D.C.: U.S. Government Printing Office, 1958), p. 151; cf. Mehdi, *A Nation*, p. 95.

14. Examples cited as evidence of this view can be gleaned from American political history concerning the region. They go back to President Roosevelt, who during the presidential campaign of 1944 sent a message to the Annual Conference of the Zionist Organization of America in which he promised that "if elected I shall help to bring about its [Israel's] realization." Shortly afterwards, as a follow-up to a meeting with King Abdul Aziz of Saudi Arabia, he wrote: "I assure you that I would take no action . . . which might prove hostile to the Arab people." Seth P. Tillman, *The United States in the Middle East: Interests and Obstacles* (Bloomington: Indiana University Press, 1989), p. 15.

15. Eisenhower, Public Papers, p. 151.

16. When Henry Kissinger was unable to get any concessions from the Israelis, the Ford Administration declared a "reassessment" of its policy. More than three-fourths of the Senate objected, forcing Kissenger and Ford to withdraw their plans.

17. Quoted in *A Select Chronology and Background Documents Relating to the Middle East*, 2nd rev. ed., Committee on Foreign Relations, U.S. Senate, February 1957 (Washington, D.C.: U.S. Government Printing Office, 1975), pp. 249–50.

18. Richard Nixon, *The Memoirs of Richard Nixon* (New York: Gosset and Dunlap, 1978), p. 479.

19. See, for example, Naseer Aruri, "The United States and Israel: That Very Special Relationship," in Nasser Aruri, Fuad Moughrabi, and Joe Stork, *Reagan and the Middle East* (Belmont, Mass.: Association of Arab–American University Graduates, Inc, 1983), p. 1, where he writes: "What was achieved at Camp David in 1978 and in Washington the following year was at best a separate peace between Egypt and Israel—the fulfillment of a long-cherished Zionist dream."

20. *Weekly Compilation of Presidential Documents, Jimmy Carter*, 1977, 13, 12, March 21, 1977.

21. When Israel accelerated the establishment of settlements in the occupied territories, a matter not allowed under the Camp David agreement, the administration of incumbent Jimmy Carter supported the UN Security Council resolution calling for a halt to such illegal activities. Ambassador Charles Yost said the following: "The United States considers that the part of Jerusalem that came under the control of Israel in the June [1967] war, like other areas occupied by Israel, is occupied territory and hence subject to the provisions of international law governing the rights and obligations of an occupying power. . . . The occupier must maintain the occupied areas as intact and unaltered as possible, without interfering with the customary life of the area, and any changes must be necessitated by immediate needs of the occupation. I regret to say that the actions of Israel in the occupied portion of Jerusalem presents a different picture, one which gives rise to understandable concerns that the eventual disposition of East Jerusalem may be prejudiced, and the rights and activities of the population are already

being affected and altered." This prompted Mayor Koch of New York City to express his fear that Carter would lose the New York State primary. Consequently, Carter carefully reiterated a U.S.–Israeli policy that included "an undivided Jerusalem." Even this apparently did not satisfy the Jewish leadership as Robert S. Strauss, his campaign manager, and Sol M. Linowitz, his special ambassador to the Middle East negotiations, informed him. It was only after he left office that Carter was candid about letting Sadat down on the issue of Jerusalem through this compromise.

22. Richard B. Strauss, a former member of the American Israel Public Affairs Committee wrote that "U.S. Middle East Policy under President Ronald Reagan and Secretary Shultz has 'shifted so dramatically in favor of Israel' that it amounts to nothing less than a 'revolution'. . . " Mr. Strauss quoted an unidentified former State Department official as saying, "We used to have a two-track policy. Now only Israel's interests are considered." Donald Neff, "Reagan Administration Called Most Anti-Arab and Pro-Israel in U.S. History," *Middle East Times* 4: 18 (May 18–24, 1986), 1 and 20. Neff also quotes one former U.S. diplomat who refused to be identified as saying, "There has never been an administration that has so completely supported Israel and so completely ignored America's interests in the Arab world."

23. Bob Woodward of the *Washington Post* broke the story that Larry Speaks, White House spokesman, misled the press with disinformation about Libya's role in international terrorism to justify the bombing of that nation.

24. The Arab-American Anti-Discrimination Committee accused the Reagan administration of "Arab-bashing" and documented a substantial rise in hate-violence directed against Arab-Americans and their institutions in the United States. "Beginning with the very night of the April 14 bombing [of Libya] a sharp increase in reports were received amounting to 28.6 percent of the annual calls. All these reports were directly attributable to the Libya bombing backlash. The total reports related to the pre and post Libya bombing attack amount to 38.1 percent of the overall reports received in 1986. Albert Mokhiber, *1986 ADC Annual Report on Political and Hate Violence* (Washington, D.C.: ADC, April 1987), p. 25.

25. The Council of Masajid condemned the statement as a "slanderous travesty of and a fallacious distortion of the teachings of Islam." They cabled Reagan, saying "We consider this matter as transcending politics and a flagrant violation of Muslim rights as enshrined in the U.S. Constitution." "Mosque Council Condemns Reagan's Attack on Islam," *Majallat al-Masajid* 2: 2 (Feb. 1981), 17–18.

26. Three Palestinian women survivors of the massacre sued General Yaron under the Nuremberg Principles, drafted by the United Nations' International Law Commission, as being responsible for war crimes and crimes against humanity. The American court agreed with his defense lawyers that he could not be brought to trial because of diplomatic immunity. "Shatila Survivors Contest Yaron's Immunity Defense," *ADC Times* 8: 5 (July 1987), 3. See also Bob Tutt, "Lawsuit May Put Focus on Arab Plight," *Houston Chronicle*, May 8, 1987, Section 1, p. 30; *ADC Newsletter* 5: 1 (June 1987), 1; *ADC Times* 8: 2 (Feb. 1987), 9.

27. Janice Terry, professor of Middle East history at Eastern Michigan University, spoke about the biased press reporting at a media panel during the Third National Convention of the Arab-American Anti-Discrimination Committee in 1987. "The terrorist murder of Arab-American Alex Odeh in October 1985 did not win the same kind of media attention as the terrorist murder of Leon Klinghoffer during the Achille Lauro incident; the terrorist attack against Palestinian students at the Hebron Islamic College in 1983 got far less press than the terrorist attack on an Istanbul synagogue in 1986. "The Media and Arab-Americans," *ADC Times* 8: 3 (April 1987), 10.

28. "ADC Out in Front to Stop Anti-PLO Bill," *ADC Times* 8: 5 (July 1987), 1.

29. "Mokhiber: ADC Goes to Court," *ADC Newsletter* 5: 1 (June 1987), 1. See also "New Hearing Due in L.A.; ADC vs Meese Going to Appelate Court," *ADC Times* 8: 5 (July 1987), 3.

30. Murphy, "Current Political," p. 11.

31. Paul Findly, "The American Political Process and U.S. Middle East Policy," *American–Arab Affairs* 16 (spring 1986), 5. Findly adds, "in respect to Middle East policy, our government is not a superpower—not even a minor power—in its capacity to fend off pressures by a lobby devoted to the interests of a foreign government" (p. 5).

32. Philip Groisser, *The United States and the Middle East* (Albany: State University of New York Press, 1982), p. 170.

33. See, for example, Nadav Safran, *Israel: The Embattled Ally* (Cambridge, Mass.: Harvard University Press, 1981); Groisser, *The United States.*

34. In 1972, the rights of the Christian inhabitants of Berem and Iqrit were confirmed by the Israeli High Court allowing them to return to their villages from which they were removed after 1948. The Israeli government destroyed all their homes. Golda Meir rejected the Court's decision because "the villagers were gentiles—Maronite and Greek (Melkite) Catholics. Their lands were now occupied by Jewish immigrants. Allowing the original residents to return and rebuild, she noted, would therefore be an 'erosion of Zionist values.'" Edwin M. Wright, *A Tale of Two Hamlets* (Cleveland: The Northeast Ohio Committee on Middle East Understanding, Inc., position paper No. 4, 1973), p. 1. See also Sabri Jiryis, *The Arabs in Israel* (New York: Monthly Review Press, 1976).

35. Not too long ago, a twenty-year Druze veteran of the Israeli Border Guards was denied the right to open a business in a village designated for Jewish residents, even though it had been an Arab village until the 1960s when it was expropriated by the state. Noam Chomsky, *The Fateful Triangle*, p. 159.

36. U.S. Department of State, *Current Policy*, No. 475 (April 11, 1983), 4. See also Harold H. Saunders, *The Middle East Problem in the 1980s* (Washington, D.C.: American Enterprise Institute, 1981), p. 9.

37. See Adeed Dawisha, "Comprehensive Peace in the Middle East and the Comprehension of Arab Politics," *Middle East Journal*, Winter 1983, p. 50; cf. Zeev Schiff, "Dealing With Syria," *Foreign Policy*, summer 1984, p. 102; Robert G. Newmann, "Assad and the Future of the Middle East," *Foreign Affairs*, winter 1983–84, p. 247.

38. Cyrus Vance, *Hard Choices: Critical Years in America's Foreign Policies* (New York: Simon and Schuster, 1983), p. 167; Talcott Seelye, *Christian Science Monitor*, April 9, 1983; William Quandt, "Reagan's Lebanon Policy," *Middle East Journal*, spring 1984, p. 253.

39. Yvonne Y. Haddad, "The Muslim Experience in the United States," *The Link* 12: 4 (Sept.–Oct. 1979).

40. El-Kholy quotes a woman in Detroit who told a Jordanian official accompanying King Hussein in 1959 as saying, "Whenever a party is opened in the name of the Prophet, no one is particularly moved. If it is opened in the name of God, no one cares either. But the name of Gamal Abdul-Nasser electrifies the Hall." Abdo A. Elkholy *The Arab Moslems*, p. 48, See also *An Islamic Lebanese Community*, pp. 37, 87; Said Muhammad Massoud, *I Fought as I Believed* (Montreal, 1976).

41. Edward Said, professor of English and comparative literature at Columbia University, said at the Third Annual Convention of the ADC, "It was a result of 1967 that for the first time, the Arab-American identity came to a crisis of collective self-knowledge. There would [be] no Arab-American organization had it not been for 1967.

And it was because of 1967 and 1973 and 1982 that Arab-Americans discovered that the main issue confronting every Arab-American in this country was the issue of Palestine." Quoted in "Said, Robinson, Conyers: Justice Knows No Borders," *ADC Time* 8: 3 (April 1987), 20.

42. Haddad, "Nationalist" pp. 141–59.

43. Yvonne Haddad, "The Impact of the Islamic Revolution in Iran on the Syrian Muslims of Montreal," in Earle Waugh, Baha Abu-Laban, and Regula Qureshi, eds. *The Muslim Community in North America* (Edmonton: The University of Alberta Press, 1983), pp. 165–81.

44. A visitor to the mosque in Houston will find it has a shelf with hundreds of copies of two books: *The Qur'an* and *They Dare Speak Out*. The latter highlights some of the victories the Israeli lobby has won against any one seeking an independent policy for the United States.

45. For a report on the Hasbara Project whose supporters include key U.S. media executives who support the State of Israel and have used the American media to propagate Israeli interests, see Robert I. Freedman, "Selling Israel to America," *Mother Jones* 12: 11 (Feb./March 1987), 20ff.

46. For a typology of Muslim identity in the United States, see Yvonne Yazbeck Haddad and Adair T. Lummis, *Islamic Values in the United States* (New York: Oxford University Press, 1987), pp. 170–72.

47. Noor al-Hussein, "Peace Efforts: Principles Versus Practices," *American–Arab Affairs* 8 (Spring 1984), 2–3.

16

Convergence and Divergence in an Emergent Community: A Study of Challenges Facing U.S. Muslims

Sulayman S. Nyang

The history of Islam in the United States is not only a story of immigrants searching for economic opportunities in a strange land. It is also the experience of conversion by a small but growing body of indigenous men and women in American society who discover a new way of life and a new belief system that fills a void in their spiritual lives. Islam has also received support from students visiting the United States since the 1930s. But if the main difference among the immigrants has been their sectarian interpretations of the Qur'an and of the life and example of the Prophet Muhammad, the perennial and significant question of race has continued to serve as a wedge between the followers of the Nation of Islam and other heterodox groups, and the orthodox Muslims. This American dilemma, as Gunnar Myrdal described the racial question in U.S. society before the enforced desegregation became the law of the land, manifested itself in the early encounter between immigrant Islam and local groups in American society.[1]

Different reactions to the challenges and opportunities in American society have been described elsewhere as the Elijahian and Webbian approaches to Islamic *da'wa* in American society.[2] An approach is Elijahian when it follows Elijah Muhammad's teachings on the effective and rigid separation of the races; it is Webbian when it takes Muhammad Alexander Russell Webb's view of Islam as a color-blind religion that addresses itself to the plight of all persons in this world. As we show later, the evolution of both the immigrant and indigenous segments of the Muslim *umma* (community) in America reveals these two tendencies. Whereas the majority of the indigenous and immigrant Muslims have embraced an Islam that is color-blind, a pocket of heterodox and sometimes orthodox Sunni Muslims still remains, especially among African–Americans, who see Islam as an ideological weapon in the fight against white racism.[3]

In this chapter our attention is focused on the emerging American Muslim community, which is now estimated to be between 3 million and 5 million.[4]

The constituent elements of this community are immigrants from virtually all parts of the Muslim World and native-born Americans who converted to the faith of Islam (or as these American Muslims themselves like to put it, "they return to their natural religion [*fitra*]"). The history of the immigrant segment of the emerging Muslim community goes back to the last century, as does the rise of Islam among native-born Americans. But Islam among Americans became a national phenomenon only in the 1960s.

Our task here is to show how challenges facing Muslims in the United States, some of which can be traced back to the nineteenth century, affect the nature of Muslim life in America and the responses of the Muslim *umma* to these challenges. Working on the assumption that the Muslim community is not a monolithic group, and taking note of the fact that the indigenous and the immigrant segments of the Muslim community respond differently to some of the challenges facing Muslims, we argue that the differential rates of assimilation to American culture and society have affected the perceptions and attitudes of the different members of the Muslim community in the United States. This study addresses the following challenges: (a) to *maintain an Islamic identity*; (b) to *project and defend Islamic institutions*; (c) to *build Muslim economic structures*; and (d) to *participate in American political life.*

Challenge to Maintain Islamic Identity

One of the most crucial elements in the history and development of a social group is the maintenance of its identity. American Muslims find themselves in a country where identification is defined politically, linguistically, culturally, and ethnically. An American Muslim is therefore, first of all, a U.S. citizen and for this reason carries an American passport that distinguishes him from nationals of other countries in the Muslim world. He is also looked on by his fellow Americans as a member of a racial group and is further classified culturally and religiously as a member of one of the multiple cultural and religious groups of America. Although American social scientists speak much about the civic religion that now dominates the larger American society, the political and cultural pluralism it gives rise to does not necessarily put an end to the feelings and perceptions of religious identity and affiliation. Because of these sociological realities, one can argue that to define properly and maintain effectively a strong identity the American Muslim must recognize that he lives in four concentric circles. He is a U.S. citizen whose political loyalty is to these United States, and he affirms this, accepting all duties expected of citizens and asserting his rights guaranteed by the U.S. Constitution. The loyal response to any national call to serve in the armed forces and the bold assertion of the freedom of speech to do da'wa for Islam are two critical examples of the acid test of the Muslim American identity.

But the American Muslim also lives in other circles of identification. If he were not mindful of the nonracial nature of Islam in its ideal form, the American Muslim, by virtue of his early conditioning in a racially conscious society, could easily trap himself in a world of racial consciousness that cuts him off from other Muslims in different racial groups. This is a major challenge to the emerging Muslim umma. It should be pointed out that other American religions are still grappling with this racial problem. Muslim Americans are neither racially homogeneous nor ethnically monolithic. Because of this sociological fact, one challenge to Muslims is to attempt to build the bridges within the Muslim communities necessary to spare the Muslim Americans the racial divide that presently splits the other Abrahamic religions into multiple ethnic/racial islands.

Since one's identity in American society is not only defined by common national origin and racial similarities, a third factor had developed among American Muslims called ethnic consciousness. This ethnic identity within the Muslim community provides a subtler form of differentiation among the immigrant Muslims. It manifests itself as the number of Muslims from abroad increases and the process of self-identification and self-differentiation begins to be felt. For example, as the number of Arabic-speaking members of a Muslim community increases, a natural segmentation or grouping along national lines begins to take place. The Syrians begin to branch off from the Egyptians, and the Saudis from the Moroccans. The same phenomenon is observable among the South Asians. The Bengalis may regroup themselves in distinction to other South Asians as their numbers increase. Although many Muslim observers of the American scene may argue that this splinterization process is an American phenomenon, it can be argued that it is a natural human tendency. Efforts by Muslim leadership need to be directed to the positive use of such ethnic islandization of the Muslim umma through the creation of bridges between leaders and members of such groups.

In the Muslim segment of the African-American community ethnicity is virtually synonymous with raciality. Because of this peculiar situation in the black community, two tendencies have developed among converts to Islam, which can be called the assimilationist and the simulationist tendencies toward Islamization. The assimilationist approach is what makes the American Muslim convert totally change his way of life to the point that he adopts an Islamic name, an Islamic code of dress to reflect the cultural origins of those who introduced him to Islam, an Islamic code of ethics, and an Islamic consciousness, which negates a great deal of what he was previously socialized to accept as American culture. The assimilationist African-American Muslim begins to see his membership in the Muslim community as an alternative, and sometimes superior, identity to his original ethnic identity. Such a person may come to feel that his Islamic identity is in conflict with his American identity. However, other types of assimilationist African-American Muslims are better able to reconcile their Islamic identity with the secular culture that American sociologists called "Americanity." Two other types can be identified here. One is the assimilationist who immerses himself in Islamic culture but still recognizes his African-American identity. Though he now sees himself as a part of a subculture within the African-American community, he identifies totally with that community in matters that are not related to religion. Such a person usually has a Muslim name and is active in African-American community life. The other is the African-American Muslim who assimilates totally into the Islamic culture, but for a variety of reasons opts for the Americanization of his Islamic culture. This type of African-American Muslim, by virtue of his previous positive attitudes toward American culture and American constitutionalism, sees his new Muslim identity as a way of shedding what he perceives as negative characteristics of his past identity in American society that Islam has helped eliminate in his personal life. Such a person usually has a Muslim first name and an American last name.

In contrast to the assimilationists identity are the simulationists who take a totally different view of Islam. Their decision to embrace the new religion is determined largely by utilitarian considerations. They usually see Islam as a political weapon, a strategy for physical and spiritual survival, and a way of life that can be effectively appropriated in their struggle for racial justice and ethnic freedom. The simulationist is determined to simulate everything within the Muslim community as long as his purpose of self-definition is served. Like the assimilationist he adopts an Islamic name, an Islamic code of dress (not an assimilationist mode of dress), and an Islamic orthodox or sometimes heterodox view of the world. What distinguishes the simulationist in his view and use of Islam in American society? Two types of simulationists can be identified. One redefines his African-American identity in such a way that his new religion makes him different and separate from both the Muslim community and his fellow African-Americans of non-Islamic faith. This was the nature of the relationship between the Nation of Islam and the African-American community, on the one hand, and the Muslim community, on the other. This state of affairs continued up to the transformation effected by Imam Warith Deen Muhammad in the late 1970s. The other simulationist group consists of those who embrace Islam as a religion while still insisting strongly on a black nationalism that calls for the unity of all black people regardless of religion.

In looking at the evolution of the Nation of Islam (NOI), one can see the transformation of that movement from a simulationist group with a heterodox interpretation of Islam to a bona fide Muslim group with an assimilationist philosophy of Islamism and Americanism.[5] In fact, one can argue that this movement, which the late Honorable Elijah Muhammad (1897–1975) inherited from Abdul Wali Farad Muhammad Ali (1897–1929?) in the 1930s has spawned elements that can be placed on the spectrum of identity of both the assimilationists and the simulationists. The two major groups that now claim the legacy of Honorable Elijah Muhammad, that is, the former American Muslim Mission of Imam Warith Deen Muhammad and the reconstituted Nation of Islam under Minister Louis Farrakhan, are good examples of these two views of Islam.[6]

The Challenge to Build and Defend Islamic Institutions

Second in importance only to the question of identity is the challenge to build and defend Islamic institutions. Muslims have been aware of this since the early years of their sojourn in the United States. Both Muslim immigrants and native-born Muslims have tackled this question, although historically they have encountered great difficulty. Most of the Muslim immigrants in the early period were not intending to stay in this country. Because they wanted to strike it rich quickly and return home at the earliest opportunity, their minds were not directed toward institution-building. Furthermore, the overwhelming majority were illiterates, without the intellectual and social resources and leadership potential necessary for dealing with the challenges of building institutions. Efforts toward creating Muslim institutions were half-hearted and sporadic. Organizations formed to deal with such needs generally did not last. There were, however, some notable efforts.

In Ross, North Dakota, a small Muslim community thrived for a while. Historians of Islam in America now identify the first *masjid* (mosque) in that city as the oldest in America.[7] Pittsburgh, Pennsylvania, was the birthplace of the African Muslim Welfare Association of North America (AMWANA)[8] in the late 1920s. We now know that the AMWANA tried to teach Arabic to its members and to provide them with basic instruction on Islam and that a Sudanese Muslim served for a short while as the imam. By the 1930s along the eastern seaboard of the United States and in the Midwest, where Arab, southern European, and other Muslim immigrants settled, the collective efforts of Arabs, Serbians, Turks, Bosnians, Albanians, Ruthenians, and indigenous African-Americans laid the foundations for a Muslim umma. The coming of the Ahmadiyya Movement to America was a major challenge to American Muslims, particularly to those Arab-Americans who felt that their leadership was being usurped by a heterodox group of South Asian Muslims. Its activities in Chicago and Detroit would somehow link some of its early African-American converts to the Nation of Islam.[9] Despite the existence of such orthodox and not so orthodox manifestations of Islam in the Midwest, the fact remains that advocates of Islam among southern European and Middle Eastern Muslims demonstrated very little strength in their efforts at Muslim institution-building.

The period beginning with the end of World War II serves as a new chapter in such efforts. Two factors can be cited as causes of changes in Muslim self-perception and strategies. The first was the decision of a group of second-generation Arab Muslims and their coreligionists from elsewhere in Dar al Islam to organize a national organization, in large part as a result of the impact of events in the Middle East on Arab-Americans, both Christian and Muslim, and the gradual but strong popularity of Gamal Abdul Nasser in Arab communities in America. Many Arab-Americans began to take pride in their heritage and to pay greater attention to events in that part of the world.[10]

The second factor was the emergence of a small but growing body of students from the Muslim world who started their academic sojourn in the United States in the early 1930s. Most of these early students were adventurous young men from colonized regions of Dar al Islam who aspired to secure places in British or European universities and colleges. After World War II, the rivalry between the United States and the USSR as the dominant superpowers led to a cultural contest that resulted in the establishment of a number of educational exchange programs for students from the newly independent Muslim states of Asia and Africa. This, together with the official policies of the individual Muslim countries to send students here, led to a dramatic increase in the Muslim student population in the United States. There soon developed a tension between the Americanized Arab Muslims and their visiting cousins on the American campuses, particularly in the Midwest, where there is a heavy concentration of Arab-American descendants of earlier immigrants. The Muslim Student Association (MSA) developed out of this situation, and its founding fathers included several students who objected to the brand of Islam identified with the host community of Americanized Muslims.[11]

Faced with Americanized Muslims from the Arab world and elsewhere whose knowledge of Islam was very limited, and determined to deal with the challenges from the dangers of both "Americanized Islam" and heretical brands of Islam of the NOI and Ahmadiyya varieties, the young MSA leadership proceeded to establish chapters. These Muslim students were not originally interested in a large-scale institutionalization drive. Rather, they see their task as that of Muslims in a strange environment where their brief sojourn as seekers of knowledge demanded certain sacrifices.

This original attitude toward the American environment changed as the institutional competition between the MSA and the home-grown Arab Muslim organizations became intense. With a large pool of students from different parts of the Muslim world to recruit from, the MSA soon found itself a national organization with many chapters across the United States and Canada. These chapters would gradually serve as nuclei of an emerging professional class of Muslims. Such a phenomenon has been most evident in big urban areas where the Muslim students have made the successful transition from student life to professional life.[12] The origins of many of the present Muslim national organizations can be traced back to the Muslim Student Association. For the roots of some of the other organizations and institutions now present in American Muslim Society, we must look at the histories of the Nation of Islam, the Ahmadiyya Movement, the various Sufi groups, and the network of Arab Muslim organizations grouped under the Federation of Islamic Organizations (FIA).[13]

The transformation of the NOI by Imam Warith Deen Muhammad, the son and successor of the late Honorable Elijah Muhammad, has significance for Muslim efforts at institution-building on two grounds. First, it brought the movement into the fold of orthodox Islam and made the facilities of this social movement available to many orthodox Muslims who previously were either unwelcome or too aggravated by Elijah's teachings to join the NOI members in developing their institutions. Second, the new teachings of the Imam opened the movement to all Americans, regardless of race, and at the same time made it categorically clear that both the African-American Muslims under Imam Muhammad and the MSA have a common responsibility of safeguarding Muslim identity through institutionalization. Although a variety of circumstances going back to the 1930s led to the present division of labor between immigrants and native-born Americans, events of the late 1970s and early 1980s seem to suggest new ways of constructing bridges between the two communities.

Three different types of persons are now involved in the task of institution-building. The first are the custodians of the MSA heritage. They are now mainly professionals who seek social security and a sense of stability and continuity in the work of their national organizations, the Islamic Society of North America (ISNA), and their local mosques or Islamic centers affiliated to it. The second are the African-American Muslims in the old NOI who followed Imam Warith Deen Muhammad in 1975. They can now be described as the builders of Islamic institutions that embody the imam's serious attempts to foster simultaneously Islamism and Americanism in the whole society. Third are those small orthodox Muslim groups that have existed in African-American society well before Warith Deen's transformation of the NOI. Many of these Muslims, in their own way, tried hard to build institutions to maintain Islamic identity in the United States. Among others mention should be made of Shaykh al-Hajj Daud Faisal (1891–1980), founder of the Islamic Mission of America in 1928, in Brooklyn, New York; the leaders of the Islamic Party of North America; the leaders of the Ansarulla in New York; the leaders of the Islamic Brotherhood, Inc., in New York, which once published the *Western Sunrise*; and the leaders of the Hanafi Movement.[14]

When we examine the role and contributions of Arab-American Muslims in the creation and maintenance of Islamic institutions in America, we must again remind ourselves that these Muslims embarked on this delicate task of institution-building out of a concern for self-preservation and a quest for cultural and religious continuity. The second- or third-generation immigrant Muslim is different from the MSA rank and file because he is separated from the source of his own culture and religion by both time and space. Because of these factors he sees in his Muslim institutions and organizations an embodiment of his hope to remain Muslim and his will to reconcile his Muslim identity. He hopes to accomplish this as effectively and as successfully as his American Christian and Jewish counterparts. But while working to make his own dream come true, this Americanized Muslim must recognize the presence of both his African-American Muslim neighbor, who is also laboring to construct an Islamic identity and the structures that would give it meaning, and the nonimmigrant student whose Islamic da'wa efforts are either remembered later as those of a transient worker of Islam in the United States or as the first installment of service given by a former MSA member who has graduated into the ranks of the emerging Muslim professionals in America.

The Challenge to Build Muslim Economic Structures

In looking at the points of convergence and divergence within the Muslim community, one finds that the issue of Muslim economic activity in the United States has become a problem for some leaders. There is the issue of Muslim attitudes toward interest (*riba*). There is the question of ownership of property and the need to remain faithful to the Islamic precepts, which are likely to be subverted by Muslim involvement with the rules and practices of capitalist materialism. There is still the problem of trading in goods such as alcohol, pork, and other items considered forbidden (*haram*) to Muslims. Strict orthodox Muslims can easily find themselves condemned to a marginal existence in the current American social and economic system.

At least three areas can be identified as of mutual interest to the entire Muslim community in the United States. The first area is the collective desire of Muslims to survive as individuals, as families, and as a community, which demands that they participate in their different ways in the American economy. Evidence for the different degrees of involvement with the American economy can be drawn from the activities of the old Nation of Islam the Darul Islam Movement, the Islamic Party of North America, the Ansarulla, the Hanafi, and ultraorthodox Muslim organizations located in American cities. Regardless of their differences, however, all of these groups can be seen as active or passive participants in the American economy. Here these African-American groups join their immigrant brothers in the game of economic survival.

The second area of mutual interest is in the selling of Muslim products or merchandise useful to Muslims. Muslims have found in the creation of their own businesses the best avenues to self-protection and the reduction of cultural trauma from the encounter with American society. Evidence for this point of convergence between the foreign-born Muslims and their native brethren can be gleaned from the number and types of businesses established by these two subgroups in the Muslim community. All these Muslim groups have seen, in the creation of businesses, opportunities to assert themselves and to demonstrate their independence from the majority culture's power of hiring and firing.[15]

The third point of convergence between the immigrants and locals is the common Muslim interest in increasing Muslim cultural presence in American society. This interest, in my view, is inextricably linked to the economic question. By asserting their cultural presence, Muslims hope to win over non-Muslim entrepreneurs to make concessions to their community by not trampling on their sensitivities. It should be stressed, however, that despite this concern small business owners would not like to see competition from other non-Muslim businesses. Such rivals could reduce the independence of Muslim businessmen who specialized in providing services to fellow Muslims. These "neighborhood stores," in areas where Muslims are numerous, are definitely appreciated by Muslims, although only a few Muslims might entertain the illusion that they protect Muslims from the economic penetration of the capitalist market.

The Muslim community diverges on other economic questions. The problem of interest in financial transactions remains the great divide between the rigidly orthodox Muslims and their brethren who are willing to make adjustments to American society. Although it may be dangerous, without a proper sample, to generalize about Muslims all over the United States, one can argue that most of the practicing immigrant Muslims from the Old World and a sizable number of strict orthodox African-American Muslims tend to view interest (riba) with suspicion. These Muslims differ from their more accommodating brethren in two ways. First, they disagree over whether to participate actively in the United States economy and to take or pay interest. Second, they differ in their perceptions of the American Dream. To the strictly orthodox, the American Dream is not defined exclusively in terms of owning creature comforts and material things considered status symbols in the larger society. The Dream, if it has any significant place in his mental horizon, is a symbolic encapsulation of divine blessing (*baraka*) bestowed on American society and its inhabitants by a generous God who grants this favor as a trial.

The accommodationist Muslim embraces the American Dream unhesitatingly. Like his Christian or Jewish neighbors who adjust their religions to face up to the challenges of the secularization of society, he maintains his commitment to his faith but makes minor concessions that more rigidly orthodox coreligionists would not accept. The accommodationist sees his presence in American society as a God-given opportunity to better himself and family and to demonstrate to the larger society that American Muslims do belong, no matter what religious bigots or Muslim fanatics think of his relationship to the American Dream.

When we apply the categories developed earlier in our interpretation of the identity question among Muslims in the United States, and particularly among African-Americans, we find that attitudes toward and opinions on the American economy and the American Dream tend to be defined by how one fits on that spectrum of self-definition. Among the assimilationists who embrace Islam as a total way of life, a negative perception of and attitude toward the United States economy tends to develop. This ideological posture is brought about by the convert's dissatisfaction with American society and by his perception and belief that much of what goes on around him is haram and un-Islamic. Such a convert would join the bandwagon of the Muslim faithfuls who seek alternatives to live with riba (usurious interest) in the United States.[16] The second category of ethnic Americans who embrace Islam are those who totally assimilate themselves into Islamic culture but still recognize their ethnic origins. African-Americans and Latinos of this type do not shy away from participation in the U.S. economy. They definitely embrace the American Dream and see no serious conflict between their religion and the dream.

Opposed to these are the simulationists, earlier described as Elijahian. Concerned with the maintenance of identity separate from the larger community, the simulationists and the rigidly orthodox Muslims share the common attitude of rejection or isolation from the mainstream of society. Though the simulationists may, in the realm of theological purity, be dismissed as heretical or heterodox, in the realm of economic life and activity they share the attitude toward the corporate economic system of the rigidly orthodox Muslim. Both groups believe that any deep and abiding interaction with the larger economic system erodes and undermines the pillars of their separate existence and identity—hence the attempts to promote economic independence through the creation of economic and business networks. In the case of the old NOI, the quest for a separate state was the ultimate solution to the economic problem. The greatest success story of a simulationist drive was that of the old Nation of Islam, which was reported to own $75 million in assets when its spiritual leader passed away.[17]

The Challenge to Participate in American Political Life

Attitudes similar to those about the economy are manifest in the political arena, where the accommodationists have shown no hesitation to participate. During World War II when the followers of Elijah Muhammad and of Sunni Muslim leader Shaykh al-Hajj Daud Faisal of Brooklyn, New York, claimed Islam as the religion that prohibited them from fighting with the U.S. military, American Muslims from the Middle East and southern and east Europe signed up for the war zones, where they would later collect medals of valor.

The African-American Muslims opposed the war because they felt they were being used as cannon fodder by European and American Christians for the settling of their scores. The followers of Shaykh Daoud joined the military in the late 1950s and 1960s.[18] When Imam Warith Deen Muhammad took over the leadership of the NOI he redefined attitudes toward America and her military establishment. Unlike his father, who authored a book entitled *The Fall of America*, Imam Muhammad urged his followers to accept their American as well as their Islamic identity. He moved his father's organization from the simulationist to the assimilationist position by transforming it into a body of men and women who take pride in their American citizenship and remain steadfast in their practice of Islam in American society. Imam Muhammad demolished the "idol of the tribe" by telling his followers that race should no longer determine membership, that their responsibility is to God who brought them to this life. Implicit is his teaching that Muslims should participate in American politics. This theme has been repeated over and over again in the imam's lectures around the country. His reconstituted organization, known respectively as the World Community of Islam in the West and the American Muslim Mission, was later disbanded and authority transferred to the local mosques. But before he effected this radical transformation of the old Nation of Islam, the imam managed to plant the seeds of political participation among his flock around the country.

As a result of Warith Deen's policy changes Muslims have now made some serious efforts to engage in political life in the United States. The Muslim Political Action Committee in Greater Washington received recognition from Washington, D.C., Mayor Marlon Barry when in his victory speech he listed Muslims after Christians and Jews as supporters of his successful campaign. Similar efforts have been made elsewhere in the country. The mosques of the American Muslim Mission have created a platform for political education of Muslims interested in politics, and conferences dealing with political issues continue to be held in different locations in the country.

As a result of these changes in attitudes and perceptions, many African-American Muslims with political ambitions no longer hesitate to seek elective office within the American political system. Though the number of Muslim politicians within the larger black community is negligible, there is reason to believe that, as the attitude change becomes more and more deeply felt in Muslim African-America and in the larger Muslim community, some American politicians with Muslim names will begin to make the roster of U.S. elected officials.

But while the orthodox and not so orthodox African-American Muslims stayed away from politics in America because of their perception of and attitudes toward the white society and its controlling establishment, the immigrant Muslims of the first, second, and third generations reacted to the politics of the society differently for an entirely different set of motives and reasons. Coming from countries where little or no democracy prevailed, most of the immigrant Muslims remained apathetic about politics in the United States. This attitude underwent a significant change in the second generation of Muslims because of their greater identification with and assimilation into American culture. Their new sense of patriotism, when skillfully tapped by urban or rural politicians in the Midwestern and Northeastern parts of the country, led to greater politicization of these Muslims. But in making this point, we should hasten to add that though these individuals were Muslims in their names and their identities within their local communities, the politicians who sought their votes appealed to them as American voters of a particular ethnic background. This is an important point, because up until the late 1970s American Muslims did not organize or mobilize themselves as a political force within the American universe of political lobbies.

The earliest efforts of Muslims to seek political recognition from the leadership of this country came from the leaders of the FIA. Composed primarily of descendants of Middle Eastern Arabs, the FIA made some efforts to register the Muslim presence by appealing to President Eisenhower to allow Muslim members of the armed forces to have the letter "I" on their dog tags as Christians have their crosses and the Jews their stars of David. This was accomplished thanks to the efforts of Abdullah Igram, a World War II veteran, so that Muslims now have the letter "I" as their badge of religious identification in the multireligious U.S. military.[19]

In analyzing the question of Muslim involvement in American politics, and the divergent positions taken by the numerous groups within the community, one must also note the changes in the Muslim population that resulted from the immigration of a large number of highly educated Muslims from various parts of the Muslim world and most particularly from the Middle East and South Asia. While the implications of this influx of new and better educated Muslims are not yet properly understood, we can identify some of the factors responsible for changes in attitudes toward the American political process. The first is the emergence of national Muslim organizations committed to the assertion of a Muslim American identity. Unlike the FIA which continues to be perceived in Muslim circles as an organization catering to descendants of Arab

Muslims from Lebanon and the Fertile Crescent, the new organizations, such as the Islamic Society of North America, are led and financed by recent immigrant Muslims. They project their organizations as continental societies for all Muslims. Whatever its shortcomings, ISNA still serves as one of the very few Muslim organizations connected to thousands of Muslims around the country. Over the last five years, because of their growing self-confidence and the increase in anti-Muslim harassments and attacks in the media and in the larger American community, some members of the ISNA leadership have now begun to take seriously the option of greater and more active Muslim involvement in the American political process. This option is now being pursued at both the national and local levels. At the national level, there is talk of a national Muslim Political Action Committee.[20]

This decision to engage in political activities in North America has been debated within ISNA since the late 1970s. The idea won majority support in 1986 when the majilis al-shura of ISNA decided to lobby politically for Muslims and to call on all Muslims to become more involved in the American and Canadian political processes.

Thus, the political option is now shared by the followers of Imam Warith Deen Muhammad and the members of the Islamic Society of North America. These two organizations represent a significant portion of the Muslim community, and their involvement in the American political process could give Muslims and issues of interest to them greater visibility.

The identity question is central to the Muslim presence in the United States. The American Muslim can maintain his identity only by holding steadfastly on to the rope of *tawhid* (unity of Allah). This is definitely not an easy task, because numerous forces are at work which are likely to make life difficult. Though Muslims differ on some of the burning issues of American society, however, their sense of unity is evident in their common faith in tawhid, in their collective practice of Muslim rituals and in the expression of solidarity on matters affecting all Muslims living in America. To put this another way, one could say that, though divergence exists in the realm of perceptions of and attitudes toward American society, convergence exists in the realm of rituals and fellow feelings toward one's coreligionists.

Institution-building among Muslims has been slow. This has been due largely to the type of immigrant Muslim who came to America and the slow pace of conversion of native-born Americans who were intellectually and socially equipped to take the leadership in this process. Again it should be stated that those immigrants who could have founded Muslim institutions were primarily interested in making money in the shortest possible time and returning to their respective countries. Related to this is the fact that in the late nineteenth and early twentieth centuries, Muslims were on the defensive in their relationship with the Western countries, and Muslim immigrants were not psychologically prepared to settle permanently outside of Darul Islam.

Muslim economic structures are beginning to emerge, and their success is going to depend on the availability of capital within the Muslim community and on the attitudes of Muslim business people toward the American capitalist system. The divergent attitudes identified in our classification of different definitions of the Muslim identity in the United States will have significant effects on the future role of Muslims in the economy. Assimilationist Muslims will fare very much like assimilationist members of other religious traditions operating within the U.S. economy. They will develop intellectual justifications for dealing with banks that charge interest and with home-building companies that include interest in their mortgage rates. The simulationists, on the other hand, will in the coming years create economic structures that are faithful to Islamic economics and reassuring to those who believe in God and the Sunna of Prophet Muhammad.

The rise in Muslim self-confidence and the increase in the number of Muslims in the country will lead assimilationist Muslims to participate more and more in the American political system. Related to this is the fact that the trends in interreligious relations in America and the Muslim world could affect not only the image of Muslims in the United States, but also their self-perception in American society. The future of Muslim survival in American society is inextricably linked to the future of religious pluralism in this country. Any radical alteration in this pattern could threaten not only Muslim Americans but all other minorities who are targeted for discrimination. If the present and recent past are significant guides to the future, it is possible to hope that Islam as a minority religion has a promising future and Muslims will be as well adjusted in the coming years as any other religious minority. Their religion will join Christianity and Judaism as the third branch of the Abrahamic tradition. Were this to occur, Will Herberg's statement on American religion could be amended to read that being American means that one may be a member of the Christian, Jewish, Muslim, or any of the other religious traditions in American society.

Notes

1. For some insights on the racial situation in the United States at the time Gunner Myrdal wrote his book, see his *An American Dilemma*, Anniv. Ed. (New York: Harper & Row, 1964).

2. See my editorial in the *American Journal of Islamic Studies* 1: 1 (spring 1984), v–ix.

3. Included in this category are groups like the Ansarullah; the Islamic Party of North America; the Islamic Brotherhood, Inc., of New York; the Darul Islam Movement; and the Institute of Islamic Involvement in Winston-Salem, North Carolina. For details on their views of Islam in America, read the numerous publications of the Ansars, the back issues of *al-Islam*, *The Western Sunrise*, and *Jihadul Akbar*, and *Vision*.

4. Although there is no agreement on the number of Muslims in the United States, a widely cited figure is 3 million. For latest attempts at tabulations, see Yvonne Haddad, *Islamic Values in the United States: A Comparative Study* (New York: Oxford University Press, 1987). Arif Ghayur, "Muslims in the United States: Settlers and Visitors," *Annals* ASPSS 454 (March 1981).

5. For some treatment of the history of the Nation of Islam in the United States, see C. Eric Lincoln, *The Black Muslims in America* (Boston: Beacon Press, 1961); E. U. Essien-Udom, *Black Nationalism* (New York: Dell Publishing Co., 1962). For details on the transformation of the Nation of Islam, see Clifton E. Marsh, *From Black Muslims to Muslim* (Metuchen, N.J.: The Scarecrow Press, 1984); Akbar Muhammad, "Muslims in the United States: An Overview of Organizations, Doctrines and Problems," in *The Islamic Impact*, ed. Yvonne Haddad, Bryon Haines and Ellison Findly (Syracuse: Syracuse University Press, 1984), pp. 195–218.

6. For a good survey of events within the NOI since the Honorable Elijah Muhammad passed away in 1975, see *The African Mirror*, August/September 1979.

7. See the chronology of major historical events for Muslim America in Yvonne Haddad, *A Century of Islam in America* [Occasional Paper No. 4] (Washington, D.C.: American Institute of Islamic Affairs, 1986), p. 10.

8. See my "Growth of Islam in America," *The Saudi Gazette*, October 19, 1983.

9. Richard B. Turner, "The Ahmadiyya Movement in Islam in America," Unpublished paper, p. 3.

10. Abdo El-Kholy, *The Arab Moslem in America* (New Haven, Conn.: College and University Press, 1966), p. 48.

11. For more information on the MSA and its activities, see back issues of *al-Ittihad* and *Islamic Horizons*.

12. See Sulayman S. Nyang and Mumtaz Ahmad, "The Muslim Intellectual Emigre in the United States," *Islamic Culture* 59 (1985), 277–90.

13. See Lincoln, *The Black Muslims*; Turner, "The Ahmadiyya Movement"; El-Kholy, *The Arab Moslem*.

14. For details on the activities of these Muslim groups in the African-American community, see Sulayman S. Nyang and Robert J. Cummings, *Islam in the United States* (forthcoming), especially chapter on "Islam and the Black Experience in the U.S.A."

15. In a recent issue of the *Islamic Horizons* (November 1987), one Nahid Khan writes: "After years of watching both local and national politicking from the sidelines, Muslims are beginning to realize that it's time for the community to make its entrance into the political arena. In moving in this direction, the Islamic Society of North America (ISNA) has recently filed with the Federal Election Commission to form a Political Action Committee (PAC) and is now awaiting approval, according to the ISNA Secretary General Iqbal Unus." Khan adds that the decision of ISNA is part of "a scant group of Muslim communities and organizations who have already started to test the political waters." He identified the United Muslims of America of California, the Texas-based All-American Muslim Political Action Committee (AAMPAC), and the League of Muslim Voters in Chicago. For details see my "Muslim Minority Business Enterprise in the United States," *The Search* 3: 2 (spring 1982).

16. The Ansarullah Movement and members of ultraconservative Muslim groups fall under this category. Such persons usually do not like the idea of paying interest on home mortgages, interest on credit cards, and on other ribaic activities.

17. See Linda Jones, "Nations Apart," *The Detroit News, Michigan*, July 17, 1988.

18. Interviews with Bedria Saunders, Bilal Abdul Rahman and his wife Rakiya in Brooklyn, New York (spring 1982).

19. Abdo El-Kholy, quoting an F.I.A. document, maintains that Muslims in the U.S. army were relegated to the residual X category. See his *The Arab Moslem*, p. 46.

20. See *Islamic Horizons*, November 1987, p. 13.